Belief about the Self

Belief about the Self

A Defense of the Property Theory of Content

Neil Feit

OXFORD
UNIVERSITY PRESS
2008

OXFORD
UNIVERSITY PRESS

Oxford University Press, Inc., publishes works that further
Oxford University's objective of excellence
in research, scholarship, and education.

Oxford   New York
Auckland   Cape Town   Dar es Salaam   Hong Kong   Karachi
Kuala Lumpur   Madrid   Melbourne   Mexico City   Nairobi
New Delhi   Shanghai   Taipei   Toronto

With offices in
Argentina   Austria   Brazil   Chile   Czech Republic   France   Greece
Guatemala   Hungary   Italy   Japan   Poland   Portugal   Singapore
South Korea   Switzerland   Thailand   Turkey   Ukraine   Vietnam

Copyright © 2008 by Oxford University Press, Inc.

Published by Oxford University Press, Inc.
198 Madison Avenue, New York, New York 10016

www.oup.com

Oxford is a registered trademark of Oxford University Press

Library of Congress Cataloging-in-Publication Data
Feit, Neil.
Belief about the self : a defense of the property theory of content/Neil Feit.
p. cm.
Includes bibliographical references and index.
ISBN 978-0-19-534136-2
1. Self (Philosophy)   I. Title.
BD450.F388   2008
126—dc22   2007039746

9   8   7   6   5   4   3   2   1

Printed in the United States of America
on acid-free paper

To my parents,
Hedy and Martin Feit

ACKNOWLEDGMENTS

I would like to acknowledge the comments of those who read versions of this manuscript, parts of it, or ancestors of parts of it. I am grateful to the following people for their very helpful comments: Lynne Rudder Baker, Phillip Bricker, David Denby, Andy Egan, Ed Gettier, Hud Hudson, Michael McGlone, Phillip Montague, Ted Sider, Dale Tuggy, and anonymous referees.

I am especially grateful to my friend and colleague Stephen Kershnar, who read the entire manuscript with great care and commented on it extensively.

I would also like to thank Julia Wilson, my wife, for her love, inspiration, patience, companionship, and conversation.

I have used portions of three previously published articles of mine, in modified form, in the present work. Two of these articles appeared in *Philosophical Studies*. In particular, parts of chapter 5 are drawn from Feit (2000), and material in chapter 2, section 3, is adapted from Feit (2006). This material is reproduced with the kind permission of Springer Science and Business Media. The other article appeared in *Philosophy and Phenomenological Research*. Chapter 6 is a modified version of several sections of this article, Feit (2001). Some other material drawn from this paper appears in chapter 4, section 4. I am grateful to Blackwell Publishing for permission to reproduce this material.

CONTENTS

INTRODUCTION

This book is a study of the nature of the representational, mental content of our cognitive attitudes. A cognitive attitude is a mental state such as a belief, desire, hope, fear, expectation, or the like. When a subject adopts any one of these attitudes, there seems to be a *content* that represents things as being a certain way. For example, if you believe that all good people are happy, then what you believe—i.e., the content of your belief—seems to represent good people as being happy. The term "content" is a bit vague and elusive. However, we can get clearer on the notion of content by thinking about the roles it needs to play. Let's briefly consider three such roles.

The first role has to do with truth and falsehood. Cognitive attitudes seem to have contents that are capable of being true or false. For example, suppose I believe that the earth revolves around the sun. The content of my belief, in this case, seems to represent things as being the way they actually are, and so it seems to be true. One of the roles for content, then, consists in accounting for the truth or falsehood of certain types of attitude, and for analogous features of other types of attitude. (This is the second time an instance of belief has served as an example, and that is no accident. Following tradition, I shall focus my discussion on belief and, to a lesser extent, on desire. But my conclusions about the nature of belief and desire will carry over to the other attitudes as well.) Talk of truth and falsehood might not readily apply to our desires, hopes, expectations, and so on, but there are analogous notions for these attitudes, e.g., the notion of a desire being satisfied or unsatisfied.

The second role that content plays has to do with the logical relations between various attitudes. For example, a police detective might suspect that a certain Mr. X committed a burglary in her precinct on Friday night. When the detective learns, a few days later perhaps, that Mr. X was nowhere near her precinct on Friday night, she will conclude that Mr. X was not the burglar after all. This is a successful inference. If we assign to the detective's attitudes contents that are capable of standing in the appropriate logical relationships to one another, we can account for the inference and its success.

The third role has to do with purposeful behavior or action. We often explain why someone did this or that by pointing out that she had certain beliefs and desires. Let's consider a trivial example. We might explain why Ms. Y opened her umbrella when it began to rain by appealing to her desire to stay dry and her belief that she will stay dry only if she opens her umbrella. Another role for content, then, is explanatory. We appeal (correctly, it seems) to the contents of cognitive attitudes to explain why we act in certain ways. The three roles just discussed are related in fairly obvious ways.

One way of doing justice to the idea that content plays these roles is to take the traditional view that the content of an attitude is a *proposition*, something that is true or false in an absolute sense. On this view, when you believe something, what you believe is a proposition; when you have a desire, the content of your desire is a proposition; and so on. The various cognitive attitudes, according to this traditional view, are properly called "propositional attitudes." However, the main thesis of this book is that the traditional view is mistaken and must be replaced with another theory of content.

Why is the traditional view mistaken? The short answer is that it cannot make sense of a special class of cognitive attitudes. Let's take belief again as an example. Some of our beliefs are beliefs that are fundamentally about ourselves. These are beliefs that we typically express, in English, with the use of the first-person pronoun "I." For example, I believe that I am left-handed, that I am a philosopher, that I am married, and so on. These beliefs have been called *self-locating*, *egocentric*, or *de se* (about the self). Why do these *de se* beliefs force us to reject the traditional view about the contents of the attitudes? Well, consider again my belief that I am left-handed. One possibility is that my believing myself to be left-handed consists in my believing the proposition *that Neil Feit is left-handed*. But it seems that if I were somehow to fail to realize that I am Neil Feit, then I could believe this proposition without believing myself to be left-handed. Another possibility is that my believing myself to be left-handed consists in my believing some proposition by means of which I single myself out with a description, such as the proposition *that the philosopher who lives at 26 Curtis Place is left-handed*. However, it seems clear that I might forget my address, for example, and somehow come to believe this proposition without believing myself to be left-handed. There do not seem to be any other viable possibilities, and this spells trouble for the traditional view. Moreover, *de se* attitudes are ubiquitous. From the point of view of theorizing about cognitive content, the class of such attitudes cannot be cast aside and ignored.

The theory of content that I shall be defending is not new. It was developed by Roderick Chisholm and David Lewis (independently) in the late 1970s. According to this theory, the content of my belief that I am left-handed is not a proposition; it is a *property*. In particular, it is the property *being left-handed*. This property—like all others—is not something that is true or false, at least not in the absolute sense in which a proposition is true or false. On the view I shall defend, every cognitive attitude (including the attitudes that do not cause trouble for the traditional view) has a property as its content. On this account, then, every instance of an attitude turns out to be a *de se* attitude. This view is the *property theory of content*. The property theory differs from the traditional view in two important ways. The first way is obvious, i.e., the contents assigned to the attitudes are properties rather than propositions. The second difference consists in the fact that the property theory builds *reflexivity* into the relations between a conscious subject and the contents of his or her attitudes. Believing, for example, is taking-oneself-to-have some property. Consider again my belief that I am left-handed. According to the property theory, my having this belief consists in my reflexively taking-myself-to-have the property *being left-handed*; it does not consist in my accepting any proposition.

Despite its impressive pedigree, the property theory has not caught on like wildfire. One of my hopes is that this book will help to remedy this (at least as I see it) sad state of affairs. In the book, I lay out the case in favor of the property theory, defend it against objections, and apply it to some important problems in the philosophy of mind. I will conclude this introductory section by providing a brief overview of the seven chapters to come.

The first chapter contains some more discussion of the cognitive attitudes, the notion of content, and the traditional view of the nature of cognitive content (also known as the *doctrine of propositions*). It also contains a somewhat more detailed discussion of the problem that *de se* beliefs, and *de se* attitudes in general, pose for the traditional view that such attitudes always have propositional contents. The chapter concludes with an examination of the property theory of content. In particular, I argue for a version of the property theory that upholds a kind of *individualism* or *internalism* about the mind. The property of having a belief with a certain content, on this view, is one that supervenes on, or is completely determined by, what is going on inside the head of the one who has it.

The second chapter contains the bulk of the positive case for the property theory. I review John Perry's (1979[1988]) argument against the traditional doctrine of propositions, based upon his classic case of the messy shopper. I also review Lewis's (1979) case of the two gods, and discuss an argument for the property theory based upon it. The remainder of the chapter is devoted to some different arguments in favor of the property theory. I argue that the traditional view, on which the content of every belief is a proposition, is incompatible with the internalist view of the mind and also with a very plausible version of physicalism. That is, the traditional view begs important questions concerning the relations between psychological properties and certain physical properties. I argue that the property theory does not beg these questions, and moreover, since we have good reasons to think that both internalism and physicalism are true, we should accept the property theory. Finally, I discuss and extend a line of argument given by Chisholm (1981), which suggests that the property theory provides the best explanation of a range of phenomena associated with cognitive attitudes and our discourse about them.

In the third chapter, I consider the main rivals to the property theory of content and evaluate each of them with respect to the property theory. The chapter is largely devoted to only two rival views, but each of them comes in several varieties. One of these views is a simple version of the traditional view. This is *dyadic propositionalism*, which holds that belief, for example, is simply a dyadic or two-place relation between a believer and a proposition, and that there is nothing more to believing something than standing in this relation. The other main rival, at least as I see it, is the *triadic view of belief*. On this account, the belief relation also relates a believer and a proposition, but there is more to belief than just that. In order to believe something, on this view, one must be related not only to a proposition but to something else besides, i.e., a triadic or three-place relation must obtain among the believer, a proposition, and something else. I argue that both of these general rivals to the property theory have costs that the property theory does not have, and fail to bring any additional benefits. Along the way, I discuss some other accounts that do not fall neatly into the dyadic or triadic families of views.

The fourth chapter consists of a sustained defense of the property theory in light of a battery of criticisms. Here is a sampling of the objections: The property theory is implausible because *de se* attitudes require a rather sophisticated kind of self-awareness, which not every subject of an attitude needs to have; the property theory cannot plausibly account for certain attitudes that entail the nonexistence of their subjects nor for certain other attitudes that can be evaluated in possible situations where their subjects do not exist; the property theory has trouble accounting for the communication of our thoughts to others; and the property theory cannot account adequately for the validity of certain intuitively valid inferences that involve the attribution of cognitive attitudes. I will try to show that, in each case, there are plausible property-theoretic answers to the objections.

The rest of the book is an extended discussion of the applications of the property theory to some important issues and problems in the philosophy of mind. In the fifth chapter, the topic is *de re* belief. Our *de re* beliefs are the beliefs that we have about particular things in our environment, e.g., my belief, of my cat Virginia, that she is presently curled up beside me. I sketch out a general, property-theoretic account of *de re* belief and argue that this phenomenon does not pose any special problems for the theory. That is, every problem that is associated with *de re* belief (including the general problem of accounting for the conditions under which a given belief is about a given object in the relevant way) is equally problematic for every theoretical perspective on the attitudes.

The final two chapters concern more specific problems. The sixth chapter is devoted to Saul Kripke's (1979[1988]) puzzle about belief, and the final chapter is devoted to the evaluation of Twin Earth examples and arguments based upon them. I view these chapters as a kind of supplement to the earlier case in favor of the property theory. In particular, I argue that the property theory gives us the resources to provide an extremely satisfying way to solve Kripke's puzzle, and a very plausible way to rebut the standard Twin Earth arguments against the internalist view of cognitive content.

The issues concerning the nature of the contents of attitudes are, in some sense, at the intersection of the philosophy of mind and the philosophy of language. This book is focused chiefly on certain issues in the philosophy of mind. (In ch. 1, sec. 1, I shall discuss some of these issues and highlight the most relevant ones.) However, from time to time, some philosophy of language will be required. For example, questions about the content of *de se* beliefs are closely bound up with questions about the correct analysis of certain locutions used to report such beliefs, especially the "he-himself" and "she-herself" locutions. How are we to analyze, e.g., belief reports such as "Roger believes that he himself is clever" and "Maria believes that she herself is a millionaire"? Issues in the philosophy of language concerning the correct analysis of our attributions of belief and the like will come up also in the final three chapters. For now, however, I would like to emphasize that my primary focus will be more metaphysical than semantic. And again, my primary goal will be to defend the thesis that the content of every cognitive attitude is a *property* to which the subject is related in the appropriate psychological way.

Belief about the Self

CHAPTER ONE

MENTAL CONTENT AND THE PROBLEM OF *DE SE* BELIEF

Suppose that a given person is believed by herself and another to be a spy. For example, consider the case of Joe and Valerie. Suppose that Valerie believes that she herself is a spy, and suppose that Joe, who is acquainted with Valerie and knows her by name, believes that Valerie is a spy. In this case, Valerie has a *de se* or *egocentric* belief about herself, a belief about the way she herself is. The traditional view about the content of our beliefs holds that the content of a belief is a *proposition*, i.e., something that can be true or false. (We shall soon examine this view, in sec. below.) It might seem natural to say that, in this case, Joe and Valerie believe the same thing, e.g., the proposition *that Valerie is a spy*. There are good reasons, however, to think that this cannot be the case. Moreover, identifying the precise content of Valerie's *de se* belief is not a trivial matter. There are good reasons to think that it cannot be a proposition at all.

In the situation above, Valerie believes something and, in virtue of believing it, she believes herself to be a spy. I just suggested that Joe and Valerie do not believe the same thing in this situation. To see why this is the case, consider Joe's belief that Valerie is a spy. What precisely does Joe believe when he has this belief? That is, what is the *content* of his belief? Call the content X. Joe believes X partly in virtue of background beliefs, and partly in virtue of his perspective on Valerie. For example, we might imagine that Joe thinks that everyone who wears a trench coat is a spy, and he has seen Valerie wearing a trench coat. Now, it seems possible that *Valerie* should believe *X* without believing that she herself is a spy. This is because it seems possible that Valerie should have a perspective on herself that matches Joe's perspective on her, while she thinks that she has this perspective on somebody else. She might see herself wearing a trench coat (on video, perhaps, or in a mirror), but fail to realize that she is looking at herself; or she might see various documents on which her name appears, but suffer from amnesia and not realize that she is a spy named "Valerie." It seems natural to say that Joe has a "third-person belief" about Valerie, and Valerie could have any such belief without the "first-person belief" that she herself is a spy. Whatever *X* is, then, it is not a belief such that, in virtue of having it, Valerie would believe herself to be a spy. So, Joe and Valerie have different beliefs.

In fact, it appears difficult to imagine a proposition that will serve as the content of Valerie's *de se* belief that she herself is a spy. For example, it seems that, for any property *F*, she could believe the proposition *that the F is a spy*, but fail to believe that she herself is the one and only individual who has *F*. It also seems that she could believe that Valerie is a spy—whatever exactly that amounts to—but fail to believe that she herself is Valerie (she might have amnesia, or might not realize that she is looking at herself in a mirror, and so on). We will soon return to this puzzle about *de se* belief.

1. Cognitive Attitudes and Content

An important feature of the human mind is its ability to have various attitudes about things. Sometimes, people have different attitudes about the same thing. For example, Jones might hope that it will snow while Smith dreads that it will snow. Sometimes, people have the same attitude toward different things. For example, Jones might desire chocolate ice cream while Smith desires pound cake. I shall use the term "cognitive attitudes" for such things as our beliefs, desires, hopes, fears, and so on. There are at least two questions we might ask about the contents of our cognitive attitudes. First, we might ask: What makes it the case that a given instance of an attitude has the particular content that it has (for example, what makes it a belief that coal is black rather than a belief that London is pretty)? Second, we might ask: What kind or kinds of thing can serve as the content of an attitude (for example, sentences, propositions, ice cream, pound cake)? This book is largely about the second question.

Cognitive attitudes are representational mental states. They seem to have contents that can be true or false, and that represent the world as being one way or another. When I believe something, I represent things to myself in a certain way, a way that I take them to be. When I desire something, I also represent things in a certain way, a way that I would like them to be. And so on for my other attitudes. The *content* of a cognitive attitude characterizes how that state represents things. Beliefs and desires are central cases of cognitive attitudes largely because of the role they play in (the explanation of) our purposeful behavior. Again, I will focus on them throughout the book, but every conclusion about their content can be applied to the other attitudes as well.

One major question about the nature of representational mental content has to do with whether such content is *narrow* or *wide*. The content of a given attitude is narrow provided that the property of having an attitude with that content supervenes on intrinsic (micro-structural) properties of the conscious subject of the attitude. If the content of a belief, for example, is narrow, then the property of having that belief is itself an intrinsic property of the believer. Any doppelgänger or molecule-for-molecule duplicate of the believer will have a belief with the same content. Narrow content, as the saying goes, is in the head. The content of a given attitude is wide provided that it is not narrow. I will defend the view that all cognitive attitude content is narrow. This view is a version of what is called "internalism" or "individualism" about psychological properties (I have a slight preference for the first label). Since a solid majority of philosophers of mind probably take the opposite position, I will explain and defend this view in due course.

There are several issues concerning content that I plan to sweep aside. One of these, already mentioned, is the question about what makes it the case that an attitude has one content rather than another. A second issue involves degrees of belief and desire. These attitudes seem not to be all-or-nothing affairs; instead, they admit of degrees. We believe certain things more strongly than we believe others, and we want certain things more than we want others. With respect to belief, we might assign a number between zero and one (inclusive) to represent the credence that a subject has in a given content. With respect to desire, we might assign any positive or negative finite number, thereby allowing a subject to disvalue a content by giving it a negative value. None of this has any bearing on the nature of the contents themselves. So, for simplicity, I shall treat belief and desire as if they were all-or-nothing affairs rather than things that (probably) come in degrees. Everything that I have to say about content can be adapted to the strategy of assigning values to believed and desired contents.

Another issue involves the way in which beliefs and desires are stored in our brains. Some philosophers say that mental representations in the brain have a kind of sentential or quasi-sentential structure, i.e., that there is a *language of thought*. On this view, each belief is an independent entity "written" somewhere in one's brain, and its content is the meaning of what is written. Others say that each of us has some sort of system of representation (like a map, perhaps) that incorporates a total belief state and a total desire state, but that cannot be broken down into individual representations that count as beliefs and desires. I wish to remain neutral between these two broad accounts of the form that mental representations take. Nothing that I say about content forces a commitment one way or another on this issue.

One final issue concerns the distinction between the metaphysics of the attitudes and the semantics of attitude reports, e.g., sentences of the form "S believes that p." This book is primarily about the metaphysics of belief, desire, and the like. Some of the main questions are as follows: Is belief a relation between a conscious subject and an abstract proposition? Is it a two-place relation? Is it, or can it somehow be analyzed in terms of, a three-place relation? I shall hold that belief is a two-place relation between believers and properties that they *self-ascribe*. Obviously, views about the metaphysics of the attitudes will have consequences for the semantics of attitude reports, where the main questions might involve identifying the semantic content or, perhaps, truth conditions of sentences that report our beliefs, desires, and so on. For example, consider the following simple view about the semantics of belief sentences: A sentence of the form "S believes that p" is true if and only if the bearer of the name S stands in the two-place belief relation to the proposition that is semantically expressed by the *that*-clause "that p." If belief relates subjects to properties rather than to propositions, then this simple semantic view is incorrect. The semantic issues are not my main concern here, and I do not have a general theory to offer, but again, I will occasionally have to draw conclusions and make suggestions about the semantics of attitude reports.

I mentioned in the introduction and at the beginning of this chapter that the traditional view of mental content holds that the contents of our cognitive attitudes are propositions. It is for this reason that many of us continue to use the Russellian term "propositional attitudes" for our beliefs, desires, and the like. In the next section, we take a look at the traditional view.

2. The Doctrine of Propositions

The standard view about cognitive attitude content is the doctrine of propositions, which says, in effect, that when you believe or desire something, the content of your attitude is a proposition.[1] This view is so entrenched in our way of thinking about the attitudes that the quasi-technical term "proposition" is often defined on its terms. That is, a proposition is commonly defined, at least in part, as something that can be the object of an attitude. If a definition were needed, I would prefer to define propositions as being the primary bearers of truth and falsity. (I would also like to leave open the possibility that not every proposition has a truth value, and so even this definition needs tweaking.) However, I do not think that we really need to define the notion of a proposition here. I shall assume only that propositions exist, and that they have truth values in an absolute way, which does not vary from person to person, place to place, time to time, and so on.[2] So, as I use the term "proposition"—and this usage is standard—a proposition cannot be true for one person and false for another (unlike the way in which the property *being a spy*, for example, can be true of one person and false of another).

Theorizing in semantics gives us good reason to believe in propositions, however exactly we might conceive of them. It seems that, if Peter says "snow is white" and Pierre says "la neige est blanche," then

---

1. Sometimes, this claim is expressed by saying that the *object* of your attitude is always a proposition. I will sometimes follow this terminology. However, we will need to be careful to avoid confusing the object of belief in this sense from the sense in which, e.g., London is the object of your belief when you believe something about London. More on this in chapter 5.

2. If the future is open in the very strong way that some believe, then we should allow for a certain kind of variation in the truth value of a proposition from time to time. However, once a proposition takes on a truth value of true or false, it retains that truth value forever. As for the very existence of propositions, one who is skeptical about their existence (and the existence of properties, for that matter) might be able to recast much of what I say in more agreeable terms.

Peter and Pierre have said the same thing (in different languages). If we take this literally, it entails the existence of something that would seem to be a proposition, viz., the proposition *that snow is white*. Like propositions generally, this proposition has possible-worlds truth conditions, i.e., it is true at a given possible world or situation if and only if snow is white in that world or situation. Propositions make appealing semantic theories possible, and this certainly counts as a reason to admit them. Propositions also seem to be the things we think of as being *necessarily* the case or *possibly* the case, and things that can stand to one another in the relation of *entailment*.

Before moving on to a brief discussion of some conceptions of propositions, I would like to consider a somewhat precise formulation of the doctrine of propositions:

> *Doctrine of Propositions*: Necessarily, all the contents of one's beliefs, desires, and other cognitive attitudes are propositions, i.e., entities with truth values that do not vary from object to object, place to place, or time to time.

According to this view, when Peter expresses one of his beliefs by uttering the English words "snow is white," the content of the belief that he expresses is a proposition. We might report this belief by saying that Peter believes that snow is white. By itself, the doctrine of propositions is silent on precisely which proposition Peter believes. It might be the proposition *that snow is white*, or it might be some other (related) proposition.

There are several competing conceptions of propositions. With respect to the problem at the heart of this book, the differences among these conceptions do not really matter, and so I shall officially be uncommitted about the debate. However, since I shall be discussing the views of philosophers who take one conception over the others, it will be useful to review the conceptions briefly here. The conceptions fall into two general groups: those that attribute a certain kind of internal structure to propositions, and those that do not.

The structured view of propositions holds that a proposition has a structure that basically mirrors the structure of a sentence. A structured proposition has constituents that are ordered in a particular way. For example, the proposition *that Shaq is taller than Mugsy* might be identified with a structure like this: <<Shaq, Mugsy>, *being taller than*>. Order matters here, and so this proposition is distinct from the proposition *that Mugsy is taller than Shaq*. There are various versions of the structured view of propositions. On one account—often called "Russellian"—a proposition can have properties, relations, and ordinary concrete particulars as constituents (the example above has one binary relation and two concrete particulars). A proposition that contains a concrete particular as a constituent is a *singular proposition*. Not every version of the structured view allows for singular propositions. For example, on a broadly Fregean view, the only constituents that a proposition can have are Fregean senses (modes of presentation, concepts).

On other conceptions, propositions are structureless, or at least they lack the kind of structure that mirrors the structure of sentences. For example, Bealer (1993, 1998) defends the view that a proposition is an eternal, metaphysically simple entity. A more popular view identifies propositions with sets of possible worlds or situations (although different defenders of this conception have different accounts of possible worlds). The proposition *that some cats purr*, on this view, is the set of worlds where some cats purr. The possible-worlds conception of propositions allows us to think of belief as a matter of ruling out possibilities. Your total belief state can be thought of as the intersection of all your beliefs, and so the more you believe, the fewer possibilities are consistent with your beliefs. However, when it comes to mental content, this approach has serious problems. Here is one example. Suppose that propositions are sets of worlds, and that proposition p logically implies proposition q. In this case, the conjunctive proposition p *and* q is the same proposition as p itself, since the conjunction is true in all and only the worlds where p is true. However, it is surely possible for somebody to fail to realize the implication and to believe p without believing p *and* q. Another case involves necessary truths, e.g., since there is only one necessary truth (the set of all possible worlds) on the present conception of propositions, if you believe one of them you thereby believe them all.[3]

The notion of a singular proposition was briefly mentioned above. Only the proponents of structured, Russellian propositions can maintain that we sometimes believe singular propositions. (This claim is extremely controversial, and we will consider it at times in what follows.) However, the other conceptions might be able to provide certain

---

3. For a nice discussion of these closure-related problems for the possible-worlds conception of propositions, see Richard (1990: 9–16). Stalnaker (1984) provides a sustained defense of possible-worlds propositions as mental contents.

propositions that have the same *truth conditions* as singular propositions, and thereby provide a kind of substitute for belief in singular propositions. We might call these "pseudo singular propositions."[4] Instead of a proposition that contains Bill Gates, for example, we might have one that contains his individual essence or haecceity, *being (identical to) Bill Gates*. The proponent of Fregean structured propositions might try to use special sorts of object-dependent "*de re* senses" or modes of presentation to mimic Russellian singular propositions.[5] And the possible-worlds theorist might make use of the set of worlds where Bill Gates is rich (or, perhaps, where one of his counterparts is rich) to mimic the singular proposition <Gates, *being rich*>. From now on, I will assume that, if an ordinary proper name occurs in a term that designates a proposition, then what the term designates is a singular or pseudo singular proposition. So, for example, the proposition *that Bill Gates is rich* is either a singular proposition about Gates, or a pseudo singular proposition that is true if and only if Gates is rich.

Before concluding this section, I would like to make a few remarks about what the doctrine of propositions does *not* entail about cognitive attitudes. The doctrine of propositions says that, if something, x, is the content of somebody's belief, then x is a proposition. One might think this entails that belief is a dyadic, or two-place, relation between believers and propositions. But this is not the case. The assertion that belief is such a dyadic relation goes beyond what is claimed by the doctrine of propositions. I shall reserve the phrase "dyadic propositionalism" for the stronger view:

> *Dyadic Propositionalism*: Belief is a dyadic relation between a subject and a proposition, which is the content of the subject's belief. No other property or relation need be instantiated for a subject to have a belief.

As we shall see in chapter 3, section 1, there is a view about belief that is consistent with the doctrine of propositions, but not with dyadic propositionalism. Following Richard (1983[1988]), I shall call this the "triadic view of belief," since it implies that someone believes something if and only if a three-place relation obtains among a sub-

---

4. We should not confuse these with the "quasi-singular propositions" of Schiffer (1978) and Recanati (1993), where objects are paired with modes of presentation of them.

5. As in Evans (1982) and McDowell (1984). I will briefly discuss this view later.

ject, a proposition, and something else (often called a "guise" or "belief state"). The idea here is that people can believe the same proposition in different ways, and people can believe different propositions in the same way. (This will be discussed more fully in ch. 3.) Since those who hold the triadic view typically say that the *content* of a given belief is the proposition, this view is consistent with, and can be seen as a version of, the doctrine of propositions. However, since the triadic view holds that belief is a three-place rather than a two-place relation, one who holds this view must reject dyadic propositionalism.

Things are actually a little bit more complicated. Salmon (1986) defends the triadic view, but he also holds that belief is a two-place relation between a subject and a proposition. But Salmon also needs to reject dyadic propositionalism. The reason is that, on Salmon's view, in order for somebody to believe a proposition, a three-place relation among subject, proposition, and guise must be instantiated. On Salmon's account, the two-place belief relation is *analyzed* in terms of this three-place relation, which he calls *BEL*. That is, a subject S believes a proposition P if and only if there exists an x such that $BEL(S, P, x)$.[6] Since the three-place *BEL* relation needs to be instantiated for a subject to have a belief, Salmon's version of the triadic view is also inconsistent with dyadic propositionalism. (I have formulated dyadic propositionalism to get this result, because on Salmon's view there is more to the concept of belief than the concept of a two-place relation between subjects and propositions.)

One way to consider the problem of *de se* belief is to think of it as a challenge to dyadic propositionalism. This strategy will be adopted in the next section. Later, I will argue that the property theory of content provides a simple and theoretically satisfying solution to the problem, a solution that fares much better overall than does any version of the doctrine of propositions.

3. The Problem of *De Se* Belief

Let's reconsider the case of Joe and Valerie presented at the beginning of this chapter. Valerie has the *de se* belief that she herself is a spy, i.e., she believes herself to be a spy. Joe, on the other hand, has a

---

6. The expression "$BEL(S, P, x)$" means something like "S grasps P by means of x and assents to P when grasped by this means."

belief that he would express by saying "Valerie is a spy" or, perhaps, "She [pointing to Valerie] is a spy." For concreteness, let's suppose that Joe has read in the newspaper that Valerie is a spy, and that he sees Valerie wearing a trench coat, and thinks that everyone who wears a trench coat is a spy. For comfort, let's assume that Joe knows Valerie by name and is acquainted with her in some ordinary sense. In this case, the following two claims are true:

(1) Joe believes that Valerie is a spy.
(2) Valerie believes that she herself is a spy.

Let's start by taking dyadic propositionalism as our theory of belief content. The problem, then, is to identify a proposition such that Valerie believes it and her believing it makes (2) true. This is the belief she would express by uttering the words "I am a spy." However, it seems that Valerie could believe the proposition *that Valerie is a spy* without believing that she herself is a spy (she might somehow fail to realize that she is Valerie), and that for any qualitative property *F*, she could believe the proposition *that the F is a spy* without believing that she herself is a spy (she might not think that she is the *F*). So, it seems that there is more to Valerie's *de se* belief that she herself is a spy than her belief in any of these propositions. How, then, is such a belief to be characterized? This is the problem of *de se* belief.

To get a bit clearer on this presentation of the problem, we might consider claim (1) above. What makes this true? Which proposition might Joe believe, and thereby believe that Valerie is a spy? There seems to be a dilemma: Either (a) Joe believes some singular or pseudo singular proposition about Valerie, viz., the proposition *that Valerie is a spy*; or (b) there is some property *F* that Valerie and only Valerie has, and Joe believes the proposition *that the person with F is a spy*. If we take option (a) and say that the proposition *that Valerie is a spy* is what Joe believes, it seems that Valerie's believing this proposition would not make (2) true. For example, suppose that Valerie gets amnesia and then reads in the newspaper that Valerie is a spy, not realizing that she is reading about herself. Or, suppose that Valerie also thinks that anybody who wears a trench coat is a spy, and sees herself in a mirror wearing a trench coat, not realizing that she is looking at herself. If we take option (b), we have the same problem. Valerie could believe the proposition *that the woman in a trench coat at the corner of C and 20th streets is a spy* without believing that she herself is at that corner, and hence without (2) being true. Whatever Joe believes, he believes it in virtue of a *third-person perspective* on Valerie. So, it seems possible for Valerie to believe the same thing in virtue of a third-person perspective on herself, and hence without the *de se* belief and the first-person perspective associated with it.

According to the reasoning above, the content of Valerie's *de se* belief cannot be identified with the proposition *that Valerie is a spy*, and it cannot be identified with any proposition that might be expressed with words of the form "the *F* is a spy." This is a big problem for dyadic propositionalism, since on this view her belief consists in a binary relation to a proposition that is its content, and these propositions seem to exhaust the suitable candidates. The dyadic propositionalist might be tempted to respond to the puzzle as follows. Perhaps only Valerie is capable of believing the proposition *that Valerie is a spy* (or some such proposition) and, in believing it, she thereby believes that she herself is a spy. Nobody except Valerie, Joe included, can believe (or even consider) this proposition. Roughly following Chisholm (1981), I shall use the phrase "first-person proposition" for a proposition that a given person expresses by uttering sentences with a first-person pronoun such as "I," and that no other person can express, believe, or grasp at all. For example, one might say that my first-person propositions contain my individual essence or haecceity, while your first-person propositions contain your individual essence or haecceity. We will consider this suggestion in some detail in chapter 3, section 3. For now, let's just consider a couple of potential worries about it.

On this view, what makes (1) true is that Joe believes an appropriate proposition that is not a singular or pseudo singular proposition about Valerie, e.g., the proposition *that the woman named "Valerie" wearing a trench coat at the corner of C and 20th is a spy*. On the other hand, what makes (2) true is that Valerie believes a proposition that only she can believe, the proposition *that Valerie is a spy*. One worry here involves the very idea of a first-person proposition, which is able to characterize the content of only one person's attitudes. Do we have any independent reason to admit propositions that are accessible to the thought of one and only one individual? We might also wonder why Valerie's believing this proposition makes (2) true. Why is it that, in virtue of believing the proposition *that Valerie is a spy*, Valerie believes herself to be a spy? Why isn't it possible that she should believe this proposition, but not believe *herself* to be a spy?

Frege (1918[1988]) defended a view about the contents of the beliefs that we express when we use the word "I," and Russell wondered for many years about the nature of one's acquaintance with oneself and its impact on self-knowledge. However, I think it is fair to say that the problem of *de se* belief was given its first explicit statement by Geach (1957), who put it like this: "[I]f we say of a number of people that each of them believes that he himself is clever, what belief exactly are we attributing to all of them? Certainly they do not all believe the same proposition, as 'proposition' is commonly understood by philosophers" (1957: 23).

The problem is sometimes presented in a way that emphasizes a subject's ignorance of certain *de se* information. For example, Castañeda (1968) describes an example in which a man writes the most authoritative biography of the only war hero who was wounded a hundred times, yet does not know that he himself is the war hero.[7] Perry (1977), inspired by Frege, describes the following similar case:

> An amnesiac, Rudolf Lingens, is lost in the Stanford Library. He reads a number of things in the library, including a biography of himself, and a detailed account of the library in which he is lost.... He still won't know who he is, and where he is, no matter how much knowledge he piles up, until that moment when he is ready to say, "*This* place is aisle five, floor six, of Main Library, Stanford. *I* am Rudolf Lingens." (1977: 492)

Lingens, in some perfectly ordinary sense, does not know who he is or where he is. He lacks beliefs that he would express with indexical terms such as "this place" and "I," like the ones expressed at the end of the quotation above. The problem is to characterize the nature of the beliefs that Lingens lacks.

Because of the indispensability of indexical expressions like "I" and "this" in capturing the content of beliefs of this sort, Perry calls our problem "the problem of the essential indexical." Some of the information Lingens lacks is information about his spatial location, about *where* in the world he is. We can take this to be a special kind of *de se* information. The belief Lingens would express by saying "*this* is Main Library" could be expressed by saying "the place where *I* am is Main Library." Similar problems arise when we consider informa-

---

7. Castañeda was not primarily interested in the metaphysics of belief and the like. He was primarily interested in the logical features of attitude reports whose *that*-clauses contain locutions like "he himself," which Castañeda famously abbreviated "he∗."

tion that is about a specific time. Consider this example from Perry (1979), reprinted in Salmon and Soames (1988):

> [A] professor, who desires to attend the department meeting on time, and believes correctly that it begins at noon, sits motionless in his office at that time. Suddenly he begins to move. What explains his action? A change in belief. He believed all along that the department meeting starts at noon; he came to believe, as he would have put it, that it starts *now*. (1979[1988]: 84)

The professor's new belief is an instance of what is sometimes called belief *de nunc* (of now). On my view, which comes from Lewis, *de nunc* information can also be taken to be a special kind of *de se* information. The idea is that we persist through time by having different stages, or temporal parts, that exist only at particular times. Person stages are the fundamental subjects of the attitudes, and persisting, four-dimensional persons have attitudes in virtue of having parts (stages) that have those attitudes, much like a building that is on fire in virtue of its first few floors being on fire. So, the belief the professor expresses by saying "the meeting starts *now*" could be expressed by saying "the meeting starts at the time when *I* am." And this brings back our old problem, the problem of *de se* belief. (For those who do not accept temporal parts, *de nunc* beliefs raise new, but similar, problems for the doctrine that the contents of our beliefs are propositions whose truth values do not vary from time to time.)

Some philosophers are inclined to maintain that the problem of *de se* belief is a minor, technical problem. I disagree. As I see it, the problem forces us to abandon the dominant conception of the attitudes, viz., dyadic propositionalism, and arguments based upon it ultimately lead us to reject the doctrine of propositions itself. Moreover, *de se* attitudes are neither unimportant nor unusual. As I claimed earlier, they are ubiquitous. There are good reasons to think that our perceptual beliefs are typically *de se*, e.g., my belief that there is a white coffee mug in front of *me*. Commonsense psychology, in its quest to provide explanations of purposeful behavior, must reserve a central role for *de se* attitudes. Think of your belief that you have a pain of a certain sort, your belief that your flight takes off at noon, your desire for a cup of coffee, your desire to be healthy, and so on. The problem suggests that a correct account of belief, desire, and the other cognitive attitudes must, in some sense, reach beyond the realm of propositions. The account I will defend is presented in the next section.

4. The Property Theory of Content

Let's begin this section by reconsidering Geach's question. Suppose we say of a number of people that each of them believes that he himself is clever. What belief are we attributing to all of them? The question incorporates a kind of presupposition. It assumes that what we say of the people is true only if there is something that all of them believe. The view to be discussed in this section entails that such a presupposition is correct. This is the property theory of content, the view that belief, although it is a dyadic relation, is not (in general) a relation between subjects and believed-true propositions. Instead, the contents of beliefs are properties. Properties do not have the kind of truth conditions that propositions have. The property *being clever*, for example, is not the kind of thing whose truth value does not vary from person to person. However, talk about truth is appropriate for properties, insofar as we speak of properties as being true of their instances, e.g., *being clever* is true of every individual who is clever, and false of every one who is not.

What belief, then, are we attributing to the people of whom we said that each one believes himself to be clever? According to the property theory, we are attributing a belief the content of which is the property *being clever*. In general, the content of a *de se* belief is a property that the subject takes himself or herself to have. The presupposition of Geach's question is therefore correct. If we say that each one believes himself to be clever, we are attributing a single belief to all of them. We are characterizing them as psychologically similar in an important way. This should be contrasted with the doctrine of propositions, according to which the people are not said to share any belief, since each one has a distinct belief about himself (e.g., each person might believe the singular proposition, about himself, to the effect that he is clever).

The same goes for Valerie's *de se* belief that she herself is a spy. The content of this belief is the property *being a spy*, which Valerie takes herself to have. This is how the property theory solves the problem of *de se* belief. The contents of such beliefs are properties that the subjects believe themselves to have, not propositions that they believe to be true. Following Lewis (1979), I shall use the term "self-ascription" for the relation between subjects and the properties that they believe themselves to have. Each person in Geach's example, then, is said to self-ascribe the property *being clever*, and Valerie self-ascribes the property *being a spy*. The self-ascription relation is in an important sense necessarily reflexive. To self-ascribe a property is to ascribe it *to yourself* and not to any other thing. This is especially clear on Chisholm's version of the theory, which employs the phrase "direct attribution" rather than "self-ascription." For Chisholm, the most basic form of a belief report is "the property of being F is such that x directly attributes it to y" (1981: 27), which seems to make direct attribution a three-place relation. However, he also affirms this principle concerning direct attribution: "For every x, every y and every z, if x directly attributes z to y, then x is identical with y" (1981: 28). So it is impossible for one person to attribute directly a property to somebody else.

The version of the property theory that I will defend maintains that, in general, belief can be understood as the self-ascription of properties. There is no good reason to restrict self-ascription to special beliefs like Valerie's. For example, when you believe that the smallest mountain is bigger than the largest bicycle, you self-ascribe a property, and when Joe believes that Valerie is a spy, he self-ascribes a property.[8] So, on the view I am defending, all belief turns out to be *de se* belief. Even more generally, properties serve as the contents for all of the so-called propositional attitudes.

Before taking a closer look at this strategy, I would like to consider briefly the nature of properties. To get started on this, let's consider Lewis's property-theoretic diagnosis of the Lingens case, in which Lingens lacks certain *de se*, allegedly nonpropositional, information:

> The more he reads, the more propositions he believes, and the more he is in a position to self-ascribe properties of inhabiting such-and-such a kind of world. But none of this, by itself, can guarantee that he knows where in the world he is. He needs to locate himself not only in logical space but also in ordinary space. He needs to self-ascribe the property of being in aisle five, floor six, of Main Library, Stanford; and this is not one of the properties that corresponds to a proposition. (1983a: 138)

On Lewis's modal realism, a proposition is a set of possible worlds (the worlds where the proposition is true) and a property is a set of possible individuals (those that have the property). A property

---

8. This version of the theory has been defended by Chisholm (1981) and Lewis (1979, 1986: 27–40). Page references to Lewis (1979) will be to the reprinted version in Lewis (1983a). Loar (1976) proposes a more restricted version of the view, according to which certain beliefs, but not all of them, are to be understood in terms of a self-ascription relation between believers and propositional functions.

corresponds to a proposition provided that it contains all and only the inhabitants of every world contained in the proposition. The property *being in Main Library, Stanford*, on Lewis's view, is the set of all actual and possible things that are in (a counterpart of) Main Library, Stanford. Since this set contains certain things in a given world but not others, it does not correspond to a proposition. The content of the information that Lingens lacks, then, is a certain property rather than a proposition.

It seems that, to capture the potential contents of thought, we will have to admit what Lewis (1986) calls an *abundant* conception of properties: "The abundant properties may be as extrinsic, as gruesomely gerrymandered, as miscellaneously disjunctive, as you please. They pay no heed to the qualitative joints, but carve things up every which way" (1986: 59). On Lewis's view, this has the result that any set of possible individuals is a property. The content of my belief that I am left-handed, for example, is the set of possible people who are left-handed. This approach enables Lewis to characterize a person's *total* belief state in terms of her "doxastic alternatives" (1986: 28), i.e., the set of possible people who are all as she believes herself to be.

I prefer to take a more Platonistic view of properties, even the abundant ones, partly because I do not accept Lewis's brand of realism about (merely) possible worlds and individuals. Beyond maintaining that there are such things as properties or attributes, however, I wish to say as little as possible about their nature. Indeed, many nominalists will be able to accept my claims about mental content, although perhaps in a somewhat modified form. But there are reasons to take some sort of realist view about abundant properties, reasons that parallel those for believing in propositions. For example, such properties serve well as the meanings of certain linguistic items. The meaning of the predicate "is round," for instance, is conveniently taken to be the property *being round*, which is exemplified by all round things. While we might not want to say that every predicative expression expresses or designates a property, abundant properties simplify semantics in the way that propositions simplify semantics.

Many philosophers take properties to be *universals*, or entities that can be exemplified by numerically distinct things. This seems to rule out properties such as *being Bill Gates* (or *being identical to Bill Gates*), which could only be exemplified by one individual. I do not mind admitting that such properties exist; perhaps they are the exceptions to the general rule that properties are universals. A similar property is the previously mentioned property *being in Main Library, Stanford*.

These properties entail the existence of particular individuals, in the sense that, if they are exemplified, then some particular individual exists (Gates, Main Library, etc.). However, as will become clear later in this section, I deny that these properties ever characterize the contents of our attitudes, and so I would also be happy with an account that denied the existence of properties of this sort. (These are the properties that either are, or contain in some way, individual essences or haecceities.)

The guiding insight behind the property theory is that some cognitive attitudes are not adequately characterized by the assignment of propositions as their contents. Some philosophers of mind, who do not like to talk of properties, might be able to shape this insight into an analogue of the property theory. For example, if in addition to or instead of properties, there exist Fregean senses or concepts, e.g., in the sense of Peacocke (1992), then the property theory could be recast in terms of senses or concepts. What is important is the *non-propositionality* of at least some attitude content. There must be some attitudes the contents of which are merely the senses of predicative expressions, for example, and not the senses of entire sentences (i.e., Fregean thoughts).

On the strong version of the property theory that I favor, the content of every instance of a cognitive attitude is a property. On a weaker version, properties are the contents of some, but not all, of our attitudes. For example, the content of one of my beliefs might be a property that I self-ascribe, while the content of another might be a proposition that I accept. The argument for the strong version of the theory is primarily methodological. It is necessary to refer to the logical relationships between the contents of attitudes in the systematization of our commonsense psychological explanations of behavior, inferences, and so on. If the contents of our beliefs and other attitudes are uniform in nature rather than varied, these relationships will be much simpler to characterize.

In addition to the methodological considerations that favor the uniformity of contents, there are some other reasons to prefer the strong version of the property theory. In a single act of believing, for example, I might believe that many people are wealthy but I am not. My belief in this case seems to have a single content. If the weak version of the property theory is true, the content of my belief that I am not wealthy is a property (since this belief is irreducibly *de se*). As a result, if we are to preserve the idea that my belief has a single content, we should say that the content of my belief that many people are wealthy is a property too. Moreover, it seems intuitively clear that belief is a single phenomenon. However, self-ascribing a property, on the one hand, and accepting or believing a proposition, on the other, seem to be different kinds of thing, i.e., different relations. In light of the problem of *de se* belief, this gives us good reason to analyze belief in a proposition in terms of the self-ascription of a property.

Suppose I believe that there are spies. According to the doctrine of propositions, let us suppose, the content of my belief is the proposition *that there are spies*. In this case, I wish to follow Lewis and Chisholm and say that the content of my belief is the property *being such that there are spies*. This is how the strong version of the property theory provides uniform contents for belief. Whenever the doctrine of propositions says that the content of a belief is a proposition, *P*, the property theory says that the content is the property *being such that P*. This is a kind of global property that corresponds to the relevant proposition. (Different accounts of propositions and properties might have somewhat different ways of describing this correspondence between all propositions, on the one hand, and some properties, on the other.) The treatment of the other attitudes is analogous to that of belief. Special conceptual repertoires or psychological abilities are not needed for these properties to be assigned as mental contents. That is, if you can believe the proposition *P*, you can self-ascribe the property *being such that P*.

The strong version of the property theory thus requires that there are properties like *being such that there are spies, being such that not all swans are white*, etc., but on the abundant conception of properties, this is not problematic. Again, such properties enable us to provide a unified account of the contents of cognitive attitudes. (As we will see in chapter 5, attitudes about particular objects, or *de re* attitudes, can also be assigned properties as contents and therefore be represented as attitudes *de se*.) So, as I shall take it, the property theory accounts for *de se* beliefs and desires in a way that is unified with beliefs and desires generally. Given that many of our beliefs and desires are *de se*, this gives us the advantage of having a single account on which the logical relationships among attitude contents are conveniently described.

From this point on, I shall suppose that the property theory simply is the strong version of the theory just sketched. Let's formulate the view as follows:[9]

---

9. As with dyadic propositionalism, I am here formulating the property theory as a theory about the nature of *belief*. However, we should take these views to be intended to apply in an analogous fashion to the other cognitive attitudes as well.

Property Theory of Content: Necessarily, a subject, *S*, believes
something if and only if there is a property *F* such that *S* self-
ascribes *F*. Belief is a dyadic relation—viz., self-ascription—
between a subject and a property. The content of a belief is
the property that the subject self-ascribes.

The remainder of this book will be devoted to considering arguments in favor of the property theory, comparing it with alternative
views about the nature of mental content, defending it against objections, and applying it to some important issues and problems in the
philosophy of mind.

My view of the cognitive attitudes is an internalist one, insofar
as I think that the contents of attitudes are narrow. That is, on my
view, the psychological property of having an attitude with a certain
content is narrow, in the sense that it is completely determined by,
or supervenes on, the intrinsic properties of the subject (in particular, the microstructural properties of the subject's brain). On such a
view, we explain behavior not by attributing beliefs whose content
is wide (i.e., not narrow in the sense defined above), but by using
narrow-content beliefs together with facts about the relevant subject's relation to his or her environment. For example, suppose we
explain why I opened my refrigerator by pointing to the facts that I
wanted a beer and believed that some beer was in it. Proponents of
wide content are inclined to put my refrigerator into the content of
this belief. Proponents of narrow content are not so inclined, since
I could have been in the very same mental state even if somebody
had previously swapped my refrigerator for a qualitatively identical one. We explain my action in terms of beliefs and desires with
narrow content (e.g., wanting beer and believing that I am related
in such-and-such ways to something with beer in it), together with
the nonpsychological fact that I am related in such-and-such ways
to my refrigerator.

My project, then, is to motivate and defend the conjunction of
the property theory of content and a version of internalism, or individualism, about mental content. Let's use the following formulation
of such a view:

Internalism: Our psychological properties supervene locally on
our intrinsic, physical properties, in the sense that any two
individuals who share all of their intrinsic, physical properties
(molecule-for-molecule duplicates) must share all of their
psychological properties as well.

Experiencing a sensation, having a perceptual experience, and having a belief with a certain content are all psychological properties. I will be particularly concerned with belief-content properties, i.e., properties that consist in having a belief with a certain content. According to internalism, such properties are intrinsic to the individuals who have them, and so, as the saying goes, belief is in the head. What you believe is fully determined by your intrinsic properties, and so any molecule-for-molecule duplicate of you will have all and only the beliefs that you have. I take this to be the commonsense view. However, at present, it is held by probably only a small minority of philosophers of mind. Later in the book, especially in chapter 2, section 4, and also in chapter 7, I will explore and defend this view more thoroughly.

For now, let us just note one consequence of internalism for the theory of mental content. A while ago, we considered the property *being in Main Library, Stanford*. According to Lewis, this is the informational content that Lingens, who is lost in the Stanford Library, lacks. If he were to self-ascribe this property, perhaps in virtue of asking someone nearby about his location, he would thereby come to know where he is. As I see it, however, this property is not quite the information that Lingens lacks, and not quite what he would self-ascribe were he to discover his location. Perhaps this is really Lewis's view as well, and perhaps Lewis was using this property merely for illustrative purposes.[10] The reason for this is the internalist view of intentional states and their contents.

To see this point clearly, let's imagine a Twin Earth example. Suppose that Lingens has a doppelgänger, a molecule-for-molecule duplicate, on Twin Earth. Since Lingens and Twin Lingens are intrinsic duplicates, internalism entails that they share all of their belief-content properties. Given the property theory, this means that, for every property, Lingens self-ascribes it if and only if Twin Lingens does. So, either they both self-ascribe the property *being in Main Library, Stanford*, or neither of them does. It is hard to see how Twin Lingens could self-ascribe this property, however, since he is on Twin Earth and has had no causal interaction whatsoever with Stanford. So, it seems reasonable to conclude that neither of them self-ascribes this property and, as a result, that the property does not characterize the information Lingens lacks in his ignorant state.

---

10. This is because Lewis himself was an internalist of a certain sort, although perhaps not quite the sort characterized in the text. See, e.g., Lewis (1979, 1994).

The argument can be made more forcefully by stipulating that Lingens and Twin Lingens are so careful with their beliefs that whatever they believe is true. This is clearly metaphysically possible. Suppose that Lingens and Twin Lingens come to have beliefs that they express by uttering the words "I am in Main Library, Stanford." Now, assume for *reductio* that Lingens and Twin Lingens both self-ascribe the property *being in Main Library, Stanford*. Given our stipulation, they are both correct, and hence they both have this property. But Twin Lingens is not in Stanford; he is millions of miles away in Twin Stanford. So, our assumption entails that Twin Lingens has and lacks a certain property, which is a contradiction. We are thus led to conclude that Lingens and Twin Lingens do not both self-ascribe the property *being in Main Library, Stanford*. Internalism then implies that neither of them self-ascribes this property, and again we must conclude that the information Lingens lacks in Perry's example is not given by this property.

The upshot of all of this is that, if internalism is correct, we do not self-ascribe properties that contain or entail individual essences, like the property *being in Main Library* or the property *being Bill Gates*. These properties are importantly similar to singular or pseudo singular propositions. Just as the internalist who accepts the doctrine of propositions maintains that we do not believe singular propositions, the internalist who accepts the property theory must say that we do not self-ascribe properties relevantly like the ones above. What property, then, would Lingens come to self-ascribe were he to find out where he is? One possible way to answer this question is to go metalinguistic. For example, we might say that Lingens would self-ascribe the property *being in a library called "Main Library" at a school called "Stanford,"* or some such property. Lingens and Twin Lingens could both self-ascribe this property, and both would be correct. We need not take a metalinguistic approach here; the crucial point is that the properties we self-ascribe are purely qualitative properties, i.e., ones that do not involve or incorporate particular individuals or individual essences.

Earlier in this chapter, we noted that cognitive attitudes like belief and desire seem to have contents that can be true or false. (Again, we tend not to speak of desires as being true or false, but we do say that desires are satisfied when their contents are true and unsatisfied otherwise.) One might think that the property theory has a problem with accommodating this fact. After all, properties are not things that can be true or false. The doctrine of propositions has no problem here. To have a true belief is to have a belief the content of which is a true proposition; to have a false belief is to have a belief the content of which is a false proposition. I would like to conclude this section by suggesting that the property theory can do justice to the intuition that beliefs have contents that can be true or false. We have already seen that truth talk applies to properties. A given property is true of the things that have it, and is false of the things that do not. So, on the property theory, a subject has a true belief (i.e., believes truly) when she self-ascribes a property that she has, and a subject has a false belief when she self-ascribes a property that she does not have. In this way, the property theorist can make sense of the intuition or platitude that the contents of our beliefs and desires are capable of being true or false.

CHAPTER TWO

IN FAVOR OF THE
PROPERTY THEORY

This chapter sets out the case for the property theory of content. In the first section, we take a look at an argument based upon Perry's widely discussed case of the messy shopper. This is an argument against dyadic propositionalism, which implies that change in belief is always change in a believed-true proposition, and will pave the way for the property theory. In the second section, we consider Lewis's fascinating case of the two gods. This example serves as the basis for a compelling argument for the property theory. In the third section, I present arguments from psychological internalism and physicalism in favor of the property theory. The idea is that the doctrine of propositions is logically incompatible with internalism and with physicalism, and so the proponent of either of these views needs to reject this doctrine together with any view that entails it (including the triadic view of belief). This leaves a void that is best filled by the property theory. Finally, in the fourth section, I argue that the property theory provides the best explanation of the various phenomena associated with *de se* attitudes. This includes Chisholm's suggestion that the theory provides the best way to make sense of the logical relations between certain types of belief attribution, and more besides.

1. Perry's Messy Shopper and the Argument
from Explanation

Perry (1979) presents his case of the messy shopper as a puzzle for the view that belief is irreducibly a dyadic relation between a subject and a proposition, the view that we are calling dyadic propositionalism. Perry suggests that certain features of some of our attitudes about ourselves tell against this view. He calls these attitudes "locating beliefs" and describes them as "one's beliefs about where one is, when it is, and who one is" (1979[1988]: 85).[1] He describes the case of the messy shopper as follows:

> I once followed a trail of sugar on a supermarket floor, pushing my trolley down the aisle on one side of a tall counter and back along the aisle on the other, seeking the shopper with the torn bag to tell him he was making a mess. With each trip around the counter, the trail became thicker. But I seemed unable to catch up. Finally it dawned on me. I was the shopper I was trying to catch. (1979[1988]: 83)

The proponent of dyadic propositionalism needs to pick out two propositions: first, the one Perry believed before his epiphany, viz., the content of the belief he would have expressed by saying something like "the shopper who left this trail of sugar is making a mess"; and second, the one he later comes to believe, the content of the belief he would express by saying "I am making a mess." Perry makes this need more vivid by noting that the second belief must explain a change in his behavior, a change that the first belief cannot even partly explain:

> I believed at the outset that the shopper with a torn bag was making a mess. And I was right. But I did not believe that I was making a mess. That seems to be something I came to believe. And when I came to believe that, I stopped following the trail around the counter, and rearranged the torn bag in my trolley. (1979[1988]: 83)

We explain why Perry stopped to rearrange the bag of sugar in part by conveying information about the relevant change in his beliefs. Since this change in belief (partly) explains his clean-up behavior, the proponent of dyadic propositionalism must be able to provide the propositions to give a plausible account of the change. However, identifying the proposition Perry believes when he finally says "*I* am

---

1. All page references for Perry (1979) are to the reprinted version in Salmon and Soames (1988).

making a mess," the proposition that allegedly explains his clean-up behavior, is no easy task. We have already reviewed the reasoning for this, at least in large part, when we considered the problem of *de se* belief in chapter 1, section 3. So, we are in a position to formulate and discuss the following argument against dyadic propositionalism based on the case of the messy shopper.

The Argument from Explanation

1. If dyadic propositionalism is true, then whenever an agent's behavior is partly explained by the acquisition of a new belief, there is some proposition such that the agent's coming to believe it partly explains his or her behavior.
2. Perry's clean-up behavior is partly explained by the acquisition of a new belief.
3. There is no proposition such that Perry's coming to believe it partly explains his clean-up behavior.
4. ∴ Dyadic propositionalism is not true (from 1–3).

Here, the key premise is line 3. Before we review the reasoning in favor of premise 3, however, let's take a moment or two and briefly discuss the first two premises. Premise 1 follows from the claims made by dyadic propositionalism. If this view is true, there is nothing more to one's acquiring a new belief than one's coming to believe a proposition that one did not previously believe. If Perry's *de se* belief that he himself is making a mess is an instance of a dyadic relation between Perry and a given proposition, then his coming to believe this proposition must explain his behavior if the behavior can be explained partly in terms of his beliefs. Premise 2 asserts that his behavior can in fact be explained, in part, by his coming to have a new belief. This is extremely reasonable, although philosophers will no doubt disagree about the details of the explanation. It is hard to deny, however, that an adequate explanation of Perry's clean-up behavior would make essential reference to his belief that he himself was the mess maker, or some such *de se* belief. For simplicity, let's assume that the clean-up behavior can be completely explained with a certain belief-desire pair, e.g., by attributing to Perry the belief that he himself was making a mess, and the desire to avoid making messes. (Note that these are both instances of *de se* attitudes.) The argument thus hinges on the explanatory role of Perry's belief that he himself is making a mess. Given his standing desire to be neat, his coming to have this belief explains why he stops his pursuit and starts cleaning up.

Premise 3 claims that there is no proposition such that Perry's coming to believe it explains his behavior. The reasoning here is essentially the same as the reasoning given earlier, during the discussion of the problem of *de se* belief. The dyadic propositionalist, it is alleged, cannot meet the challenge of providing a proposition that will allow Perry's belief that he himself is making a mess to play the relevant explanatory role. Before we pursue the reasoning in a bit more detail, let's eliminate one way of trying to meet the challenge. One might say that it is easy to identify the needed proposition, in particular, that the proposition the belief in which explains Perry's behavior is simply the proposition *that I am making a mess*. However, there is a big problem with this suggestion, since there is no such proposition. This is because the sentence type "I am making a mess" expresses a proposition only relative to a context in which it is or might be uttered by a speaker. Different speakers will express different propositions in uttering this sentence, some of them true and others false. The linguistic meaning of "I am making a mess" is more like a function from speakers into propositions, or a *property* of speakers, than a proposition. But the use of indexical pronouns like "I" or "he himself" seems essential to explaining Perry's behavior. For this reason, Perry (1979[1988]: 88) claims that propositions lack an "indexical ingredient" that his belief must have, given its explanatory role.

Premise 3 relies upon the claim that the explanatory role of Perry's belief that he himself is making a mess cannot be played by belief in any proposition. The rationale for premise 3 goes as follows: If Perry's coming to believe a certain proposition is what explains his behavior, then the proposition must be singular or pseudo singular, on one hand, or purely descriptive or qualitative, on the other. (Purely descriptive propositions, on the structured-propositions perspective at any rate, are those whose constituents are standard Fregean senses, or concepts, or properties, or the like. Such propositions do not contain particular individuals or nonqualitative individual essences.) However, neither alternative yields a plausible candidate, since belief in every such candidate is consistent with the lack of the sort of *de se* belief that the explanation of Perry's behavior requires.

Let's take purely descriptive propositions first. Suppose a dyadic propositionalist were to identify a purely descriptive proposition, *P*, and claim that Perry's coming to believe P partly explains his clean-up behavior. We know a bit about what P must be like, given that it is alleged to be both purely descriptive and the content of Perry's *de se* belief that he himself is making a mess. Proposition P must somehow pick out Perry by means of some qualitative property, set of properties, or individual concept, and associate this with the concept or property *making a mess*. This means that we should be able to give the truth conditions for P along these lines: For some property F, P is true if and only if exactly one thing has F, and whatever has F has the property *making a mess*.[2] In this case, Perry must pick himself out in thought (correctly) as the one and only thing that has property F, i.e., by means of grasping F or the concept of F.

Let's suppose that the dyadic propositionalist has identified this qualitative property or individual concept, F. In a nutshell, then, such a dyadic propositionalist's claim is that the belief that partly explains Perry's clean-up behavior is his belief in the proposition *that the F is making a mess*. However, it is extremely implausible that such a belief could, in conjunction with his desire to avoid mess making, explain why he begins to clean up. Perry makes this point as follows:

> [E]ven if I was thinking of myself as, say, the only bearded philosopher in a Safeway store west of the Mississippi, the fact that I came to believe that the only such philosopher was making a mess explains my action only on the assumption that I believed that I was the only such philosopher, which brings in the indexical again. (1979[1988]: 88)

The point here is that it seems quite clear that Perry could believe the proposition *that the only bearded philosopher in a Safeway west of the Mississippi is making a mess* without believing that he himself is making a mess, since he could fail to believe himself (uniquely) to have the property *being a bearded philosopher in a Safeway store west of the Mississippi*. And the same goes for any qualitative property or individual concept. So, belief in some purely descriptive proposition could not play the explanatory role of Perry's *de se* belief that he himself is making a mess, i.e., it could not provide the belief component of the belief-desire explanation of his clean-up behavior.

The dyadic propositionalist cannot say that Perry's coming to believe some purely descriptive proposition partly explains (in the

---

2. Here, F might very well be a complex disjunction or conjunction of more basic properties.

relevant sense) his clean-up behavior. The other option is to say that what explains his behavior is his coming to believe a singular or pseudo singular proposition, where the truth conditions are not completely determined by descriptive information. In this case, let's take singular propositions first. Might the dyadic propositionalist say that Perry's clean-up behavior is explained by his coming to believe the singular proposition *that Perry is making a mess*? (We might represent this proposition with the structure <Perry, *making a mess*>.) Even granting the externalist perspective required here, there are a few reasons that we should resist this alternative.[3]

First, the most common views according to which people can believe singular propositions entail that Perry believed <Perry, *making a mess*> before it finally dawned on him that he himself was the mess maker. When he started following the trail of sugar, for example, he came to believe that the shopper who was leaving the trail was making a mess. Since he himself was this shopper, he formed a belief about himself, to the effect that he was making a mess. This, on the most common views allowing belief in singular propositions, means that he believed <Perry, *making a mess*>. Even views on which it is more difficult to believe a singular proposition, e.g., views on which perceptual contact with the object of belief is necessary, are in trouble here. This is because we can imagine that Perry perceived himself in some way and took the person he perceived to be making a mess, without believing himself to be making a mess. In fact, Perry imagines just this:

> Suppose there were mirrors at either end of the counter so that as I pushed my trolley down the aisle in pursuit I saw myself in the mirror. I take what I see to be the reflection of the messy shopper going up the aisle on the other side, not realizing that what I am really seeing is a reflection of a reflection of myself. I point and say, truly, "I believe that he is making a mess." (1979[1988]: 92)

---

3. Instead of <Perry, *making a mess*>, we might want to identify some token sensory or perceptual experience of Perry's—call it E—and say that he believes the proposition *that the subject of E is making a mess*. This is a singular proposition about E, not about Perry. In addition to sharing some of the difficulties discussed in the text, this suggestion lacks an important sort of psychological realism. Certainly, Perry can think to himself "I am making a mess" and not identify himself as the unique person who is having a particular experience. So this suggestion is a nonstarter from the psychological point of view.

Of course, if Perry believed the proposition <Perry, *making a mess*>, and he believed it *before* the truth finally dawned on him, then his coming to believe it cannot explain his clean-up behavior. The issues here are similar to certain ones discussed in relation to the problem of *de se* belief. If following a person's trail of sugar, or seeing him in a mirror, are relations that are sufficient for believing a singular proposition about him, then someone with merely a third-person perspective on Perry could believe the singular proposition <Perry, *making a mess*>. And if this is the case, then Perry could believe this proposition without believing *de se* that he himself is making a mess, and belief in this proposition cannot play the explanatory role of that *de se* belief.

So, the dyadic propositionalist who attempts to explain Perry's clean-up behavior in terms of his belief in the relevant singular proposition must say that *only* Perry could believe this proposition and, in general, that any given person can believe propositions that no other person can believe (i.e., singular propositions about himself or herself). This is to admit the existence of first-person propositions.[4] The claim that Perry can believe the proposition *that Perry is making a mess*, for example, but nobody else can grasp or believe it, even in principle, seems implausibly ad hoc. Moreover, this version of the dyadic propositionalist view cannot explain why believing this proposition should make it the case that Perry believes *himself* to be making a mess. Why is it impossible for Perry to believe the proposition *that Perry is making a mess* without believing himself to be making one? For example, if Perry does not know who he is, it seems that he could know exactly which individual is making a mess, and know every bit of information about this individual down to the last detail (including his name, rank, and serial number) without believing *himself* to be this individual.

We will consider these issues again, especially when we take a look at dyadic propositionalism as an alternative to the property theory in chapter 3, section 3. For now, let's think about whether pseudo singular propositions, in some form or other, might do the job better than either purely descriptive or singular propositions. We characterized a pseudo singular proposition as a proposition that has the same

---

4. Perry (1979[1988]: 95–96) considers and dismisses propositions of this sort, which he calls "propositions of limited accessibility." In chapter 3, section 3, I argue that all forms of dyadic propositionalism are committed to first-person propositions.

truth conditions as some singular proposition. For example, the singular proposition *that Perry is making a mess* is true if and only if Perry is making a mess, and there might be a proposition that has the same truth conditions but does not contain Perry himself as a constituent. We are trying to determine whether the dyadic propositionalist can supply a plausible propositional content for Perry's *de se* belief that he himself is making a mess, and thereby supply a proposition the belief in which partly explains his clean-up behavior. I take it that such a proposition must be true if and only if Perry is making a mess, since the propositions we are considering are not purely descriptive and there seems to be no other plausible truth condition. In any case, if the dyadic propositionalist offers a proposition with different truth conditions, she must surely explain away the strong intuition that Perry's belief is true if and only if he is making a mess.

One way to construct a pseudo singular proposition along these lines would be to use Perry's individual essence or haecceity, assuming that he has one. Such an essence would have to be a property that is not wholly qualitative, even if it contains or entails qualitative properties such as *being human*. This is because it has to distinguish Perry from his possible doppelgängers. We might take such a proposition to look something like this: <*being Perry, making a mess*>. Or, perhaps we might take it to look like this: <*the x such that x is identical to Perry, making a mess*>. In any case, these propositions face the same drawbacks and problems as singular propositions do. They must also be first-person propositions, or private propositions that could be grasped and believed by only one person. Moreover, assigning such a proposition as the content of Perry's belief requires that he can, in some sense, conceive or grasp his own haecceity or individual essence, even while not giving undue thought to himself. This seems doubtful, to say the least. A similar criticism applies, of course, to the use of singular propositions.

I would like to discuss briefly one final version of the pseudo singular proposition strategy, this time along Fregean lines. (We will return to it in ch. 3, sec. 3.) While he was discussing the sense of the word "I," Frege (1918[1988]: 42) maintained that "every one is presented to himself in a special and primitive way in which he is presented to no one else."[5] Applied to Perry's *de se* belief, this suggests that the content is a proposition that only Perry could believe, in vir-

---

5. This quotation is taken from the version of Frege (1918) that is translated as "Thoughts" in Salmon and Soames (1988).

tue of its containing a mode of presentation of Perry that only Perry could grasp. This in turn seems to suggest that the mode of presentation, or sense, does not contribute purely descriptive information to the proposition. (At any rate, if the proposition were purely descriptive, we would be led back to the problems for that view discussed previously.) So, on this view, what Perry believes is a proposition that contains his "self-concept"—i.e., a nonqualitative mode of presentation that presents or designates Perry, but not in virtue of any descriptive fit—along with the sense of the predicate "is making a mess." In addition to postulating first-person propositions, this strategy also seems ad hoc and mysterious, since it is unclear what nonqualitative modes of presentation are and how they do their work.

We can sum up this discussion as follows: Perry believed himself to be making a mess; but he did not believe this merely in virtue of believing the proposition *that the F is making a mess* (for any qualitative property *F*), or of believing the singular proposition *that Perry is making a mess*, or of believing a corresponding pseudo singular proposition. It is therefore very plausible to think that premise 3 of the argument from explanation is true. There is no proposition such that Perry's clean-up behavior is explained in the relevant way by his coming to believe it. So, it is very plausible to think that the argument from explanation is sound. This is my view. It is also my view that the property theory provides the most satisfying solution to the messy shopper puzzle. What explains Perry's behavior, in conjunction with his desire for cleanliness, is the fact that he comes to self-ascribe the property *making a mess*, which he did not self-ascribe until the truth finally dawned on him.

Perry's own solution to the puzzle is different. It is a version of the triadic view of belief. (Indeed, it is reasonable to think that accepting the argument from explanation leaves one with a dilemma: Accept either the property theory or the triadic view.) Perry distinguishes between the proposition he believed, and the *belief state* in virtue of which he believed it. We will examine the triadic view in chapter 3, section 1, but for now we can illustrate Perry's account by saying that, on it, belief is a relation among a subject, a proposition, and a sentential meaning, or *character*, in something like Kaplan's (1989) sense. When a given proposition serves as the content of your belief, you believe that proposition under some sentential meaning, which characterizes your belief state. In the case of the messy shopper, what explains Perry's cleaning-up behavior is his coming to believe the proposition *that Perry is making a mess* under the meaning of the sentence "I am making a mess." This meaning can be taken to be the sentence's character, a function from a context to a singular proposition about the agent or speaker S of the context, to the effect that S is making a mess. Before the truth finally dawned on him, Perry might have believed this same proposition, but only under a different sentential meaning (perhaps the meaning of "he is making a mess," if Perry had pointed to the man in the supermarket mirror). So, what explains Perry's clean-up behavior is a change in his belief state, and not his coming to believe a new proposition.

The argument from explanation, as I see it, eliminates what is probably still the dominant conception of the attitudes and one of the property theory's chief rivals, viz., dyadic propositionalism. The argument also gives some indirect support to the property theory, when we begin to compare its explanation of the messy shopper case with those of alternative accounts. We now turn to more direct arguments for the property theory.

2. Lewis's Case of the Two Gods

In this section, we shall consider an argument based upon an example given by Lewis (1979). Lewis presents a case that, he alleges, shows that the contents of some beliefs cannot be propositions, and hence that we should not in general consider belief to be a propositional attitude. As we shall see, this case proves troublesome for any view that entails the doctrine of propositions, and even for versions of the triadic view that deny the doctrine of propositions. The example is truly a thought experiment for the ages, the case of the two gods:

> Consider the case of the two gods. They inhabit a certain possible world, and they know exactly which world it is. Therefore they know every proposition that is true at their world. Insofar as knowledge is a propositional attitude, they are omniscient. Still I can imagine them to suffer ignorance: neither one knows which of the two he is. They are not exactly alike. One lives on top of the tallest mountain and throws down manna; the other lives on top of the coldest mountain and throws down thunderbolts. Neither one knows whether he lives on the tallest mountain or on the coldest mountain; nor whether he throws manna or thunderbolts. (1983a: 139)

This is a somewhat bizarre example, but it does seem that the gods "inhabit a certain possible world," i.e., that this is a metaphysically possible scenario. How could the gods suffer ignorance in this case? Well, we can imagine that the gods always have qualitatively identical experiences. Lewis suggests that the gods might lack the beliefs that they do because "they have an equally perfect view of every part of their world, and hence cannot identify the perspectives from which they view it" (1983a: 139). This also seems possible, and if it were the case, then neither perspective would allow its subject to self-ascribe an identifying property like *being the one and only god on top of the tallest mountain.*[6] Since the gods believe every proposition that is true at their world but could still truly believe more than they in fact do, the argument goes, the contents of the missing beliefs cannot be propositions.

I think it would be useful to examine a formally valid version of this argument in favor of the property theory. Let's consider this one:

The Two Gods Argument

1. Each of the two gods believes every true proposition, but could have a true belief that he does not actually have.
2. If (1), then there can be beliefs the contents of which are not propositions.
3. If there can be beliefs the contents of which are not propositions, then the property theory is true.
4. ∴ The property theory is true (from 1–3).

On Lewis's view, a proposition is a set of possible worlds. Let's accept this conception, at least for the time being, and review the reasoning for the premises above in light of it. (We need not accept Lewis's account of the nature of possible worlds.) After that, we will consider whether moving to a different conception of propositions makes the argument any less persuasive. I shall suggest that it does not.

The first premise is a conjunction of two claims about the example. As Lewis sees it, the first premise is true because each of the gods knows exactly which world is his. The idea is that each god's total belief state is given by the set whose only member is his own possible world. This set is the intersection of every proposition that each god believes. Although this type of omniscience is extraordinary, it does seem possible. (In

---

6. The case probably also requires that the gods lack a certain kind of self-consciousness, or access to their own thoughts or utterances, that we typically have. For discussion, see O'Brien (1994: 280–281) and Robbins (2004: 66–73). Nevertheless, the example seems coherent.

claiming that the gods know exactly which world is theirs, Lewis is implying that they can distinguish it from qualitatively indiscernible worlds, if there are any. More on this shortly.) The second conjunct of premise 1 is also true in the thought experiment. Even though the gods live atop their mountains, neither one knows whether he is on the tallest or the coldest mountain. So each god could come to have a true belief that he does not actually have (whether such a belief could be justified is another matter). In possible-worlds talk, premise 1 can be summed up by saying that each god knows exactly where he is located in logical space, but not exactly where he is located in ordinary space.

The second premise seems compelling. Every true proposition is already an object of each god's beliefs. The class of true propositions is exhausted in this way, but for each god there are true beliefs that he could have but doesn't. So, anything that could serve as the content of one of the missing beliefs cannot be a proposition. If true beliefs are true in virtue of their contents, which seems undeniable, then premise 2 is secure.

According to premise 3, if there can be beliefs the contents of which are not propositions, then the property theory is true. The support for this claim comes in two stages. First, it is extremely plausible to think that, if the content of a belief is not a proposition, then it is a property (or something very much like a property). One way to have a true belief is to take yourself to have a property that you have. For example, if the god on the tallest mountain were somehow to come to believe that he himself lived on the tallest mountain, his belief would consist in his self-ascribing the property *living on the tallest mountain*. Second, if there can be beliefs the contents of which are not propositions, then the doctrine of propositions is false. This, in turn, rules out dyadic propositionalism and the triadic view as accounts of belief content.[7] The only other serious alternatives would seem to be the property theory and its weaker cousin, a bifurcated theory according to which some content is given by propositions and some is given by properties. The (strong) property theory provides uniform contents for attitudes and is intuitively more satisfying, as was argued in chapter 1, section 4.

The two gods argument seems sound, if we take propositions to be sets of worlds. However, the argument has been criticized even on this conception of propositions. One such critic is Stalnaker (1981),

---

7. That is, it rules out any version of the triadic view that takes contents to be propositions. Other variants will be discussed in chapter 3, section 1. As we will see, all such variants have disadvantages that the property theory does not have.

who thinks that if the gods really do suffer ignorance, they do not know *every* proposition that is true at their world. (We shall take a closer look at Stalnaker's dyadic propositionalism in ch. 3, sec. 3, but it will be helpful to sketch his view of the case of the two gods here.) According to Stalnaker, the two gods example is

> a case of ignorance of which of two indiscernible possible worlds is actual. One of these possible worlds is the actual world (assuming that the theologian's story is true), while the other is like it except that the god who is in fact on the tallest mountain is instead on the coldest mountain, with all the properties which the god on the coldest mountain in fact has (1981: 143).

Let's call the world that Lewis describes *W*. Let's also use *TM* and *CM* as names for the god on the tallest mountain in *W* and for the god on the coldest mountain in *W*, respectively. According to Stalnaker, there is a world that is qualitatively exactly like *W* but differs in that the gods have swapped places and properties. Let's call this world *V*. In *V*, *TM* is on the coldest mountain and *CM* is on the tallest mountain. Stalnaker relies on a distinction between purely descriptive or qualitative propositions, on the one hand, and pseudo singular or nonqualitative ones, on the other. If we allow Lewis to stipulate, for example, that *TM* is ignorant in *W* about his location, then this must mean that he doesn't know which of *W* or *V* is actual. So, on Stalnaker's view, he is ignorant of at least one nonqualitative proposition (one that is true at *W* but false at *V*). In a nutshell, then, Lewis cannot claim both that the gods are ignorant about their locations, etc., and that they are omniscient with respect to *all* propositions, qualitative and nonqualitative.

Stalnaker's position involves a doctrine called "haecceitism" and a technique called "diagonalization." Haecceitists maintain that individuals have nonqualitative essences, or haecceities, and that qualitatively indiscernible worlds can be distinct; but they make an even stronger claim. We can take haecceitism to be the view that things have nonqualitative essences, but do not have any qualitative properties essentially.[8] This is how *TM* can inhabit world *V* with all the

---

8. It is often characterized in other ways. For example, there is Lewis's (1986) formulation that there exist possible worlds that are qualitatively indiscernible but differ with respect to representation *de re*, i.e., with respect to which individuals are represented as existing. Lewis (1979) notes that haecceitists can distinguish *W* and *V*, in which the two gods have traded places, and thereby claim that the gods (in *W*) do not know *every* proposition that holds at their world (1983a: 140). Stalnaker (1981) embraces this haecceitist strategy.

qualitative properties that CM has in W. What makes him TM there is his nonqualitative haecceity, *being TM*.

Diagonalization is a bit trickier, and I will say more about it later. The basic idea can be illustrated by considering the following sentence:

(1) I live on the tallest mountain.

In world W, an (actual or possible) utterance of (1) by TM would express a proposition that is true at W but false at V, since his token of "I" rigidly designates himself and he lives on the tallest mountain in W but not in V. In world V, too, an (actual or possible) utterance of (1) by TM would express a proposition that is true at W but false at V, since his token of "I" again rigidly designates himself. Given that W and V are the only worlds relevant to attributing attitudes to TM in the present context, we can form a matrix, or *propositional concept*, of (1) like this:

$$\begin{array}{ccc} & W & V \\ W & T & F \\ V & T & F \end{array}$$

Here, the *diagonal proposition* is true at W but false at V. It is $\{W\}$. (So are the horizontal propositions; see the next example.) According to Stalnaker, this diagonal proposition is the belief that TM would express by uttering a token of (1). It is what TM would believe if he were to believe that he himself lives on the tallest mountain. So, on Stalnaker's view, if TM can distinguish W from V, he would know this proposition and hence know his location. In this way, Stalnaker argues that Lewis cannot assume both that TM knows he is in W rather than V and that he is ignorant of his spatial location.

The example above might not make the point of diagonalization clear. So let's consider another example. Suppose that, in W, TM looks upon the world and somehow demonstrates the god on the tallest mountain, and in so demonstrating utters a token:

(2) He lives on the tallest mountain.

What belief does TM express? By diagonalizing, Stalnaker arrives at the result that the content of this belief is the proposition that contains both W and V. In W, TM's utterance of (2) expresses a proposition that is true at W but false at V, since his token of "he" refers directly to, and rigidly designates, TM, who lives on the tallest mountain in W but not in V. But the utterance of (2) occurs in V as well as in W. In V, the utterance expresses a proposition that is true at V but false at W, since this token of "he" refers directly to, and rigidly designates, CM, who lives atop the tallest mountain in V but not in W. On this view, then, the content of the belief that TM expresses in uttering (2) is the diagonal proposition represented in the propositional concept below, which is true at W and V:

$$
\begin{array}{ccc}
 & W & V \\
W & T & F \\
V & F & T \\
\end{array}
$$

Haecceitism and diagonalization thus provide Stalnaker with an objection to premise 1 of the two gods argument. As Stalnaker puts it: "One cannot just stipulate that the god knows that he is in W and not in V, for on the proposed explanation, that amounts to the assumption that he knows which mountain he is on" (1981: 144). What should we make of this objection? I would like to suggest that it is not persuasive. As far as claims concerning essence or representation *de re* go, haecceitism is extremely implausible. And there is good reason to believe that diagonalization does not help to account for the nature of the gods' ignorance about where they are. Let's take these points in turn.

According to the kind of haecceitism required by Stalnaker, in order for some individual at another possible world to be you, it needs only your haecceity and it could have any other properties. For instance (to borrow an example from Lewis), you could have been a poached egg. This is how TM can inhabit world V with all the qualitative properties that CM has in W. However, this is extremely implausible, since we might imagine that, in W, TM and CM are as different from each other as are Frank Sinatra and Sammy Davis Jr., or much more different. Surely, some moderate form of essentialism is much more plausible than haecceitism is. Even one who is inclined toward haecceitism must admit that the fact that Stalnaker's view of content is committed to haecceitism is a disadvantage for it, especially relative to views, like the property theory, which make no similar metaphysical commitments.

The next point concerns Stalnaker's analysis, achieved with diagonalization, of TM's (possible) knowledge that he himself is on the tallest mountain as knowledge of $\{W\}$. Having anticipated a reply like Stalnaker's, Lewis put the point like this:

Let's grant, briefly, that the world W of the gods has its qualitative duplicate V in which the gods have traded places. Let the god on the tallest mountain know that his world is W, not V. Let him be omniscient about all propositions, not only qualitative ones. How does that help? Never mind V, where he knows he doesn't live. There are still two different mountains in W where he might, for all he knows, be living. (1983a: 141)

Lewis's point is that it is possible that TM should believe the proposition that contains W but not V, and at the very same time wonder about whether or not he lives on the tallest mountain, i.e., he could know exactly which world is actual without knowing where he is located within it. Since this is possible, it is incorrect to analyze his coming to believe that he himself lives on the tallest mountain as his coming to believe the proposition containing W alone instead of the one containing both W and V. This point seems correct. Let TM know all the nonqualitative facts in addition to the qualitative ones. Let him know that W, and not V, is actual. What follows is that TM knows that TM is on the tallest mountain (if you like, he knows the nonqualitative proposition *that TM is on the tallest mountain*, since this is a fact at W). However, it does not follow that TM knows that *he himself* is located there. This does not follow unless he knows that he himself is TM, i.e., unless he knows that *his* haecceity is *being TM*, and not *being CM*. But knowing exactly which world is actual, as impressive as this is, does not give him this knowledge.

Again, the two gods argument seems sound, if we take propositions to be sets of worlds. But what if we hold to the structured conception of propositions instead? One might view the case of the two gods as yet another reason to favor structured propositions over sets of possible worlds.[9] However, I am inclined to think this would not be correct. The salient difference between the two types of proposition is a difference in *grain*. On the possible-worlds conception, if propositions P and Q are logically equivalent, then they are identical; but this is not the case on the structured conception, and so propositions are more fine-grained entities on this conception. The possible-worlds conception is challenged by the fact that the cognitive attitudes are not, in general, closed under logical consequence, which was briefly discussed earlier. However, it does seem that *if* all

---

9. Robbins (2004: 77–78) hints at this, but he does not identify the allegedly propositional contents of the ignorant gods' missing beliefs.

subjects of thought were ideally rational—perfectly consistent and fully aware of all logical relationships between propositions—then possible-worlds propositions would do as well as structured ones with respect to attitude content. But Lewis has shown that when the nature of propositions is exhausted by their possible-worlds truth conditions, propositions are not sufficient to characterize mental content. This is the case even for ideally rational creatures, since we may take the two gods to be such creatures. So, if possible-worlds propositions cannot account for all possible beliefs of ideally rational subjects, it is implausible to think that structured propositions can.

One might think this begs the question against the structured view by assuming that closure-related difficulties are the *only* drawback for the possible-worlds conception relative to more fine-grained conceptions of propositions. Even if this is right, the fan of fine-grained propositions faces the task of identifying which proposition each god would believe, were he to come to know his spatial location. Given the problems discussed in the last section, concerning Perry's belief that he himself was making a mess, this is no easy task. Moreover, in the case of the two gods, it seems that, for every possible-worlds truth condition, each god believes a true proposition with that truth condition (since each one knows which world is actual). So, the proposition that each god is missing, in virtue of his ignorance, must be logically equivalent to one he already believes. But this is not plausible, since we may stipulate that the gods are ideally rational.

The fine-grained propositionalist might follow Stalnaker and claim that the gods do not know exactly which world is actual because each god fails to know certain nonqualitative, first-person propositions that he can know. (I will discuss this further in ch. 3, sec. 3, where I will argue that the dyadic propositionalist must accept first-person propositions.) This brings up Lewis's difficult question, i.e., how would nonqualitative knowledge help? It would also make genuine omniscience impossible, since no subject could know the true, first-person propositions of another.[10] And there is good reason to think that nonshareable attitude content is a cost that we should not be willing to pay.

It might be thought that, in my discussion of the two gods argument, I have been overlooking the triadic view of belief. I am going to

---

10. Strictly speaking, what becomes impossible is that there should be two or more subjects of cognitive attitudes, at least one of which is omniscient. See, e.g., Grim (1985) for an argument against omniscience along these lines.

postpone a good bit of the discussion of what a triadic theorist might say about the two gods until chapter 3, section 1, where the triadic view will be discussed at length. But here is a preview. For concreteness, let's take the triadic view to say that belief is, or can be analyzed in terms of, Salmon's three-place *BEL* relation among subjects, propositions, and guises. The triadic theorist should probably treat the two gods case as follows: Each god believes every true proposition under some guise or other, but neither god believes every truth under every guise. There seems to be some sense, then, in which each god is missing true beliefs. This account is consistent with premise 1 of the two gods argument, i.e., each god believes every true proposition but could have a true belief that he does not actually have. However, triadic theorists should probably reject premise 2, which claims that, if premise 1 is true, there are beliefs the contents of which are not propositions. This is to say that the content of a belief is the believed-true proposition and not the guise under which it is accepted.

This account complicates the notion of omniscience, since true propositions can be known under multiple guises. Moreover, I am not sure that the account I have put into the mouth of the triadic theorist adequately captures the way in which the two gods are *missing* true beliefs. It seems that a true belief would have to be a true proposition to which one is related via *BEL*; but each god is already related to every truth via *BEL*. The triadic account is also complicated. It incorporates propositions, guises, and a three-place relation to account for the gods' ignorance. By contrast, the property theory provides a much simpler account, according to which each god's ignorance consists in his failure to self-ascribe properties that he actually has.

3. Arguments from Internalism and Physicalism

I will argue that psychological internalism, or individualism, is incompatible with the doctrine of propositions, and that the truth of internalism thereby tells in favor of the property theory as an account of cognitive content.[11] Moreover, the mere fact that the doctrine of propositions is inconsistent with internalism shows that it involves more philosophical commitments regarding the nature of thought.

---

11. This argument, and some of the other material in this section, is based upon Feit (2006), which contains further discussion of some of the issues.

According to internalism, as we have seen in chapter 1, section 4, psychological properties strongly supervene on the intrinsic properties of the subjects who have them. One's psychology is purely a matter of one's intrinsic nature. I do not have much new to add to the case for internalism here, but I should review some of the considerations in its favor.

I have the intuition that intrinsic twins, whether actual or counterfactual, have beliefs in common. Suppose that I see an apple, point to it, and sincerely utter the words "that is green." I express a certain belief. I think that it is clear, intuitively, that if the apple in question had been replaced by a distinct but qualitatively indiscernible apple before I cast my gaze in that direction, then (other things being equal) I would have expressed the same belief. My beliefs seem to be a matter of what is going on inside my own head, and switching certain things in the environment would not, in itself, seem to alter my psychological characteristics. Of course, these considerations will not sway those who do not share these intuitions, and so I cannot put too much weight on them.

Another point in favor of internalism has to do with the relationship between belief (as well as certain other cognitive attitudes) and purposeful behavior. This general point can be made in several different ways. For example, consider the following line of reasoning from Lewis (1979):

> The main purpose of assigning objects of attitudes is, I take it, to characterize states of the head; to specify their causal roles with respect to behavior, stimuli, and one another. If the assignment of objects depends partly on something besides the state of the head, it will not serve this purpose. The states it characterizes will not be the occupants of the causal roles. (1983a: 142–143)

Lewis holds the plausible view that the concept of belief is implicitly defined in terms of the causal roles posited by commonsense or folk psychology. Beliefs are states that occupy certain causal roles in the network of states and roles set forth by the theory. But why think that the characterization of the states of a person's head, in virtue of attributing attitudes to her, must be made purely in terms of intrinsic properties or nonrelational states of her head? Perhaps the best reason is that it is extremely difficult to imagine how the property of having an attitude with a certain content could be at all causally relevant to a person's behavior if it were not one of her intrinsic properties.[12]

---

12. For some arguments in the spirit of this line of thinking, see Fodor (1987, ch. 2), Loar (1988), Segal (1989), and Crane (1991).

Another line of reasoning for internalism concerns the special epistemic status of self-knowledge, i.e., of one's knowledge about the very contents of one's mind. There is an enormous literature on this sort of argument and the issues that it raises. I cannot go very deeply into the matter here.[13] The argument can be cast in terms of a challenge to the externalist, who says that having a cognitive attitude sometimes involves standing in a certain relation to something external (or to a singular proposition, for example, whose identity depends partly upon its external constituent). However, it seems that, if thinking a particular thought involves standing in a relation to something contingent and external to one's mind, then one cannot have a priori knowledge of, or any sort of privileged access to, the fact that one is thinking that thought rather than another. This seems to violate a plausible Cartesian view about the transparency of the mind.

I find these considerations to be compelling evidence in favor of the internalist view of the mind. (I also think internalists have a very plausible response to the standard arguments against internalism, but that will have to wait until ch. 7.) Before turning to the argument concerning internalism and the doctrine of propositions, I would like to say a few things about the notion of a psychological property, in terms of which our version of internalism is cast. Internalism implies that psychological properties are intrinsic. I shall be especially concerned with belief-content properties, properties that entail that a subject has a belief with a certain content. Belief-content properties are psychological properties par excellence. But how should we conceive of psychological properties in general? One simple way is to maintain that a psychological property is a property that entails consciousness, i.e., that a property F is a psychological property if and only if, necessarily, anything that has F is conscious.

However, this conception of a psychological property is too broad, especially given our abundant conception of properties. Consider an object external to all of our minds, e.g., Vermeer's painting *The Concert*. On our conception of properties, there exists the property *wanting to own The Concert*. This property entails consciousness, but it

---

13. For discussion, see Burge (1988), Davidson (1988), Heil (1988), McKinsey (1991), Brueckner (1992), and Boghossian (1997), among others. Boghossian's paper is reprinted in Wright, Smith, and Macdonald (1998), which contains other fine papers.

is clearly not intrinsic. Anyone who has this property must be related to this particular painting, and an intrinsic duplicate of one who has the property need not be so related. So, there are clear cases of relational properties that entail consciousness. As a result, to define psychological properties as consciousness-entailing properties would trivialize the debate concerning the intrinsic or extrinsic nature of these properties.

Psychological properties are things like experiencing a sensation, having a perceptual experience, having an attitude with a certain content, and the like. Genuine psychological properties form a more interesting class than properties that merely require consciousness. We might want to reserve the term "mental properties" for this second class of properties. For now, we can conceive of psychological properties as mental properties to which essential reference is made in our commonsense psychological explanations of behavior, change in belief, and so on. Internalists claim that these are intrinsic properties. For example, when we explain somebody's action in terms of her beliefs, we make essential reference to narrow but not wide belief-content properties.

We are now ready to consider the argument from internalism in favor of the property theory. I will present this argument in two stages. The first stage establishes the logical incompatibility of internalism and the doctrine of propositions. Let's review these two claims quickly:

> *Doctrine of Propositions*: Necessarily, all the contents of one's beliefs, desires, and other cognitive attitudes are propositions, i.e., entities with truth values that do not vary from object to object, place to place, or time to time.

> *Internalism*: Our psychological properties supervene locally on our intrinsic, physical properties.

Let's use the phrase "narrow-minded propositionalism" to refer to the conjunction of internalism and the doctrine of propositions.[14] The number of adherents to this view is probably small, and that is good, since narrow-minded propositionalism is an inconsistent position. My argument is based upon a standard example of *de se* belief. Consider the following metaphysically possible situation:

---

14. With apologies to Shier. See Shier (1996).

Tim and Tom: Two people, whom I shall call "Tim" and "Tom," inhabit a certain possible world. Tim and Tom are molecule-for-molecule duplicates; they share all of their intrinsic, physical properties. Tim comes to have a belief that he expresses by saying "I am a millionaire." This belief is true. In fact, *all* of Tim's beliefs are true. At the same time that Tim comes to have this belief, Tom comes to have a belief that he also expresses by saying "I am a millionaire." However, Tim and Tom differ with respect to relational properties. Even though Tim and Tom are intrinsically indiscernible twins, Tom is not a millionaire. So, Tom's belief is false. All the while, Tim and Tom remain duplicates of one another.

This example is inspired by Lewis's discussion of Perry's (1977) case of the mad Heimson, who believes he is David Hume. Lewis supposes that "Heimson may have got his head into perfect match with Hume's in every way that is at all relevant to what he believes" (1983a: 142). This suggests that there is a sense in which Heimson and Hume believe alike, i.e., that Heimson believes exactly what Hume did. The problem for the propositionalist is that Hume is right and Heimson is wrong. Hume believes he is Hume, and he is right; but Heimson believes he is Hume, and he is wrong. A single proposition cannot be both true and false. Yet we should want to hold that Hume and Heimson share all of their beliefs. My plan here is to extend and refine some of the internalist considerations Lewis deployed in arguing for the property theory.

The case of Tim and Tom will form the basis of an argument for the logical incompatibility of the doctrine of propositions and internalism. This is the first stage of my general argument from internalism. The argument begins by assuming, for *reductio*, that the two doctrines are both true, and proceeds to a contradiction. Here is a relatively clear, semiformal version of the argument:

The Argument from Internalism: Stage One

1. Assume for *reductio* that (a) internalism and (b) the doctrine of propositions are true.
2. ∴ Tim and Tom share all of their psychological properties (from *Tim and Tom*, 1a).
3. ∴ Tim has a belief with a given content if and only if Tom does (from 2).

4. ∴ For every proposition P, Tim believes P if and only if Tom believes P (from 1b, 3).

5. All of Tim's beliefs are true (fact from *Tim and Tom*).

6. ∴ All of Tom's beliefs are true (from 4, 5).

7. Tom falsely believes that he is a millionaire (fact from *Tim and Tom*).

8. ∴ All of Tom's beliefs are true, and not all of Tom's beliefs are true (from 6, 7).

This argument is straightforward, and seems to be lurking just under the surface of several discussions about the nature of mental content. It seems to me that nothing about the argument is controversial. I suppose that some might question the inference from line 2 to line 3 of the argument, but the reason that line 2 entails line 3 is simply that the property of having a belief with a certain content is a psychological property.[15] Since the case of Tim and Tom is a possible one, and since line 8 is a contradiction, the argument shows that internalism and the doctrine of propositions are incompatible with one another. And since the case of Tim and Tom is nomologically possible as well as metaphysically possible, the argument succeeds no matter what degree of modal force is associated with the internalist supervenience claim (my preference is for metaphysical necessity, but I shall not argue for that here).

The second stage of the argument is just as straightforward. Of course, the first premise will be controversial, but I hope to have made at least a bit of a case for it here, and I would be content merely to persuade internalists that they ought to be property theorists as well. For the sake of completeness, here is the argument:

The Argument from Internalism: Stage Two

1. Internalism is true.

2. If (1), then the doctrine of propositions is false.

3. If the doctrine of propositions is false, then the property theory is true.

4. ∴ The property theory is true (from 1–3).

---

15. In any case, one who (implausibly) rejects this inference cannot accept internalism.

Premise 2, of course, is drawn from the first stage of the argument. Premise 3 makes essentially the same claim as the third premise of the two gods argument, and so the reasoning is analogous. The property theory also provides the most satisfying and plausible account of the case of Tim and Tom. On my view, Tim and Tom share all of their beliefs, since they are intrinsically alike. This means that they self-ascribe all of the same properties. In particular, they self-ascribe the property *being a millionaire*. This property does not correspond to any proposition. It is a *local property*, i.e., it is possible that one thing exemplifies it and another thing does not. Tim has the property *being a millionaire*, and so he believes truly, but Tom does not have it (perhaps his banker has just embezzled a large sum of his money), and this is how Tom's belief is false.

Standard versions of the triadic view of belief accept the doctrine of propositions, but it is possible to understand the triadic view in such a way that it does not entail this doctrine. However, given the internalist background here, it is hardly worth considering this position, since without some externalist account of content, there is no reason to hold the triadic view. This view does not compete with the property theory as an internalist candidate to fill the void left by the doctrine of propositions. It is also probably worth pointing out that the same goes for what is sometimes called the "multiple relation theory of belief."[16] On this view, a belief does not consist in a relation to a proposition, but rather to a plurality of entities out of which a proposition might be constructed. For example, if you were to believe that Shaq is taller than Mugsy, you would be related by the belief relation to Shaq, Mugsy, and *being taller than* severally, and not to the single proposition *that Shaq is taller than Mugsy*. This view is also false if internalism is true.

If we think that our psychological properties strongly supervene on our intrinsic, physical properties (as a matter of nomological or metaphysical necessity), then we must reject the doctrine of propositions and other doctrines that make relevantly similar claims. However, there is also a reason to prefer the property theory here, even for one who is not antecedently inclined toward internalism. The reason is this: An account of the nature of belief itself should not beg any questions regarding the supervenience, or lack thereof, of

---

16. This view was defended by Russell (1912, 1913, 1918) and has been revived by Moltmann (2003).

belief-content properties on the intrinsic properties of believers. The property theory does not beg any such questions, but all theories that entail the doctrine of propositions (and others besides, such as the multiple relation theory) do.

Other supervenience theses are also inconsistent with the doctrine of propositions. In particular, as we shall soon see, if we think that psychological properties merely globally supervene on physical ones, we must also reject the doctrine of propositions. This gives rise to an argument for the property theory with even broader appeal, because some global supervenience thesis or other is plausibly taken to be a condition of adequacy on any version of physicalism (roughly, the view that reality is exhausted by physical reality). So, if we think that some version of physicalism, or a certain global supervenience thesis, is correct, then we must also reject the doctrine of propositions, and we are again led in the direction of the property theory.

The argument here might be surprising, but it is relatively simple. Let's consider a standard version of global supervenience in the philosophy of mind, the gist of which is that there can be no psychological difference without some physical difference:

> *Global Supervenience*: For any pair of possible worlds, if the worlds have exactly the same pattern of distribution of physical properties, then they also have exactly the same pattern of distribution of psychological properties.[17]

Why is the doctrine of propositions incompatible with this sort of global supervenience? To see the answer, let's consider the following example:

> *Tim's World, Tom's World*: Imagine two possible worlds that are exactly alike with respect to their worldwide distributions of physical properties. Tim inhabits one of these worlds, and believes himself to be wise. Tom, a duplicate of Tim, takes Tim's place in the other world. Tom also believes himself to be wise.

17. This formulation is vague, but will do for my purposes here. If we wish to be more precise, we should understand this to say that psychological properties *strongly* globally supervene on physical ones. For discussion of some distinctions between kinds of global supervenience, see Stalnaker (1996), McLaughlin (1996, 1997), and Sider (1999).

Applied to this example, the doctrine of propositions entails that Tim and Tom have different beliefs, since what Tim believes is true if and only if Tim is wise, and what Tom believes is true if and only if Tom is wise. Since Tim and Tom are distinct people and it is possible that they could differ with respect to the exemplification of wisdom, these truth conditions are different. So there is a proposition, P, such that Tim has the property *believing P* (perhaps P is the proposition *that Tim is wise*), but Tom does not have the property *believing P*. However, if Tim and Tom have different belief-content properties, then the pattern of distribution of psychological properties in Tim's world is different from the pattern in Tom's world, violating global supervenience. As a result, the doctrine of propositions and global supervenience also form an inconsistent set.

This application of the example implies a certain form of haecceitism, but one that is far less extreme than the one required by Stalnaker's analysis of the two gods case. In fact, we do not need any version of haecceitism at all, since two worlds are not really necessary for showing that the doctrine of propositions is inconsistent with strong global supervenience.[18] We need imagine only a single "mirror-image world" containing both Tim and Tom, where things on Tom's side of the mirror are exactly like their analogues on Tim's side. A function from this world onto itself, which maps each thing to its mirror image and hence correlates Tim and Tom, will be an isomorphism that preserves physical properties but not psychological ones (since, given the doctrine of propositions, Tim and Tom have different beliefs). And the existence of such an isomorphism would show that psychological properties do not strongly globally supervene on physical ones.

With this in mind, we might state the argument from physicalism as follows:

Argument from Physicalism

1. Physicalism is true.
2. If (1), then psychological properties globally supervene on physical properties.
3. If psychological properties globally supervene on physical properties, then the doctrine of propositions is false.

---

18. I am indebted to Ted Sider for pointing this out to me.

4. If the doctrine of propositions is false, then the property theory is true.

5. ∴ The property theory is true.

I shall not argue for premise 1 here. In fact, we could forget about physicalism and simply begin the argument with the global supervenience claim. The doctrine of physicalism might be difficult to pin down. But it is reasonable to think either that physicalism simply amounts to some sort of global supervenience claim about psychological properties, or that it entails some such claim. And if this is the case, premise 2 is on sound footing. The *Tim's world, Tom's world* example shows that premise 3 is true, and the case for premise 4 has already been made.

I am inclined to think that something like this argument from physicalism is sound. However, perhaps premise 2 above is not quite correct. Perhaps a physicalist should hold that there is a *possible* world, maybe even a nomologically possible world, which is a physical duplicate of our world but in which there are a few stray Cartesian minds (i.e., nonphysical thinking substances). If there is such a world, then the principle of global supervenience stated above is false, and hence either physicalism is false or physicalism does not entail that principle. Holding to the first premise, I think there are ways to modify the formulation of global supervenience to allow that Cartesian minds or souls might exist, and thereby to save premise 2.

For example, Lewis (1983b) suggests that we take physicalism to be a global supervenience claim like this:

Lewisian Global Supervenience: For any pair of possible worlds where no natural properties alien to the actual world are instantiated, if the worlds have exactly the same pattern of distribution of physical properties, then they also have exactly the same pattern of distribution of psychological properties.[19]

If this is at least a necessary condition for physicalism, as I think it is, then premise 2 is correct if it is understood in terms of Lewisian global supervenience. And premise 3 is also true in this sense, since neither Tim's world nor Tom's world needs to be a world in which alien natural properties are instantiated.

---

19. This is adapted from Lewis (1983b: 364). See 363–364 for Lewis's account of alien properties. A broadly similar account of physicalism is offered by Jackson (1998).

The arguments presented in this section show that the doctrine of propositions is incompatible with each of two supervenience claims: a strong individual supervenience claim and a (strong) global supervenience claim. I think these claims are correct, and so I think we have two more good reasons to reject the doctrine of propositions and thereby to embrace the property theory of content. In the next section, I finish up the case for the property theory by arguing that it provides the best overall account of all of the phenomena associated with *de se* attitudes.

4. An Inference to the Best Explanation

Here are some important phenomena for which any adequate theory of mental content must account: the very existence and nature of *de se* attitudes, the place of such attitudes within the space of cognitive attitudes generally, the causal and explanatory roles of *de se* attitudes, statements that attribute *de se* attitudes, and the logical relations between these and other attitude reports. In this section, I shall argue that the account of all these phenomena provided by the property theory is satisfactory, and significantly better than the accounts provided by its rivals. In a sense, however, this section will not be complete until the end of the book, after the property theory and its rivals have been considered more fully.

Let's begin with an analysis of belief sentences and the logical relations between them. Chisholm (1981) suggested that the property theory gives the most plausible account of the logical relationships between certain belief sentences. For example, Chisholm provides the following attributions of belief:

(1) There is an x such that x is identical with the tallest man and x is believed by x to be wise.

(2) The tallest man believes that he himself is wise.[20]

Sentence (1) is a *de re* belief attribution according to which the tallest man has a certain belief, about himself, to the effect that he is wise. How is this sentence logically related to sentence (2), which of course is a *de se* belief attribution according to which the tallest man believes himself to be wise?

20. I have renumbered but otherwise quoted these sentences from Chisholm (1981: 18).

It seems clear that the *de se* attribution (2) logically implies the *de re* attribution (1), but that (2) is not implied by (1). More generally, utterances with the same basic form as (2) imply corresponding utterances with the same basic form as (1), but not vice versa. We have already seen several examples and arguments that motivate these claims about the logical relationships between (1) and (2). Here is an example Chisholm takes to show that (1) can be true while (2) is false:

> In this case the tallest man cannot sincerely say: "I believe that I am wise." Suppose, however, that he reads the lines on his hand and takes them to be a sign of wisdom; he doesn't realize the hand is his; and he is unduly modest and entirely without conceit. He arrives at the belief, with respect to the man in question, that he is wise. … Hence, although the tallest man cannot sincerely say: "I believe that I am wise," he can correctly express his conclusion by saying: "Well, *that* person, at least, is wise." (1981: 19)

Chisholm suggests that the property theory, which takes believing to be a two-place relation between a subject and a property, provides the simplest conception of belief that can account clearly for the logical facts about (1) and (2). By taking self-ascription to be the basic belief relation, the property theorist can give a simple analysis of sentence (2), which is true if and only if the tallest man self-ascribes *wisdom*. What about sentence (1)? On Chisholm's view, this *de re* belief report gets analyzed in terms of the basic, property-theoretic belief relation. So, in a sense, *de re* belief gets analyzed in terms of *de se* belief. What follows is a brief sketch of Chisholm's account.[21]

Recall the earlier example of Joe and Valerie. Valerie is believed by Joe to be a spy. What makes this the case? The property-theoretic answer goes as follows (to make things simple, suppose that Joe is looking at Valerie and at nobody else): Two facts are essential here. First, there is a certain relation that Joe bears to Valerie and only to Valerie (in this case, this is the two-place relation *x is looking at y* or, more simply, *looking*). This relation enables Joe to pick out Valerie by means of some definite description, e.g., "the person I am looking at," "the woman I am reading about," etc. The second fact is about what Joe believes. Joe self-ascribes a certain property, for example,

---

21. I shall not use Chisholm's terminology, and I shall simplify his account somewhat. Lewis defends a similar view about *de re* belief, which will be considered in chapter 5.

the property *looking at just one woman and at a woman who is a spy*. The basic idea here is that Joe singles Valerie out by means of some relation or other that he bears to Valerie and only to Valerie—i.e., that he bears *uniquely* to Valerie—and Joe self-ascribes the property of bearing that relation uniquely to someone who is a spy. Chisholm would say that, in this case, Joe "indirectly attributes" the property *being a spy* to Valerie. I am going to stick with the Lewisian terminology and say that Joe "ascribes" this property to her.

On this sort of view, you ascribe properties to others, and possibly to yourself, partly in virtue of self-ascribing properties. And it is possible that there is a property F such that you ascribe F to yourself, but don't self-ascribe F. On the property-theoretic account, to have a so-called *de re* belief about a thing is to ascribe a property to that thing. Here is one version of such an account, adapted from Chisholm (1981: 31):

> *De Re Belief*: Subject x ascribes property F to thing $y =_{df.}$
> There is a relation R such that x bears R uniquely to y, and x self-ascribes the property *bearing R uniquely to something that has F*.[22]

In Chisholm's example, the tallest man does not self-ascribe the property *being wise*, but he does ascribe this property to himself. How does he do this? Well, he bears the relation x *is reading the palm of y* uniquely to himself, and he self-ascribes a property such as *reading the palm of just one man and a man who is wise*. In speech, we typically express the relations we bear to others with the use of descriptions. For example, the tallest man might express his belief by saying "the man whose palm I am reading is wise." (This description literally contains the first-person pronoun, but this need not be the case.) In a sense, the tallest man has a belief about himself "under a description"—viz., the definite description "the man whose palm I am reading." It seems that, in this case, "I" is an essential indexical, and so it seems quite plausible to treat the belief in this example as a *de se* belief, which of course is exactly what the property theorist does. More generally, the picture given by Chisholm provides a plausible way to reduce *de re* belief to *de se* belief, in the sense that the cognitive

---

22. Strictly speaking, Chisholm requires only that x self-ascribe a property "*which entails* the property of bearing R to just one thing and to a thing that is F" (1981: 31; my italics). In chapter 5, we will examine this general sort of account more closely.

CHAPTER THREE

ALTERNATIVES TO THE
PROPERTY THEORY

In this chapter, we take a closer look at the main alternatives to the property theory of cognitive content. We will concentrate on belief, and see what can be said for dyadic propositionalism and the triadic view of belief. The triadic view is considered in the first section. Some philosophers might be inclined to think that, ultimately, the triadic view and the property theory are mere terminological variants of one another. However, I argue in the second section that the triadic view and the property theory are genuine rivals, insofar as they imply views about belief content that are not equivalent. I also argue that the property theory gives a better overall account of the attitudes. In the third section, I reconsider dyadic propositionalism, in both its possible-worlds and structured (in particular, neo-Fregean) forms. I argue that dyadic propositionalism faces severe difficulties, and the property theory gives a better overall account of the attitudes.

1. The Triadic View of Belief

Many philosophers have proposed one version or another of the triadic view of belief.[1] Triadic theorists claim that there is an important theoretical distinction between *what* is believed, on the one hand,

---

1. Notable examples include Kaplan (1989), Perry (1979[1988], 1980), Richard (1983[1988]), and Salmon (1986, 1989).

59

and *how* it is believed, on the other. Moreover, the explanation of purposeful behavior often involves essential reference to how things are believed or, in Perry's terminology, to our belief states. The upshot of this is that belief (or some relation in terms of which belief gets analyzed) must be a relation with more than two *relata*. In particular, it must be a three-place, or triadic, relation among a subject, what she believes, and how she believes it. It might seem odd to reify "how something is believed" in this way, but belief states must be at least roughly similar to propositions believed in order to figure into psychological explanations as they do, i.e., they must be content-like entities (or at least characterized by content-like entities) that are just as essential to the belief relation as believed-true propositions are. Earlier, I suggested that, on the triadic view, a proposition is what a subject believes, and a sentential meaning is (or characterizes) how she believes it. Propositions thus play the role of what is believed, and sentential meanings play the role of how a thing is believed. This summary of the view is given by Richard (1983),[2] who describes it as follows: "On this view…belief is a triadic relation between a person, a sentential meaning (understood as being a Kaplanesque character), and a proposition; to believe a proposition is to do so under a sentential meaning" (1988: 173).

According to triadic theorists, belief is a more complicated affair than dyadic propositionalism suggests. On their view, a subject believes a proposition by accepting, in a given context, a sentential meaning, which, in the context, has the proposition as its value. Roughly, to believe a proposition P under a sentential meaning M is to accept M in a context relative to which M has P as its value. Not all triadic theorists would put things just this way, but all share the view that the most basic relation having to do with belief is a triadic relation among believers, propositions, and some other sort of thing.

Let's return to the example of Joe and Valerie. Joe sees Valerie wearing a trench coat, and forms the belief that Valerie is a spy. At the same time, Valerie believes that she herself is a spy. At the very beginning of chapter 1, I argued that Joe and Valerie must have different beliefs. Triadic theorists can deny this conclusion, since they can say that both Joe and Valerie believe the proposition *that Valerie is a spy*. Of course, the triadic theorists might also admit that there

2. Reprinted in Salmon and Soames (1988). My page references will be to the reprinted version. Kaplan (1989) suggests that we include characters in the analysis of belief.

is a sense in which Joe and Valerie do have different beliefs, since they believe this proposition in different ways (they are in different belief states; they accept different sentential meanings). For example, Valerie believes the proposition under the character of "I am a spy," while Joe might believe it under the character of "she is a spy." If Joe were to get himself into the belief state that Valerie is in, he would come to believe a different proposition, viz., the proposition *that Joe is a spy*. Nevertheless, the sense in which Joe and Valerie would believe alike in this case is captured by their shared belief state. So we can believe the same proposition while we are in different belief states, and we can believe different propositions while we are in the same belief state. Here, we have two distinct dimensions of psychological sameness and difference, each one associated with a different sort of representational content (though triadic theorists typically claim that when we speak of the content of a belief, we are talking about the believed-true proposition).

What makes Valerie's belief *de se*, according to the triadic view, is something that has to do with the nature of her belief state. Roughly, it is the fact that the sentential meaning that characterizes her belief state is partly determined by the character of the pronoun "I." (We will sharpen this idea later in this section.) The same goes for all other *de se* beliefs. And the fact that someone's belief state is so characterized might be important when it comes to the explanation of his or her behavior. This is basically Perry's own analysis of his case of the messy shopper. On Perry's account, what often explains one's behavior is not (merely) the fact that one believes a certain proposition, but rather the fact that one believes it in a certain way, i.e., by being in a certain belief state. If this view is correct, then there is at least a sense in which change in belief is not always change in a believed-true proposition. Belief states, in order to do this work, clearly must have *some* sort of content, or something analogous to content, even if it is not (always) propositional in nature.

Let's take a quick look at how a triadic theorist such as Perry handles the case of the messy shopper. Earlier, I formulated the argument from explanation, based upon this case, as an argument against dyadic propositionalism. Since triadic theorists deny dyadic propositionalism, they need not worry about this argument. But they do need to provide an adequate account of the behavior of the messy shopper. The account goes roughly as follows: Perry's clean-up behavior is explained by a change in his belief state. Before this change, he did not believe any proposition under the character of

"I am making a mess." What explains his clean-up behavior—along
with his desire not to make messes—is simply the fact that he came to
be in such a belief state, i.e., he came to accept the meaning of "I am
making a mess" and hence to believe a proposition under this meaning. The believed-true proposition in this case is the proposition *that
Perry is making a mess*. However, Perry might very well have believed
this proposition under some meaning or other *before* he finally real-
ized that the torn bag of sugar was his own. For example, he might
have believed this proposition under the character of "he is making
a mess" when he saw the messy shopper (i.e., himself) in the supermarket mirror. His believing this proposition, then, does not explain
his behavior; the belief state is what really does the explanatory
work. A successful explanation of Perry's behavior would somehow
have to convey information about his belief state, i.e., information
about the way in which he believes this proposition.

On Perry's view, the belief state that explains his behavior is a
state that disposes him to utter, or otherwise assent to, the indexical sentence "I am making a mess." We might say that, when he is
so disposed, Perry is in an "essentially indexical" belief state. Perry
claims that such states are essential to the enterprise of psychological
explanation:

> We use sentences with indexicals...to individuate belief states, for
> the purposes of classifying believers in ways useful for explanation
> and prediction. That is, belief states individuated in this way enter
> into our commonsense theory about human behavior and more
> sophisticated theories emerging from it. (1979[1988]: 98)

For example, we use the sentence "I am making a mess" to pick
out a certain belief state, a belief state that can be shared by different people. And we might expect that people in this belief state will
behave similarly, even though they believe different propositions. All
of this seems to suggest that taking belief states to be (represented by)
sentential meanings—Kaplanesque characters—is appropriate. After
all, this view does not seem to prohibit people who speak different
languages from being in the same belief state, and it does not seem
to deny belief states to creatures without language. It also allows for
sentential meanings that do not incorporate the meanings of indexical terms. However, I am happy to let triadic theorists decide for
themselves exactly what these entities are: sentential meanings, sentences in a language of thought, natural language sentences, Fregean
or neo-Fregean modes of presentation, or what have you. This is not

a trivial task, given the role that belief states are meant to play, and to the best of my knowledge no triadic theorist has given a complete account.

It is tempting to describe the triadic view as a view according to which belief is a three-place relation. As we saw in chapter 1, section 2, however, this is not quite correct. For example, Salmon holds that belief is a binary relation between believers and propositions, but he analyzes it in terms of a triadic relation among believers, propositions, and some other type of thing. On his view, you cannot believe something without instantiating this triadic relation, and so, as an account of the nature of belief, his view should clearly be grouped together with those who say belief itself is a triadic relation. (This is not to say that there are no differences between Salmon's theory and other versions of the triadic view, but it is plausible to think that these boil down to terminological differences.) Salmon describes his account as follows:

> I take the belief relation to be, in effect, the existential generalization of a ternary relation, BEL, among believers, propositions, and some third type of entity. To believe a proposition p is to adopt an appropriate favorable attitude toward p when taking p in some relevant *way*. It is to agree to p, or to assent mentally to p, or to approve of p, or some such thing, when taking p a certain way. This is the BEL relation. I do not say a great deal about what the third relata for the BEL relation are. They are perhaps something like *proposition guises*, or *modes* of acquaintance or familiarity with propositions, or *ways* in which a believer may take a given proposition. (1989: 246)

Salmon also suggests the following sort of analysis of what it is to believe a proposition: "A believes p if and only if there is some x such that A is familiar with p by means of x and $BEL(A, p, x)$."[3] This will provide us with a formulation of the triadic view, one that is neutral about whether belief itself is a dyadic or triadic relation. On Salmon's view, the propositions we believe are structured and are sometimes singular propositions. This fits naturally with the account of the attitudes associated with triadic theorists, but I am not going to build it into my formulation of the view. I am going to assume that $BEL(A, p, x)$ implies that A is familiar with p by means of x. This will simplify our formulation of the triadic view by allowing us to omit the second locution, although that locution

---

3. Salmon (1989: 246). A similar view is expressed in Salmon (1986: 111).

proves useful to the triadic theorist in other ways. I am also going to use the term "guise" for the third *relatum* of the BEL relation.[4] Since triadic theorists all take some triadic relation such as BEL to be the most basic relation in an account of belief, I propose the following formulation of the view in terms of BEL:

> *Triadic View of Belief:* Necessarily, a subject S believes something if and only if there is some proposition P, and some guise X, such that BEL(S, P, X). Belief is either the triadic BEL relation or it is analyzable in terms of the BEL relation.

Using the term BEL(S, P, X) as a primitive or basic locution, we can define the following relation between believers and propositions:

B*: B* (S, P) $=_{df.}$ There is some guise X such that BEL(S, P, X).

Triadic theorists can disagree about which relation we call "belief." Salmon maintains that it is B*, near enough, while Perry (1977, 1979[1988]) and Richard (1983[1988]) seem to think it is BEL (but of course they do not call it that).[5] As stated, the triadic view is neutral on the matter of which relation we decide to call "belief." Moreover, as stated, the triadic view says nothing about the *content* of a belief. Triadic theorists can disagree about this as well, at least up to a point. Some might prefer to use the term "content" only for the proposition that is believed, but others might prefer to say that a belief has two contents, one a proposition and the other a guise. However, even those who restrict belief contents to believed-true propositions must acknowledge a content-like role for guises, since they ground psychological similarities and differences.

---

4. Thau (2002) calls Salmon's view "guise Millianism," partly on the basis of Salmon's semantic views. (Unfortunately, Thau does not discuss the problem of *de se* belief.) The term "guise" is better than "belief state" because of the latter's connotation of internal states of the believer, and because ultimately, the triadic analysis will have to be extended to attitudes other than belief, and "guise" applies uniformly across all attitudes. Salmon (1986: 173–174, n. 1 to ch. 9) argues that taking guises to be characters will not do. Roughly, his reason is that one can assent to a single, unambiguous sentence in different ways. To adapt a case from Kripke (1979[1988]), Peter might take "Paderewski was Polish" in different ways, so that two different guises correspond to the same sentence, which has only one character. Salmon concludes that characters are too coarse-grained to serve as guises. But why can't the two relevant guises be the characters of *other* sentences?

5. Perry (2006), however, has moved in the direction of Salmon's position. See especially 206–208.

Although Salmon thinks that the *BEL* relation can be used to help solve the problem of *de se* belief, his primary motivation for the triadic view has to do with other problems. These are problems at the intersection of the philosophy of language and the philosophy of mind, such as Frege's puzzle about identity statements and Kripke's puzzle about belief. For example, on Salmon's view, which incorporates the theory of direct reference for proper names, an utterance of "Hesperus is Phosphorus" expresses the same proposition as an utterance of "Hesperus is Hesperus," viz., a singular proposition about Venus to the effect that it is identical with itself. Moreover, according to Salmon, if it is true to say that Hal believes that Hesperus is Hesperus, then it is also true to say that Hal believes that Hesperus is Phosphorus. Salmon uses the *BEL* relation to explain away the intuitive oddity of this view. The idea is that it is possible to be familiar with a given proposition—such as the proposition *that Venus = Venus*—by means of more than one guise, and to believe the proposition under one of the guises but not the other. In saying that Hal believes that Hesperus is Phosphorus, one might (pragmatically) impart the information that Hal believes this proposition under a certain kind of guise rather than another, but what one says is true provided that Hal believes it under any guise at all.

According to Salmon, it is also possible to believe and withhold belief from the same proposition. This happens when a subject, S, is familiar with a single proposition, P, by means of two distinct guises, X and Y, and $BEL(S, P, X)$ but not $BEL(S, P, Y)$. For example, Hal might believe the proposition *that Venus = Venus* under one guise but not under another, even though he is familiar with the proposition by means of each guise. It is even possible for a consistent, perfectly rational agent to believe a proposition and its negation, so long as different guises are involved. For example, in Kripke's puzzle about belief, Pierre might believe the proposition *that London is pretty* under one guise, and believe the proposition *that London is not pretty* under a different guise. Pierre does not realize that, by means of these guises, he is familiar with contradictory propositions—but this is not his fault.[6]

6. I discuss Kripke's puzzle about belief, and various issues it raises in epistemology and semantics, in chapter 6. Salmon's solution is discussed in more detail, but the main thrust is to provide a property-theoretic solution to the puzzle and account of the issues.

It would not be misleading to say that, in providing his solution to these problems, Salmon employs Fregean senses or something very much like them, without a Fregean account of proper names or a Fregean analysis of belief sentences and the like.[7] Such senses, or something very much like them, seem to reappear as guises. According to Salmon, we believe structured propositions that contain properties and relations, and sometimes concrete particulars. But it would seem quite reasonable to say that, on his view, a belief in such a proposition is mediated by a mode of presentation of it, i.e., by something like a Fregean thought. Such modes of presentation might be nondescriptive in the sense that they might not pick their referents out by *describing* them uniquely or by means of collections of properties that each referent has. For example, when Perry comes to believe that he himself is making a mess, the relevant guise might contain some nondescriptive mode of presentation of himself.

At this point, it might be useful to see how proponents of the triadic view could respond to the arguments for the property theory given in the last chapter. The first of those arguments is the two gods argument. It is likely that the best account of the two gods case from the triadic perspective goes something like this: Both *TM* and *CM* believe every true proposition under some guise or other, and for every proposition *P* and guise *X*, *BEL(TM, P, X)* if and only if *BEL(CM, P, X)*. But neither god believes every true proposition *under every guise*. For example, *TM* does not believe the proposition *that TM lives on the tallest mountain* under the character of "I live on the tallest mountain," i.e., it is not the case that *BEL* is instantiated by *TM*, this proposition, and this guise. In this sense, each god is missing beliefs. Neither god instantiates *BEL* to the extent that it is possible for him to do so. However, the content of a belief is just the proposition that is believed, something that can be true or false in an absolute sense. So *TM* is missing true beliefs, in the sense that if he were to come to believe a proposition under the character of "I live on the tallest mountain," it would be a true proposition.

On this account, each of the two gods believes every true proposition, and each could have a true belief that he does not actually have (at least in the sense that he could believe a true proposition under a guise that he does not in fact accept). This is premise 1 of the two gods argument. However, according to the argument, if prem-

---

7. Salmon admits as much. See, e.g., Salmon (1986: 120).

ise 1 is true, then there can be beliefs the contents of which are not propositions. This is premise 2. The account just sketched implies that this premise is false, since the account holds that the contents of our beliefs are propositions.

If I were a triadic theorist, I would defend this account and thereby reject premise 2 of the two gods argument. I don't have a knockdown argument against the account, but it seems to me to face a few problems and challenges. First, it complicates the notion of omniscience. There must be a kind of omniscience that goes beyond merely knowing every true proposition and requires believing every true proposition in every *way* that it is possible for one to do so. Second, the sense in which it allows the gods to be missing true beliefs does not seem robust, since a true belief needs to be a true proposition to which one is related via *BEL*, and the gods are already related to every truth via *BEL*. There is a worry, then, that the account misdescribes the facts of the case. Finally, the account is complex. It employs propositions and propositional guises to account for the cognitive facts about the gods. A simpler account is available with the property theory.

Perhaps the triadic view has the resources to provide a cogent account of the two gods. Let's turn now to the argument from internalism. Perhaps the triadic theorist has an even easier objection to this argument. According to the argument, internalism is true. This is premise 1 of the second stage of the argument. But triadic theorists (as the name "guise Millianism" suggests) are externalists through and through. They say that some propositions are Russellian singular propositions, and that we sometimes stand in *BEL* to such propositions. So they reject internalism, and hence would reject premise 1.

At this point, I have three things to say about this response to the argument from internalism. First, I think that internalism is the correct view of psychological properties in general and belief-content properties in particular, and I would be happy to convince other internalists to adopt the property theory. Second, triadic theorists are committed to externalism simply in virtue of their account of belief, i.e., their very view of belief in terms of *BEL* entails externalism just as the doctrine of propositions does, since *BEL* is a psychological relation that relates subjects to propositions. The property theory is neutral on the issue of internalism versus externalism. So, the triadic view is at a disadvantage here in virtue of having more philosophical commitments. It also has the odd consequence of making Twin Earth arguments for externalism superfluous, since externalism is already a consequence of the theory (although Twin Earth arguments might extend the range of the beliefs whose contents are not determined by the intrinsic properties of believers). Third, the fact that the triadic view implies externalism shows that the property theory is a genuine rival to it. This issue, and some others raised in this paragraph, will be explored a bit more thoroughly in the next section.

Similar remarks apply to the next argument, the argument from physicalism. According to this argument, physicalism is true, and if it is, psychological properties globally supervene on physical properties. But the triadic theorist might just deny that physicalism is true, at least the kind of physicalism according to which psychological properties supervene globally on qualitative physical properties. However, I am inclined to think that some such kind of physicalism is correct, and I would be happy to convince other physicalists to adopt the property theory. And just like the doctrine of propositions, the triadic view is a theory of belief that rules out a priori the global supervenience of psychological properties on physical ones. The triadic view's philosophical commitment to the denial of this global supervenience claim is a serious disadvantage. This is a disadvantage that the property theory, which is neutral with respect to the truth of the global supervenience claim, does not share.

The final argument for the property theory was a very general one. The main claim was that the property theory provides the best explanation of various phenomena having to do with *de se* attitudes and their place within the realm of cognitive content. One such phenomenon was described by Chisholm, and concerned the logical relations between two different types of belief report. Let's recall Chisholm's (1981: 18) examples of (1) a *de re* belief report and (2) a *de se* belief report:

(1) There is an x such that x is identical with the tallest man, and x is believed by x to be wise.
(2) The tallest man believes that he himself is wise.

The task is to provide an adequate account of belief sentences like (1) and (2) that yields the intuitively correct judgment that (2) implies (1) but not vice versa.

I think that the property theory can provide a good explanation of the logical relationships between such *de re* attributions of belief and their *de se* counterparts. For example, Chisholm's own account, discussed in chapter 2, section 4, seems at least to be on the right track. On our version of this account, sentence (1) is true if and only if the tallest man ascribes *wisdom* to the tallest man, while (2) is true if and only if the tallest man self-ascribes *wisdom*. Given Chisholm's definition of what it is for a subject to ascribe a property to a thing (and given our claim that, in self-ascribing a property, one ascribes the property to oneself under the identity relation), it is clear that, on this understanding, (2) implies (1) but not vice versa.

However, Richard (1983[1988]) shows that the triadic view also has the resources to provide a good explanation of the fact that (2) implies (1) but not vice versa. Richard's view is somewhat complex and technical; what follows is a relatively informal sketch of his account. One way to approach Richard's proposal is to introduce the notion of what I will call an *I-guise*. To get at the idea here, let's consider a few standard cases of *de se* belief. However we conceive of propositional guises, there will be a guise associated with the sentence "I am wise." Let's imagine that there are three people—Andre, Pete, and Roger—each of whom believes some proposition under this guise. What the triadic theorist says is that, in these instances, the *BEL* relation relates Andre to the proposition *that Andre is wise*, Pete to the proposition *that Pete is wise*, and Roger to the proposition *that Roger is wise*. Each of these propositions is a structured, singular proposition about the believer. This is what makes the relevant guise an I-guise. If *BEL* relates you to a proposition and an I-guise, then the proposition must be a singular proposition about you. I propose the following definition of an I-guise in terms of Salmon's notion of a subject's being familiar with a proposition by means of a guise, which is more general than *BEL*:

> *I-guise*: X is an I-guise $=_{\text{df.}}$ Necessarily, for every subject S
> and proposition P, if S is familiar with P by means of X, then
> P is a singular proposition about S.

If our notion of an I-guise captures what it is supposed to capture, then we are in a position to approximate Richard's analysis of sentences (1) and (2). In a nutshell, a *de se* belief report is taken to contain information about *how* a given proposition is believed, i.e., under an I-guise, while a *de re* belief report contains no such information. Here is an approximation of Richard's account of (1) and (2) along these lines:

(1R) There is an x such that x is the tallest man, and there is a guise y such that $BEL(x, \text{ that } x \text{ is wise}, y)$.

(2R) There is an x such that x is the tallest man, and there is a y such that y is an I-guise and $BEL(x, \text{ that } x \text{ is wise}, y)$.

Since every I-guise is a guise but not every guise is an I-guise, (2R) implies (1R) but not vice versa. So, the triadic view of belief seems able to provide a way to analyze (1) and (2) that respects the intuitively correct views about the logical relations between them.

This triadic, Richard-style explanation of the relations between (1) and (2) does seem to be a good one, and the resulting thought that a *de se* belief is one that involves an I-guise is appealing. However, I suggest that the property-theoretic explanation is even better. There are at least three reasons for this: The property theory also provides a good account of the relations between (1) and (2); the triadic account, in terms of the *BEL* relation, is more complex than the account in terms of the property theory; and the triadic account carries the burden of the extra philosophical commitments discussed earlier in this section. Since the facts concerning (1) and (2) comprise only a part of the phenomena to be explained by an account of the cognitive attitudes, this probably gives us only a small bit of evidence for the property theory. However, if the property theory accounts for the relevant phenomena at least as well as the triadic view does, the triadic view's complexity and extra commitments should make us think that the property theory is better supported by the available evidence. In the next section, we turn to a general and final comparison of these two competing views.

2. How the Property Theory and the Triadic View Are Rivals

On the face of it, it is obvious that the property theory and the triadic view are rivals. For example, the property theory (ch. 1, sec. 4) says that belief is a two-place relation between a subject and a property, while the triadic view (sec. 1 above) says that belief is, or else is analyzable in terms of, the three-place *BEL* relation among subjects, propositions, and guises. These do not seem to be equivalent claims. In fact, they seem to be inconsistent claims. Belief cannot be fully analyzable both as a two-place relation and as a three-place relation. However, perhaps it is possible to isolate what we might call the *core* doctrines of each theory, and perhaps when this is done, it will be less clear that the two theories are rivals. Consider the following two views:

> *Core Property Theory*: Necessarily, a subject, *S*, believes something if and only if there is a property, *F*, such that *S* self-ascribes *F*.

Core Triadic View: Necessarily, a subject, *S*, believes
something if and only if there is a proposition,
P, and a guise, *X*, such that *BEL*(*S*, *P*, *X*).

The core property theory and the core triadic view are indeed
rivals. However, because neither of these views explicitly identifies
the belief relation or says what belief content is, perhaps it is less clear
that this is the case. One might try to argue that these two views
are equivalent by trying to show that, if you self-ascribe some property, you thereby believe some proposition under some guise, and
vice versa. I shall soon consider an argument along these lines, and
attempt to say where I think it goes wrong. But first, I would like
to discuss briefly why the core property theory and the core triadic
view are not at all equivalent views, and hence are rival accounts of
belief and belief content.

As mentioned previously, the reason that these two views are
rivals has to do with psychological internalism, the view that, as
a matter of some sort of necessity, one's psychological properties
strongly supervene on one's intrinsic, physical properties. From the
purely logical point of view, the (core) property theory is consistent with internalism and also with the denial of internalism, i.e.,
externalism. However, as it turns out, the (core) triadic view is not
consistent with internalism; it entails externalism. This might not be
terribly surprising, since we saw in chapter 2, section 3, that the doctrine of propositions is not consistent with internalism, and standard
versions of the core triadic view (e.g., Salmon's) imply the doctrine
of propositions. However, the core triadic view is silent about what
counts as the content of a belief, and so if I am to show that belief-
content properties cannot be intrinsic on this view, I must consider
what the defenders of the core triadic view could say about content.
They must say something about it, since they are, after all, theorizing
about the nature of content just as much as property theorists are.

Suppose that *BEL*(*S*, *P*, *X*) obtains, for some subject *S*, proposition *P*, and guise *X*. According to the triadic view, then, *S* believes
something. But what is the content of *S*'s belief? The three most
natural choices are as follows: (i) The content of *S*'s belief is *P*;
(ii) *S*'s belief has *two* contents, viz., *P* and *X*; and (iii) *S*'s belief has
a single content, but it is the ordered pair <*P*, *X*>.[8] Choice (i) is

8. It seems to me that Richard's (1990) view can be understood as a version of
the triadic view with choice (iii). There is also another, sneakier, choice, i.e., that the
content is *X*. This will be considered shortly.

Salmon's choice, and it is probably also the view of most proponents of the triadic view. On this choice, the content of a belief is always a proposition. The proposition is *what is believed*, and in some sense the *belief* just is the proposition. In saying that the content of a belief is a proposition, the triadic theorist who makes this choice is accepting the doctrine of propositions. As a result, this version of the triadic view is inconsistent with internalism, since (as we have already seen) if propositions are the unique contents of beliefs, internalism is false. (Remember the original case of Tim and Tom. If propositions are the contents of beliefs, Tim and Tom must differ in their beliefs, since all of Tim's beliefs are true while at least one of Tom's is false. But then internalism must be false, since Tim and Tom are duplicates.)

Given choice (i), then, the core triadic view entails externalism. Since the core property theory does not entail externalism, the core versions of our two views, given choice (i), are rivals. But what if the triadic theorist were to make another choice? After all, even though choice (i) is the standard choice for triadic theorists, it seems to have at least one drawback. This has to do with the fact that guises function in at least some of the ways that belief contents are supposed to function, e.g., they can play an explanatory role with respect to our behavior, and they account for certain ways in which we can believe alike (think of Perry and another person who believes himself to be making a mess). So perhaps the triadic theorist should make choice (ii) or (iii) and say that our belief-content properties are determined by guises as well as by propositions.

However, it should be clear that given choice (ii) or (iii), the core triadic view still entails externalism. It is true that these choices deny the doctrine of propositions, insofar as there are belief contents that are not propositions according to both choices. But given choice (ii) or (iii), the core triadic view still implies that, if two people share all of their belief-content properties, then they are related to the same propositions. If we applied either choice (ii) or (iii) to the Tim and Tom case, we would see that, since Tom has a false belief while Tim does not, they cannot be related to all the same propositions. As a result, they cannot share all of their belief-content properties, and the core triadic view again entails externalism. The moral here is that, if propositions enter into content even partially, as is the case on choices (ii) and (iii), internalism cannot be true. So, these versions of the triadic view, like the doctrine of propositions, entail that having a belief with a certain content implies being related (via *BEL*) to some proposition, and hence they entail that internalism is false. Again, since the core property theory has no such entailment, the core versions of the two views, given choice (ii) or (iii), are rivals.

Triadic theorists should happily admit that even the core version of their view is a genuine rival to the core version of the property theory. However, it might be worthwhile to imagine a triadic theorist who is willing to make a very sneaky move. The move is to claim that, although S believes something if and only if there is a P and an X such that $BEL(S, P, X)$, the *content* of S's belief is just X. This is choice (iv). Choice (iv) is the same as choice (i) in that one of the *relata* of BEL does not enter into the content of a belief, but it is different in that it is the proposition rather than the guise that fails even partially to enter into belief content. On this choice, sharing belief-content properties doesn't entail being related to the same propositions, and in a sense, we don't really believe the propositions at all; we believe the guises instead. This would allow for duplicates to have the same belief-content properties, and hence to share all of their psychological properties.

What shall we make of this attempt to reconcile the core triadic view with internalism? The answer is that choice (iv) is a cheat. Since the idea is to retain the triadic view, to make this choice requires one to say that, in order to have a belief, you must be related (via BEL) to a proposition. But the proposition isn't *the* content of your belief, it isn't *a* content of your belief, and it isn't even part of the content of your belief. One result of this is that propositions cannot play the role of determining whether you believe truly or falsely, since this is the job of the *content* of your belief. Since it is in virtue of our belief contents that we believe truly or falsely, propositions do not even partly determine whether we believe truly or falsely on this view. But then, there is no reason at all to bring propositions and the triadic BEL relation into the picture. This is why calling choice (iv) a version of the triadic view is cheating. On this account of belief, propositions become an idle theoretical cog.

The claim that the content of a belief is a guise does have some plausibility, *if* we forget about the triadic view as the background account of belief. (The vagueness of the notion of a guise, of course, detracts from this plausibility, but let's not worry about that right now.) What the plausibility of choice (iv) shows is that, in theorizing about belief, we ought to focus on the relationship between believers and guises. This, in turn, drives us back to a dyadic conception of belief, and toward either the property theory or dyadic propositionalism (depending on the exact nature of guises, e.g., whether they are truth-value bearers and hence fit some conception of propositions). It is interesting to note that choice (i) does not force us down the same road, and so there is a kind of asymmetry here. If we start by thinking of a dyadic relation between believers and propositions, we soon see that guises (or something like them, whatever they are) are needed to explain certain facts about our relations to these propositions. (For example, we might need to explain how Perry can believe the proposition *that Perry is making a mess* but still be trying to catch the messy shopper, or we might need to explain how a perfectly rational person like Kripke's Pierre can believe a proposition and its negation at the same time.) But, if we start by thinking of a dyadic relation between believers and guises, we should see that there is really no reason to complicate the picture by bringing in propositions. Whatever work they might do can be done without them.

I conclude that choice (iv) is not a legitimate choice for the triadic theorist to make, and hereafter I shall ignore it. The end result is that the core triadic view is really a rival to the core property theory. The two accounts of belief do not say the same thing; they are not mere terminological variants of one another; etc. The reason, in a nutshell, is that, however exactly the core triadic view is fleshed out with respect to what counts as a belief-content property, the core triadic view is not consistent with internalism. Since the core property theory is consistent with internalism, the views do not come to the same thing in the end. However, there is an interesting line of reasoning for the conclusion that the two views are in fact equivalent, and before summing up my case against the triadic view, I would like to consider it.

When a subject stands in the *BEL* relation to a proposition and a guise, it seems that there is a relation that she bears simply to the guise. There is also a relation that she bears simply to the proposition, e.g., the relation that we earlier defined as $B*$, which, on Salmon's view, is the belief relation. $B*$ was defined by existential generalization on the *BEL* relation, so that $B*(S, P)$ means that there is an X such that $BEL(S, P, X)$. Let's use the name $G*$ for the salient relation between a subject and a guise that she accepts. We shall soon consider whether $G*$ should also be defined by existential generalization on *BEL*, i.e., whether $G*(S, X)$ means that there is a P such that $BEL(S, P, X)$.

Now, the core property theory and the core triadic view would be equivalent, if the relation of acceptance $G*$ had certain features, and if there were a certain correlation between self-ascribed proper-ties, on the one hand, and guises, on the other. Here are two claims about $G*$ that would help to establish the alleged equivalence:

(a) For all S and X, if there is a P such that $BEL(S, P, X)$, then $G*(S, X)$.

(b) For all S and X, if $G*(S, X)$, then there is a P such that $BEL(S, P, X)$.

The biconditional contained in (a) and (b), together with a certain sort of correspondence between guises and properties, would allow us to derive the core property theory from the core triadic view and vice versa. Here is the sort of correspondence that I have in mind. Suppose, for example, that there is a guise associated with the sentence "I am making a mess," and that Perry accepts this guise. The property theorist will want to say that Perry self-ascribes the property *making a mess*. In a way, then, the guise that Perry is sup-posed to accept is correlated with the property that he is alleged to self-ascribe. It is initially plausible, at least, that there should be a one-to-one correspondence between guises and properties along these lines. This would mean that guises cannot (all) be propositions, on any conception of a proposition as an absolute bearer of a truth value, since there is no suitable one-to-one correspondence between properties and propositions (there is only a one-to-one correspon-dence between *some* properties—i.e., global properties of the form *being such that P*—and propositions). This would rule out thinking of guises as Fregean thoughts, for example. In any case, here is a way to characterize the correspondence:

(c) There is a one-to-one correspondence C between guises and properties, which respects the relations $G*$ and *self-ascription* in the sense that, for every subject S, guise X, and property F, if C maps X to F, then $G*(S, X)$ if and only if S self-ascribes F.

Claims (a)–(c) seem reasonable. In particular, there is an extremely simple way of making (c) true. This is to let triadic theorists help themselves to the property-theoretic notion of self-ascription and say that, if a given subject bears the primitive BEL relation to a proposi-tion and a guise, then the guise *just is* a property that she self-ascribes.[9]

---

9. This has been suggested by Brown (1986), who argues that Perry's belief states are best characterized by properties that the believer self-ascribes.

This would make the correspondence posited by (c) a simple matter of identity. But other accounts of guises might also make (c) true. For example, we have been thinking of guises as sentential meanings, which in effect are propositional functions of a certain sort. It seems quite reasonable to think that there is an appropriate one-to-one correspondence between these propositional functions and properties, and if so, (c) would seem to be true.

If claims (a)–(c) are true, however, then it turns out that the core property theory and the core triadic view are equivalent (strictly, the claims need to be necessary truths, but they would seem to be necessary if true at all). This is because claims (a)–(c) jointly imply that claim (d) is true:

(d) For every subject S, there is a P and an X such that $BEL(S, P, X)$ if and only if there is an F such that S self-ascribes F.

The left-to-right direction of (d) is established by (a) and (c), which imply that if BEL is instantiated, then so is *self-ascription*. The right-to-left direction is given by (b) and (c), which imply the converse. If (d) were necessarily true, we could derive the core triadic view from the core property theory and vice versa. If you self-ascribed a property, you would believe some proposition under some guise, and vice versa. In this strong sense, the two views would be equivalent. As such, they wouldn't be rivals. But aren't they?

Let's consider the argument that proceeds from claims (a)–(c) to claim (d). The argument does not really go through, and I want to show why this is the case. How we ought to evaluate the argument, it seems to me, depends upon exactly what the relation $G*$ is like. What we need is an answer to this question about $G*$: Does $G*(S, X)$ imply that there is a P such that $BEL(S, P, X)$? $G*$ is a relation of acceptance of *some* sort, but does it entail that there is always a proposition that the subject believes under the guise?

Let's consider the two possible answers in turn. I shall start with the answer no. On this account, it is possible that there could be a subject who bears $G*$ to a guise, but who does not stand in BEL to any proposition and that guise. So, on this account, $G*$ is a basic relation of acceptance between a believer and a guise, which is not definable in terms of any triadic relation such as BEL. A remark made by Salmon provides us with some reason for thinking that there is such a relation:

> Depending on what sort of thing serves as the third relatum of the BEL relation, it might...turn out that there are things of that sort

(e.g., ways of taking a proposition) to which there does not correspond any piece of information (e.g., such that there is no proposition which it is a way of taking). (1986: 127)

Salmon does not elaborate on which relations might hold between a subject and a guise in the absence of a proposition with which the subject is familiar by means of the guise. (On his view, *belief* could never be instantiated in virtue of such a relation, since *BEL* is required for a subject to have a belief. If this seems implausible, we have another reason to think that the propositional component of *BEL*, as grasped by triadic theorists, is inessential to belief.) In any case, if we answer the question about $G*$ by saying no, then we have no reason to believe claim (b) above. Given this understanding of the relation $G*$, we should say that the argument from claims (a)–(c) to claim (d) is unsound because (b) is false. Hence, given the answer no, the argument does not show the core versions of the property theory and the triadic view to be equivalent.

Let's turn to the answer yes. On this account, a subject who bears $G*$ to a guise must stand in *BEL* to some proposition and that guise. So, we can define $G*(S, X)$ to mean that there is a P such that $BEL(S, P, X)$ and thereby make $G*$ analogous to $B*$. Given this definition, claims (a) and (b) are analytic, and in any case they are both clearly true here. (Claim (a) is true regardless of how we answer the question about $G*$.) So the only way of defeating the argument in this case is to reject (c) and its alleged correspondence between guises and properties. And this is exactly what we should do, given the answer yes to the question about $G*$. If the answer were no instead, and a primitive relation of acceptance between a subject and a guise were admitted—i.e., one that is not definable in terms of the triadic relation *BEL*—we could agree that there is a correspondence between guises and properties as described in (c). But given the yes answer, (c) should be denied.

The reason for this is that, given the conception of $G*$ associated with the answer yes, it turns out that claim (c) would commit the property theorist to externalism. This is because (c) implies that, if you self-ascribe a property, then you are related to some guise via $G*$, but on the current conception of $G*$, this implies that you stand in *BEL* to some proposition and that guise. So, if (c) is true, then if a subject self-ascribes a property, she also stands in *BEL* to a proposition and a guise. However, as I argued earlier, the *BEL* relation must be understood in such a way that any proposition to which one is related via *BEL* is (i) the content of one's belief, (ii) one of two contents of the belief, or (iii) a part of the content of the belief. In all three cases, a proposition to which one is related via *BEL* at least partly determines which belief-content properties one has. And this means that intrinsic duplicates will not always have the same belief-content properties.

For example, in the original case of Tim and Tom, each one self-ascribes the property *being a millionaire*. If each one is also related via *BEL* to a proposition, then Tim will believe the proposition *that Tim is a millionaire* under some guise, while Tom will believe the proposition *that Tom is a millionaire* under that guise. This means that Tim and Tom, despite the fact that they are duplicates, will believe different propositions and hence will have different belief-content properties. But surely the property theorist need not say (and, in my view, should not say) that the twins have different belief-content properties. This is why claim (c) should be denied. If (c) is true, then given the present conception of G* (which sanctions the jump from G* to *BEL*), the property theorist is committed to externalism. However, in reality, there is nothing about the property theory that commits its adherents to such a view. Given the answer yes, then, the argument does not show that the core versions of the property theory and the triadic view are equivalent. No matter which way we conceive of G*, the views turn out to be rivals.

It is time to sum up this discussion of the triadic view. I think that the arguments for the property theory, presented in chapter 2, are persuasive. So, I think that we should embrace the property theory and reject the triadic view. For the moment, however, suppose we admit that the formal arguments of chapter 2 are not persuasive. We will then say that the triadic view can provide an adequate account of the case of the two gods. We will say that the truth of internalism is in doubt, and also that the truth of physicalism is in doubt. Even if we say these things, we will have to admit that the property theory is simpler than the triadic view in at least two ways. First, it implies that belief is a two-place relation between subjects and properties, which is simpler than the three-place relation posited by the triadic view. Second, it makes fewer philosophical commitments (begs fewer questions) than does the triadic view, since it is neutral on the truth of internalism and physicalism. The property theory also seems easier to understand than the triadic view, since in order to understand what it is to self-ascribe a property, one simply needs to understand what it is to believe oneself to be a certain way. The triadic view, however, makes use of the not-yet-fully-explained notion of guises, and makes one wonder about whether it is true that, for every guise X, there is always a proposition P such that X is a way of taking P (recall the last quotation from Salmon).

This is where the inference to the best explanation enters the picture. Given the relative complexity and mystery associated with the triadic view, we should accept the property theory if its account of cognitive attitude content is at least as good. I maintain that this is in fact true, and I hope to have made at least a partial case for this so far. One might think that the triadic view can make better sense of *de re* belief than the property theory can, but I shall argue in chapter 5 that this is mistaken. (We have seen a little preview of this in ch. 2, sec. 4.) If there are no persuasive objections to the property theory, and I shall try to show in chapter 4 that there are none, the triadic view ought to be abandoned.

3. Dyadic Propositionalism Reconsidered

Dyadic propositionalism has at least one virtue that the triadic view does not share, the virtue of simplicity. It is also intuitively compelling, insofar as many of our intuitions tell in favor of the idea that beliefs and other attitudes have propositional contents. As we have seen, however, there are powerful arguments against dyadic propositionalism. The very problem of *de se* belief, as we have seen, spells trouble for this view, since it does not allow for the appeal to proposition guises. In this section, I shall go a bit more deeply into this view and consider whether anything more can be said for it. I shall start with a version of dyadic propositionalism that employs structureless propositions, and then move on to a version that makes use of structured (neo-Fregean) propositions. I shall argue that each view faces specific difficulties, and at the end of the section I shall summarize the general case against the dyadic propositionalist view.

Stalnaker (1981) uses the possible-worlds conception of propositions to try to reconcile dyadic propositionalism with examples of *de se* belief and related cases of self-locating belief. Stalnaker's view was discussed briefly in chapter 2, section 2. Any attempt to defend dyadic propositionalism along structureless lines will have to look very much like Stalnaker's, and so we can focus on Stalnaker's view as a paradigmatic case. Let's begin our discussion of his analysis of *de se* belief by considering Perry's example of the amnesiac lost in the library, which Stalnaker also uses to illustrate his view. Stalnaker describes the case as follows:

> Rudolf Lingens is an amnesiac lost in the Stanford Library. He has found and read a biography of himself, and so knows quite a bit about Rudolf Lingens. He knows, for example, that Lingens is a distant cousin of a notorious spy. But he does not know that *he* is Lingens— that *he* is a distant cousin of a notorious spy. No matter how complete the biography, it will not by itself give him the information he lacks. (1981: 130)

The problem for the dyadic propositionalist is the problem of *de se* belief. The solution must have two parts. The first is to identify the proposition Lingens believes, say, when he believes—while lost and with amnesia—that Lingens is a cousin of a spy. The second is to identify another proposition, the proposition Lingens would come to believe were he to come to believe *himself* to be a cousin of a spy. This would be the content of one of the *de se* beliefs that Lingens would acquire were he to discover that he himself is Lingens and that he himself is in (a certain section of) Main Library, Stanford.

Stalnaker proceeds by distinguishing three possible worlds, which, in the context of attributing beliefs to Lingens, can be viewed as the relevant exhaustive and exclusive alternatives. Stalnaker's idea is that when Lingens believes that Lingens is a cousin of a spy, he rules out the third possible world but not the other two. The first two are among Lingens's "belief worlds." Were he to believe *de se* that he himself is a cousin of a spy, he would rule out the second possible world as well, and only the first would characterize his belief state. Stalnaker describes these worlds as follows:

> Situation *i* is the actual situation. Lingens, the amnesiac, is the subject of the biography, and is a cousin of a spy. But in situation *j*, the biography correctly describes, and was written about, a different person—call him "Lingens 2." Our Lingens, the amnesiac, has a different name, and is not a cousin of a spy in situation *j*. Situation *k* is just like situation *j*, except that in *k* the biography of Lingens 2 makes some false claims. Lingens 2's cousin is not a spy in *k*. (1981: 137)

This is where diagonalization (previewed in ch. 2, sec. 2) enters the picture. Consider a token of the sentence "Lingens is a cousin of a spy" that occurs in world *i*. (This might be a token inscribed in the copy of the biography read by Lingens, or one uttered by Lingens, etc.) The token will occur in worlds *j* and *k* as well, and Stalnaker's technique of diagonalization directs us to find, for each possible world in turn, the truth value at that world of the proposition expressed by the token as it occurs in that very world. Stalnaker uses a semantic account according to which names rigidly designate their bearers, and he evaluates the token that occurs in the actual world as follows:

> According to the...semantic account, in situation i, the name "Lingens" rigidly designates Lingens—our Lingens, the amnesiac. This person is a cousin of a spy in situation i, but is not a cousin of a spy in j or in k. So the proposition expressed by the sentence is the one that is true at i, but false at the other two situations. (1981: 137–138)

However, in the token of "Lingens is a cousin of a spy" that exists in world j, the occurrence of "Lingens" rigidly designates Lingens 2, not Lingens. Lingens 2 is a cousin of a spy at j, but not at k. Moreover, Stalnaker imagines that this man does not exist at all at i. So, the proposition expressed by the sentence as it occurs in j is the proposition that is true at j, but false at i and k. And since the occurrence of "Lingens" in world k also rigidly designates Lingens 2, this same proposition is expressed by the sentence as it occurs in k. This gives rise to the propositional concept displayed in the matrix below:

	i	j	k
i	T	F	F
j	F	T	F
k	F	T	F

In the matrix, each horizontal line represents the proposition expressed by the sentence "Lingens is a cousin of a spy" as it occurs at each of the relevant worlds. (Since we are not interested in making any distinctions that would require more specificity, we need not imagine any other possible worlds.) On Stalnaker's view, Lingens does not believe either of the first two propositions represented horizontally in the matrix, since he does not know whether he is in world i or world j.[10] However, Lingens does believe that he is not in world k, because he thinks that the subject of the biography is a cousin of a spy. So, Lingens does believe the proposition represented *diagonally* in the matrix, i.e., $\{i, j\}$. This proposition is his belief that

10. Stalnaker is assuming that world i is in the set of worlds compatible with Lingens's beliefs. On his understanding of the story, "Lingens does not believe that he is *not* Lingens. He doesn't have an opinion one way or the other about who he is" (1981: 136).

Lingens is a cousin of a spy. It is the belief that he expresses when he utters the words "Lingens is a cousin of a spy," and it is the belief that we attribute to him when we say that he believes that Lingens is a cousin of a spy.

Saying that the diagonal proposition is the content of Lingens's belief that Lingens is a cousin of a spy allows Stalnaker to say that, were Lingens to learn that he himself is Lingens, and hence that he himself is a cousin of a spy, he would come to believe the proposition represented horizontally in the first row of the matrix, i.e., $\{i\}$. This is the pseudo singular proposition that is true if and only if Lingens is a cousin of a spy. We can now summarize Stalnaker's dyadic propositionalist approach to the problem of de se belief. The problem, with respect to the Lingens case, was to distinguish two different propositions that could plausibly serve as the contents of Lingens's beliefs: first, his third-personal belief that Lingens is a cousin of a spy, and second, his (potential) de se belief that he himself is a cousin of a spy. On Stalnaker's view, the first belief is the diagonal proposition $\{i, j\}$, while the second is the horizontal, pseudo singular proposition $\{i\}$.

At the end of this section, I will press some general objections against dyadic propositionalism. But Stalnaker's account faces specific problems as well, and I would like to discuss a few of these here. First, as it turns out, Stalnaker's analysis of Lingens's belief that Lingens is a cousin of a spy is a metalinguistic one. That is to say, the relevant diagonal proposition is simply the proposition *that the sentence "Lingens is a cousin of a spy" expresses a truth*, which is true at worlds i and j but not at world k.[11] On Stalnaker's view of propositions, of course, no sentence is ever a constituent of a proposition, since a proposition is just a set of worlds. This might allow Stalnaker to distance himself from the view that Lingens's belief is a belief about the semantic value of the relevant sentence. However, that so many of our ordinary beliefs turn out to be equivalent to metalinguistic ones is surely a disadvantage for the strategy of diagonalization.

Second, it is not at all clear that Stalnaker provides an adequate solution to the problem, because it is not clear that the pseudo singular proposition *that Lingens is a cousin of a spy* adequately characterizes Lingens's de se belief that he himself is a cousin of a spy. Here we may adapt Lewis's question from the debate about the two gods: How does knowing that his world is i rather than j help Lingens know

---

11. This feature of diagonalization is important to Stalnaker's (1984) approach to the closure-related difficulties that beset the possible-worlds conception of propositions.

that it is *he himself* who is a cousin of a spy? Let Lingens know that *i*, and not *j*, is actual. Let him know that Lingens, and not Lingens 2, is a cousin of a spy. Unless he also knows that *he himself* is Lingens, it does not follow that he knows that he himself is a cousin of a spy. Stalnaker will claim that, in supposing that Lingens knows which world is actual, we are thereby admitting that he knows who and where in the world he is. However, this feature of his analysis is in need of further explanation.

The point here might be made with the help of Lewis's case of the two gods. On Stalnaker's view, just as Lingens's belief state rules out neither *i* nor *j*, the belief states of the two gods rule out neither the actual world *W*, nor world *V*, in which the gods have traded places. The acquisition of *de se* beliefs would consist in each god's ability to distinguish between worlds *W* and *V*. Since W and V are qualitatively indiscernible, the only differences between them are haecceitistic; they are differences concerning when and where distinct haecceities are instantiated. For example, *TM* might come to know that the haecceity *being identical to TM* is instantiated atop the tallest mountain, while the haecceity *being identical to CM* is instantiated atop the coldest mountain, and not vice versa. However, *TM*'s knowledge seems to be consistent with his not knowing that *his very own* individual essence or haecceity is *being identical to TM*, and so his knowing that *W* is actual and *V* is not seems compatible with his failing to believe that he himself lives on the tallest mountain. It seems that *TM* could know when and where his own haecceity is instantiated but not know that the haecceity in question is his own. He might wonder: Which one is mine, is it *being identical to TM*, or is it *being identical to CM*?

Finally, as we have seen in chapter 2, section 2, Stalnaker's account is committed to a very strong form of haecceitism. For example, in the case of the two gods, *TM* and *CM* inhabit world *W*, and each one is ignorant about his own spatial location. As a dyadic propositionalist, Stalnaker needs to maintain that *TM*, for example, does not know every proposition that is true at *W*. In particular, *TM* is ignorant of certain nonqualitative facts and cannot distinguish *W* from a qualitatively indiscernible world, *V*, in which *TM* and *CM* have swapped qualitative roles—i.e., in *V*, *TM* is on the coldest mountain and *CM* is on the tallest one. So, in *W*, *TM* knows the (diagonal) proposition $\{W, V\}$ but does not know the pseudo singular proposition $\{W\}$. This allows Stalnaker to give propositional content to the missing beliefs of the ignorant gods. Haecceitism, however, is the cost.

Remember that *TM* and *CM* are not qualitative counterparts, and we can imagine them to be quite different in kind (over and above the extrinsic differences involved in throwing manna and thunderbolts). Stalnaker needs to maintain that there exist worlds, such as *W* and *V*, that differ solely by a permutation of objects over importantly different qualitative roles. This amounts to a very strong form of haecceitism, according to which there are no limits on which qualitative properties a thing can have (e.g., *TM* can have all of the qualitative properties that *CM* actually has), so long as it has its haecceity. I find this doctrine implausible, and it is a disadvantage of Stalnaker's view that it entails such an extreme metaphysical position.[12]

So much for the dyadic propositionalist attempt to account for *de se* beliefs on the possible-worlds conception of propositions. Let's turn now to the structured conception. It should be relatively clear that, in the absence of such things as guises, the proposal that the contents of *de se* beliefs are Russellian singular propositions faces some of the same difficulties that Stalnaker's view faces. But according to some neo-Fregeans, the Fregean conception of thoughts can accommodate the phenomena surrounding *de se* attitudes. Clear accounts are given by Peacocke (1981) and Forbes (1987).[13] Forbes approaches the problem via the semantics of *de se* belief reports, and follows Frege in saying that each of us has access to a first-person mode of presentation, which is inaccessible to others and plays an essential role in *de se* belief. (I shall be concerned primarily with the neo-Fregean conception of *de se* content, rather than the semantics of our talk about attitudes. The neo-Fregean account might inherit semantic problems over and above the problems I will raise about the contents it postulates.)

Consider an utterance of "Ralph believes that he (himself) is making a mess." Forbes (1987: 23) analyzes this as follows:

$$B(\text{Ralph}, [\text{self}]_{\text{Ralph}} \,{}^{\wedge}\, \ulcorner \text{making a mess} \urcorner)$$

The analysis is Fregean in that the pronoun "he" and the predicate "is making a mess" do not have their customary references. In the regimentation, corner quotes are used to form a name of the sense of the expression within them; ^ stands for the way in which senses are

---

12. Stalnaker has moved away from the view that the content of a *de se* belief can be represented by a set of possible worlds. See, for example, Stalnaker (2006).

13. Versions of a general neo-Fregean strategy for handling *de re* and *de se* thought have also been proposed by Evans (1982), McDowell (1984), and others.

combined together to form a single complex sense; and [self]$_{Ralph}$ designates the mode of presentation of Ralph that only Ralph can employ in thought.[14] The idea is that there is a single *type* of mode of presentation, [self], tokens of which are employed in thought on specific occasions. For example, when Perry believes himself to be making a mess, he grasps a *different* token of the same first-person type of mode of presentation, which accounts for the way in which Ralph and Perry believe alike. Token senses must make up the contents of these beliefs, since different tokens of [self] determine different objects, and so this is the only way in which the beliefs could bear truth values. Fregean thoughts must have truth values absolutely (this is, perhaps, unlike the guises used by triadic theorists) if this view is to count as a version of dyadic propositionalism.

The modes of presentation or senses at issue here—we might call them "*de se* senses"—are supposedly entities that can exist without being grasped or entertained, but that depend for their existence on a given individual (for example, [self]$_{Ralph}$ would not exist if Ralph did not exist). This is a departure from Frege's thought and part of what makes the present view *neo*-Fregean. *De se* senses belong to a class of neo-Fregean entities that are supposed to present, or determine, individuals, but not (solely) in virtue of properties that the individuals uniquely possess. The entities in the broader class have been labeled as "*de re*," "demonstrative," "indexical," and "nondescriptive," and have been understood differently by different thinkers. Their exact nature remains somewhat mysterious, and an investigation into it is beyond the scope of this discussion.

What shall we make of the present attempt to reconcile dyadic propositionalism with the phenomena surrounding *de se* attitudes? Here, I shall be relatively brief and suggest just a few complaints. First, *de se* senses (and the broader class to which they belong) seem ad hoc, introduced only to solve specific problems for Fregean analyses. Second, the distinction between the various token senses—such as [self]$_{Ralph}$ and the like—and the type to which they belong adds an additional layer of complexity to the theory. (Since token senses are repeatable, type/token terminology is a bit misleading; perhaps determinable/determinate terminology would be better.) Third, the very nature of *de se* senses and the way in which they do their work are still a matter of controversy and mystery. If a given *de se* sense does not determine an individual by means of a property or cluster

---

14. Peacocke offers the same sort of analysis. For example, see Peacocke (1981: 191).

of properties that the individual has, how then *does* it determine an individual? Neo-Fregeans have had things to say about this question, but none of their answers has been entirely satisfactory.[15]

The neo-Fregean position explicitly employs first-person propositions, i.e., propositions that are accessible to the thought of only one person. For example, only Ralph can think a thought that contains [self]$_{Ralph}$ (although we might be able to think *about* such a thought and *refer* to its constituent modes of presentation). This is surely another disadvantage for the present view. In taking first-person propositions to be the contents of our *de se* attitudes, neo-Fregeanism violates what Robbins (2004) calls the "stability constraint," i.e., the idea that cognitive contents are objective, shareable entities. Since it seems to me that this is a consequence not only of the neo-Fregean view but also of dyadic propositionalism in general, I will use it as a starting point in my summary of the general case against dyadic propositionalism, a case that applies to both the structured and the structureless versions of the view.

I say that every dyadic propositionalist, whether he realizes it or not, is committed to the existence of first-person propositions. My argument rests on what I shall call the "third-person principle." To illustrate this principle, let's remember the case of Joe and Valerie. Let's suppose that when Joe has a belief about Valerie to the effect that Valerie is a spy, Joe believes the proposition *that Valerie is a spy*. It seems quite clear that if Joe really believes *this* proposition, then Valerie could believe it without believing *herself* to be a spy. Simply give Valerie a third-person perspective on herself that is similar to the perspective that Joe has on her—e.g., let her read about herself, see herself in a security monitor, etc.—but imagine that Valerie thinks she has this perspective on somebody else and, for one reason or another, does not believe herself to be a spy. The same goes for *any* proposition that Joe might believe. If Joe can believe it, then, assum-

---

15. For example, Peacocke (1983) suggests that the "constitutive role" of a *de se* sense is specified by the partly descriptive, partly demonstrative description "the person who has *these* conscious states" (see ch. 5 especially). But Peacocke realizes that it will not do to say that the *content* of a *de se* sense is given by such a description. For one thing, as I noted earlier, this is implausible from the psychological point of view. For another, why can't I have a given experience but believe that some other being also has it? See Nozick (1981: 72). Evans (1982) sketches an account of the sense and reference of the first-person pronoun. For a convincing (at least to my mind) criticism of Evans's view, see O'Brien (1995). My own advice to Fregeans would be to abandon *de se* senses and accept a Fregean property theory, according to which, e.g., the content of Ralph's belief that he himself is making a mess is simply ⌈making a mess⌉.

ing that Valerie can believe it too, we can imagine Valerie believing it without believing that she herself is a spy. And the same goes for *any* local property that Valerie might believe herself to have. (Again, a local property is a property, e.g., *being a spy*, which is possibly such that one thing has it and another does not. Restricting properties to local ones allows that the subject of a belief in proposition *P* always believes herself to have the *global* property *being such that P.*)

So, here is one way to put the point. If somebody (e.g., Joe) can believe any given proposition, then assuming that any other person (e.g., Valerie) can believe that proposition too, the other person can believe it while failing to believe herself to have any given local property. The reasoning given above in favor of this principle seems to me very strong. We might state the principle somewhat rigorously as follows:

> *Third-Person Principle*: For every proposition *P*, for every local property *F*, and for every pair of distinct people *S* and *S**, if *S* can believe *P*, then if *S** can believe *P*, *S** can believe *P* while failing to believe himself or herself to have *F*.

When we put the third-person principle together with a claim that the dyadic propositionalist needs to make about *de se* belief, we get first-person propositions. The dyadic propositionalist claim is that *de se* beliefs are to be understood as being beliefs in propositions, where the relevant proposition guarantees that the belief is *de se* (e.g., that it could be expressed in terms of the self-attribution of a local property). Here is a version of this principle:

> *Dyadic Propositionalism on De Se Belief*: For every person *S* and for every local property *F*, if *S* believes himself or herself to have *F*, then there is a proposition *P* such that *S* believes *P*, and necessarily, if *S* believes *P* then *S* believes himself or herself to have *F*.

It seems clear that dyadic propositionalists must accept this claim. For example, if I really believe myself to have *F* in virtue of believing some proposition, then it does not seem possible for me to believe this very same proposition without believing myself to have *F*. If we have these two principles, we can deduce the following conclusion establishing the existence of private, first-person propositions:

> *First-Person Propositions*: For every pair of distinct people *S* and *S** and for every local property *F*, if *S* believes himself or herself to have *F*, then there is a proposition *P* such that *S* believes *P* but *S** cannot believe *P*.

According to this conclusion, if there are at least two people and one of them has a *de se* belief, then there exists a first-person proposition (i.e., a proposition that the other person *cannot* believe). This result follows logically from the conjunction of the third-person principle, which seems to me undeniable, and dyadic propositionalism on *de se* belief.[16] So there is very good reason to think that all dyadic propositionalist theorists (not just neo-Fregeans) must countenance first-person propositions, and hence there is very good reason to think that dyadic propositionalism violates the stability constraint on content.

So, in addition to the specific problems associated with the possible-worlds and structured versions of dyadic propositionalism, there is the more general problem of the commitment to nonshareable content in the form of first-person propositions. Moreover, as we have seen in chapter 2, section 3, there are a couple of other costs associated with dyadic propositionalism. In particular, since dyadic propositionalists are obviously committed to the doctrine of propositions, their view about cognitive content entails that internalism and physicalism are both false. Even if one is inclined on independent grounds to deny one or the other of these claims, one should admit that the mere commitment to denying both of them is a disadvantage for dyadic propositionalism relative to the property theory. Finally, in addition to the extra philosophical commitments of dyadic propositionalism (and, in my view, the implausibility of those commitments), there is the lingering worry that the problem of *de se* belief is alive and well for dyadic propositionalism. That is, it is not at all clear that the propositions alleged to be the contents of our *de se* beliefs are able to characterize adequately those beliefs and account for their role in our behavior. In Stalnaker's case, there are legitimate doubts about whether knowing exactly which world is actual really amounts to knowing which local properties one has; in the neo-Fregean case, there are legitimate questions about the exact nature of *de se* senses and how they present or determine the individual who is the subject of belief.

---

16. I leave the proof as an exercise for the interested reader. Possibility operators should be used for the occurrences of "can," and a binary predicate (e.g., B^s) should be used for the self-ascriptive relation of believing oneself to have a local property. For example, the expression "$S*$ can believe P while failing to believe himself or herself to have F" might be symbolized like this: $\Diamond(Bs* \, p \, \& \sim B^s \, s* \, f)$.

Of course, the considerations above would diminish in strength if there were any good arguments against the property theory of content. Several objections to the property theory can be found in the literature. In the next chapter, I discuss the ones that I find to be the most illuminating or troublesome. I shall suggest that, in each case, the property theorist can respond plausibly to the argument or objection.

CHAPTER FOUR

ARGUMENTS AGAINST THE PROPERTY THEORY

According to the property theory of content, the belief relation is *self-ascription*, and belief contents are properties that are self-ascribed by believers. The other cognitive attitudes are understood as relations to properties as well. In the present chapter, I will attempt to answer what seem to me to be the strongest objections to the property theory. Arguments against the property theory in the literature are few and far between, and formidable ones are even rarer. In a way, this is surprising. Although the theory has been defended by philosophical giants such as Lewis and Chisholm, it seems to have been rejected by the vast majority of contemporary philosophers of mind, but without strong argument. The arguments that I shall consider raise interesting questions and might also help to illuminate the property theory. All of the arguments, however, can be defeated plausibly.

The first section deals with objections concerning our ability to understand the primitive notion of self-ascription, and other objections concerning the kind of cognitive sophistication that is needed in order to self-ascribe properties. In the second section, I consider objections according to which the property theory lacks the resources to account for certain special sorts of attitude. For example, one might argue that the theory cannot adequately account for one's desire not to exist, because such a desire seems not to be a case of wanting to have a certain property. In the third section, I consider an argument against the property theory given by Stalnaker. The argument charges that the property theorist cannot give a plausible account of the relations among belief content, assertion, and the exchange of information. Finally, in the fourth section, I consider an objection having to do with inferences that contain claims about the attitudes. According to this objection, there are certain obviously valid inferences that would not be valid if the property theory were correct. The correctness of such inferences, it is argued, can be upheld only with the doctrine of propositions.

1. Self-Ascription and Self-Awareness

Some philosophers might have concerns about our ability to understand the primitive notion of self-ascription, which is the fundamental relation of the property theory.[1] One might argue that understanding the idea of self-ascription requires a prior understanding of the idea of believing oneself to have a property, and that the property theory gets this the wrong way around. However, there is only one state of affairs in question here. This is a state of affairs that consists in a subject bearing a relation (viz., *self-ascription*) to a property. So, when somebody understands what it is for a subject, *S*, to believe herself to have a property, *F*, she already understands what it is for *S* to self-ascribe *F*. (Of course, such a person might not use the terminology of the property theory, but that makes no difference here.) In order to understand what it is for a person to believe herself to have some property, then, we must have some grasp on the relation *self-ascription*, since her believing this simply is her self-ascribing the relevant property.

At this point, we might wonder about the cognitive abilities that are necessary for self-ascribing properties. One might think that, since a certain amount of self-awareness is needed for a subject to self-ascribe a property, the property theory entails that many children and nonhuman animals fail to have any beliefs. This sort of argument has been advanced by Markie (1988: 594), who suggests that the property theory cannot allow for the possibility that "some thinkers (perhaps animals, children, or computers) could be capable of *de dicto* attitudes but lack the sort of self-awareness involved in *de se* ones." Here, Markie is exploiting the property-theoretic idea that every belief is *de se*, since all belief consists in the self-ascription of properties.

---

1. I have not seen an objection like this in print, though I have heard it in conversation.

It seems to me, however, that the property theory has no such implication about the mental states of children, nonhuman animals, and the like. Markie seems to think that the property theorist has to maintain that one must be conscious of oneself in some robust way in order to have a *de se* belief. However, one need not have this sort of self-consciousness in order to self-ascribe a property. There is no reason to think that the beliefs that require such self-awareness exhaust all of our beliefs; they might just make up a special subclass of *de se* beliefs. Perhaps nonhuman animals cannot self-ascribe many of the properties that we can self-ascribe (e.g., *being a philosopher, wanting the telephone to ring*), but this is a matter only of the peculiar contents of these beliefs. It seems to me that the property theory can allow for the possibility that a subject could be capable of self-ascribing properties that correspond to propositions while lacking the sort of rich psychology or self-awareness required to self-ascribe certain other properties.

So, it seems that the present objection has no more force than, for example, the charge that the doctrine of propositions denies beliefs to children and animals because they lack the cognitive resources required to assent to propositions. The philosopher who wishes to press this objection must show that there is a need to distinguish believing a proposition, *P*, from self-ascribing the property *being such that P*, and hence that *de dicto* belief cannot be subsumed under *de se* belief. I do not think that there is any such need. Markie does not show that *de se* attitudes require any kind of self-awareness that is not required by *de dicto* ones. Moreover, it would seem to be extremely difficult to show that believing a given proposition and self-ascribing the corresponding property must play different roles in the explanation of behavior.

Markie does try to argue against the property-theoretic identification of *de dicto* attitudes with certain *de se* ones. Again, according to this view, to believe a proposition is by analysis to self-ascribe a property that is necessarily such that a thing has it if and only if the proposition is true. Taking an example from Lewis (1983a: 137), we can say that, to believe the proposition *that cyanoacrylate glue dissolves in acetone* is simply to self-ascribe the property *being such that cyanoacrylate glue dissolves in acetone*. Here is Markie's argument against this view:

> This reduction of *de dicto* beliefs to *de se* ones keeps the theory from giving an adequate treatment of self-consciousness. On Monday, Hume is working in his laboratory and is so lost in thought as to be

unaware of himself. The only thoughts going through his head are chemical equations, descriptions of chemical reactions and the like. He comes to the conclusion that cyanoacrylate dissolves in acetone. On Tuesday, he is back in his laboratory but cannot concentrate on his work. He keeps thinking about himself. The thoughts going through his head all concern himself as he comes to the conclusion that he needs to find a new career. There is a clear difference between the two cases. Hume is conscious of himself on Tuesday in a way in which he is not conscious of himself on Monday. *De se* property theorists cannot explain this difference. (1988: 593)

Markie thinks the reason that property theorists cannot explain the difference between Hume's thoughts on Monday and his thoughts on Tuesday has to do with their reduction of *de dicto* to *de se* belief. One natural way to explain the difference would be to say that, on Monday, Hume comes to have *de dicto* beliefs about chemistry, while on Tuesday, he comes to have *de se* beliefs (about himself). Markie thinks that this natural explanation is unavailable to the property theorist, who must claim that, on Monday, Hume also comes to have *de se* beliefs. I think that the natural explanation is in fact consistent with the property theory. But Markie suggests that property theorists might try to answer his objection in another way, which he rejects:

They might say that Hume is forming *de se* beliefs on each occasion, but it is only on Tuesday that he is consciously aware of the fact that he is doing so.... We have no reason to assume that Hume is this reflective on Tuesday. On that occasion, he does not just think about chemistry; he thinks about himself, but that is not to say he takes the extra step of thinking about the fact that he is thinking about himself. (1988: 594)

Perhaps Markie is correct to reject this sort of response. However, on the other hand, Markie imagines that, on Tuesday, Hume has the belief that he needs to find a new career, which does seem to be a self-conscious or second-order mental state of some sort. It is plausible that Hume's belief on Tuesday consists in his self-ascribing the property *desiring a new career*, or the property *self-ascribing the property of needing to find a new career*, or some other property that entails having a first-order mental state. However, I am happy to go along with Markie and admit that Hume is not self-conscious in this way on Tuesday. Even if it usually happens that we have such second-order attitudes when absorbed in thought about ourselves, it might be that such attitudes are not essential to this sort of thinking. So the reply might not yield a plausible way to distinguish Hume's thoughts on Tuesday from his thoughts on Monday.

However, even supposing the above sort of reply to be inadequate, the property theorist can explain the salient difference between Hume's beliefs on the two occasions. The natural explanation—i.e., that Hume has *de dicto* beliefs about chemistry on Monday and *de se* beliefs on Tuesday—can be employed by the property theorist. This is because the *contents* of the beliefs on Monday and of the beliefs on Tuesday are materially different. The property that Hume self-ascribes on Monday (e.g., *being such that cyanoacrylate dissolves in acetone*) is of a quite different sort from the one he self-ascribes on Tuesday (e.g., *needing to find a new career*). The first property, for a start, corresponds to a proposition. It is a global property, one necessarily such that, if something has it, then everything has it. We can thus distinguish it from the second property, which is local rather than global, and explain the difference between Hume's thoughts in the natural way. On Monday, Hume has *de dicto* beliefs about chemistry, and on Tuesday, he has non–*de dicto* beliefs about himself. This seems to capture the salient difference in Hume's mental states, and the fact that his beliefs are *de se* on both days (since they consist in his self-ascribing properties) is not a cause for concern. If this does not suffice for characterizing the nature of Hume's mental state on Tuesday, we could also point to the fact that, say, the property *needing to find a new career* and the like are necessarily such that the individuals who have them are conscious subjects with beliefs, desires, projects, and so on. In light of these considerations, I suggest that the general line of argument considered in this section carries little weight against the property theory.

2. Nonexistence and Impossible Contents

Markie presents another sort of objection to the general framework of the property theory. This objection has to do with various issues surrounding the contingent existence of a given subject of attitudes. Although Markie directs the objection specifically against Chisholm's version of the property theory, he clearly intends it to apply generally to any version of the view. He introduces the argument as follows:

> Sometimes we adopt an attitude *de dicto* and the content is an impossibility; sometimes we adopt an attitude *de dicto* and the content is a possibility that includes our nonexistence. Chisholm's theory fails to capture this distinction because it requires that each *de dicto* instance of an attitude involves a *de se* one. (1984: 236)

Markie provides an example of the distinction with a pair of sentences which attribute the cognitive attitude of considering something. The sentences appear below:[2]

(1) Descartes considers its being the case that two and two does not equal four.

(2) Descartes considers its being the case that he neither exists nor has any properties but someone is wise.

The consideration attributed to Descartes in (1) is an impossibility, since it is necessary that $2 + 2 = 4$. However, the consideration attributed to him in (2) is a possibility that happens to entail his non-existence. According to Markie, the property theory cannot provide an adequate account of the distinction between the contents of these attributed considerations.

Now, to consider something is not to believe it, and so the relation *self-ascription* does not come into play here. (Indeed, it might never be correct to attribute to someone the belief that he does not exist.) The property theorist, however, wishes to say that, in general, all the cognitive attitudes are relations between subjects and properties. So, the attitude of consideration must get analyzed as a relation between subjects and properties. Markie calls this relation "direct consideration" and suggests the following property-theoretic versions of (1) and (2):

(1a) Descartes directly considers…being such that two plus two does not equal four.

(2a) Descartes directly considers…being such as to neither exist nor have any properties but to be such that someone is wise.[3]

Markie claims that, although (1a) captures the fact that (1) attributes to Descartes the consideration of something impossible, (2a) fails to capture the fact that (2) attributes to Descartes the consideration of something possible. Indeed, it looks like (2a) attributes to Descartes the direct consideration of an impossible property, a property that nothing could have. (Suppose that (2a) does in fact attribute a directly considered property, F, to Descartes. If something were to

2. These sentences are renumbered but otherwise quoted from Markie (1984: 236).

3. Markie (1984: 236). Again, I have renumbered the sentences. Markie provides another interpretation of (2) that does not treat existence as a property, but neither his objection nor my response turns on this issue.

have *F*, it would thereby have at least one property, and hence would not have *F*. So nothing could have *F*.)

What exactly is going on here? It might seem that, to answer Markie's objection, the property theorist needs to supply a plausible interpretation of (2) according to which Descartes directly considers a property that something could have. One might think that such an interpretation is available along the lines of the following:

> (2b) Descartes directly considers *being possibly such that he neither exists nor has any properties while someone is wise.*

However, the consideration attributed to Descartes in sentence (2) is something that is not actually the case, since Descartes does in fact exist, whereas the consideration attributed in (2b) seems to be a property that is actually exemplified by Descartes (if not, then the property attributed in (2b) is also an impossible property). So, (2b) fails to capture the fact that (2) attributes to Descartes the consideration of something *merely* possible.

The problem for this response seems even more troublesome if we imagine an example in which someone desires, rather than just considers, his own nonexistence. (We need to have in mind an eternal or omnitemporal sense of "nonexistence" in the context of this objection. Other senses of "nonexistence" are more easily handled by the property theory.) It seems clear that a subject who desires not to exist (in the relevant sense) is not wishing for a property that he or she actually has, like *possible nonexistence.* So, an account of such a desire along the lines of (2b) would misdescribe the facts of the case. Indeed, the desire never to have existed appears to be a desire to have no properties whatsoever. But it seems that the property theorist must treat it as a desire for some property or other, and so we have a nutshell version of the objection presently under consideration.

With this in mind, we might wonder why Markie did not use an example having to do simply with the nonexistence of the subject, such as the following:

> (3) Descartes considers its being the case that he does not exist.

The property-theoretic interpretation of (3) would appear to be the following, which seems to turn a possible object of consideration into an impossible one, just as (2a) does:

> (3a) Descartes directly considers *nonexistence.*

Given that the consideration attributed in (3) is clearly possible while the one attributed in (3a) seems not to be—since it seems to be a necessary truth that nothing has the property *nonexistence*—why doesn't Markie's problem arise for (3) and (3a)?[4]

Perhaps Markie does not use an example like (3) because he is concerned about whether or not existence is a property. Or perhaps he does not use an example like (3) because he wants to focus on *de dicto* attitudes (although it seems to me that sentence (2) attributes an attitude that has a purely *de se* component as well as a *de dicto* one). In any case, it seems to me that these concerns cut across the issues at the heart of the problem raised by Markie. I think the property theorist can give a plausible account of sentence (3), and that any plausible property-theoretic account of (3) will carry over to (2) as well.

Before suggesting a solution to the problems raised by attitudes that involve the nonexistence of the subject, I would like to consider a pair of solutions that seem to me to be inadequate. It might seem natural to think that the way to deal with sentence (3) is to find some property, distinct from *nonexistence* but similar enough to it in important ways, which will serve adequately as the content of the attributed attitude. Here is one such understanding of (3):

(3b) Descartes directly considers *being distinct from every actual thing.*

The direct consideration attributed in (3b) is possible, since it is possible that there should exist something that is distinct from every actual thing. It is also such that Descartes does not have it, since Descartes is identical to some actual thing: himself. The desire not to exist (i.e., never to have existed) might be treated along the same lines. This desire is the desire to be nonidentical with every actually existing thing. The relevant property is obtained by taking the property *nonexistence* and adding an actuality operator. It is the property *not actually existing.* On this view, we could say that to exist is to be identical with something, not to exist is to be identical with nothing, and the desire not to exist is the desire to be identical with nothing actual.

However, the view associated with (3b) is problematic in a couple of ways. First, it is unclear that the relevant property—*not actually existing,* or *being distinct from every actual thing*—is possible in a

4. Nolan (2006) argues along similar lines that the desire not to exist belongs to a class of attitudes that cause trouble for the property theory.

sense that will satisfy our intuition that (3) has Descartes considering something possible. Since Descartes exists in the actual world, he will have the property *actually existing* in whichever merely possible world he might also inhabit. So, *he* cannot have the property *not actually existing*. The second problem is related and more decisive. Intuitively, what Descartes is considering in (3) is possible. Intuitively, what Descartes is considering in (3) obtains in worlds where he does not exist. Consider a world in which Descartes does not exist, every other actually existing thing does exist, and nothing else exists. Intuitively, this world meets the condition associated with what Descartes considers in (3). However, Descartes does not have any properties in this world, and, more important, nothing in it has the property *not actually existing*. So it is hard to see how (3b) provides the correct content for the consideration attributed in (3).

Here is the other inadequate solution. One might think it is easy to capture the fact that, as Markie (1984: 236) puts it, "sometimes we adopt an attitude *de dicto* and the content is a possibility that includes our nonexistence." The idea here would be to take the proposition *that Descartes does not exist*, and use the corresponding property, thus:

(3c) Descartes directly considers *being such that Descartes does not exist*.

The global property attributed in (3c) is a possible one, and so (3c) arguably captures the fact that (3) has Descartes considering something possible that excludes his existence. However, the property attributed in (3c) corresponds to a *singular* proposition about Descartes. Alternatively, it contains or entails the haecceity *being identical to Descartes*. Since I am an internalist, I must deny that we ever self-ascribe or stand in other cognitive relations to properties that contain or entail individual essences. As a result, (3c) is not a live option for me, and I must cast it aside.[5]

There is another problem for the strategy of fiddling around with contents to account for the attitudes at issue here, which will lead us to a somewhat broader problem and to a solution. Suppose we

---

5. It might be interesting to note that Chisholm's (1981) view, against which Markie's objection is primarily directed, is also inconsistent with this response. This is because Chisholm refuses to countenance such things as haecceities and singular propositions. See especially Chisholm (1981: 4). This point casts doubt on whether Chisholm would have agreed that the attitude attributed in (2) is *de dicto*, as Markie seems to claim.

are wondering about the content of Descartes' potential desire not to exist. Now, the most natural thing for a property theorist to say about desire satisfaction is that a given subject S's desire is satisfied if and only if S has the property that S desires. However, it seems that, in a world where Descartes does not exist, he does not have any properties at all. He does not have the property *nonexistence*, and he has neither the property *not actually existing* nor *being such that Descartes does not exist*. So, it appears that Descartes' desire not to exist is not satisfied at worlds where Descartes does not exist. But that seems wrong.

That isn't all. The desire not to exist should count as *de se* by anybody's lights. For example, Descartes might somehow desire that Descartes does not exist, without desiring that he himself not exist. Nolan (2006) argues that other attitudes, purely *de dicto* ones, cause very similar trouble for the property theory. The idea is that one's desires often imply preferences concerning worlds in which one does not exist. For example, suppose I desire that all good people are happy. This seems to be a *de dicto* desire, which need not have anything particularly to do with myself. On the property theory, what I desire is the property *being such that all good people are happy*, i.e., this property is the content of my desire. Now suppose that there is a possible world where all good people are happy, but in which I do not exist. Since I do not have the property *being such that all good people are happy* in this world, it seems that my desire is not satisfied there. Moreover, it seems that, on the property theory, my desire does not involve a preference for this world over another one in which I also do not exist but some good people are not happy. These are troubling consequences for the property theory.

The general problem here is that certain of our attitudes seem to "fit" worlds in which we do not exist, but it is hard to see how the property theory can accommodate this fact. I suggest that the problem is not with the contents that the property theorist assigns to these attitudes. The problem is with the notion of what it is for an attitude to fit a given world, e.g., for one's desire to be satisfied at a possible world. The problem, as I see it, cuts across *de dicto* and *de se* (non–*de dicto*) attitudes, and hence has little to do at its heart with the property-theoretic reduction of the *de dicto* to the *de se*. In what follows, I will formulate my solution to the problem.

We want to be able to say that, although *nonexistence* is an impossible property, there are possible worlds that represent actually existing things as not existing, and so a thing can be, in a sense, "nonexistent at a world." Given a possible world w, a thing that actually exists has *nonexistence-at-w* if and only if it does not exist in w. In this sense, Descartes' desire for nonexistence can be satisfied: For any world w in which Descartes does not exist, Descartes has *nonexistence-at-w*. This account does not admit nonexistent objects, and it does not imply that *nonexistence* is a possible property. It accounts for the intuitive possibility of Descartes' wish in terms of possible worlds in which he does not exist. This will be made more precise shortly.

We also want to be able to say that, if a proposition P is true at a world w, then any actually existing thing has the property *being such that P-at-w*, even if this thing does not exist in w. This would allow for one's desire for P to be satisfied at w, which intuitively seems possible. It would also allow for one's belief in P to be true at w, which might also seem possible. Is there a unified, plausible account that will allow us to say all these things? I think that there is.

We have been concerned with the property *nonexistence*, and with properties of the form *being such that P*. Notice that these properties admit of analysis, as follows:

- S has *nonexistence* if and only if it's not the case that S has *existence*.
- S has *being such that P* if and only if P.

On the right-hand side of each biconditional is a *condition* for something's having the relevant property. Given a thing, each condition is a proposition (in the second case, of course, the given thing does not enter into the proposition). We may say that a world *satisfies* such a condition provided that the appropriate proposition is true at the world. Remember that we want to say that a subject can have the property *nonexistence-at-w* and properties of the form *being such that P-at-w*, even if the subject does not exist in w. Here is the account that allows us to say these things:

- S has *F-at-w* if and only if w satisfies the condition for S's having F.

This account applies to all properties, of course, not just those that admit of analysis. If F is an unanalyzable property, then the condition for something's having F is trivial, i.e., S has F if and only if S has F.

Suppose that w is a world in which Descartes does not exist. On this account, Descartes has *nonexistence-at-w*, since the condition (i.e., proposition) *that it's not the case that Descartes has existence* is true at *w*, and so *w* satisfies this condition. Now suppose that *w* is a world in which I do not exist, but in which all good people are happy. On this account, I have the property *being such that all good people are happy-at-w*, since *w* satisfies the condition *that all good people are happy* (i.e., this proposition is true at *w*). Now, we can formulate the new account of fit as follows:

- If the content of a subject *S*'s attitude is the property *F*, then the attitude *fits* a possible world *w* if and only if *S* has *F-at-w*.

This makes Descartes' desire fit every world in which he does not exist, and it thereby makes it possible that this desire is satisfied. It makes my desire fit every world where all good people are happy, whether or not I exist in such a world, and it thereby makes my desire satisfied at all such worlds.

This account of fit can apply to true belief as well as to satisfied desire. Earlier (in ch. 1, sec. 4), I said that a subject has a true belief when she self-ascribes a property that she has. We can now give an account of a belief being true at a world, in terms of fit. A subject's belief is true at a world *w* provided that it fits *w*. This allows for one's belief to be true at a world where one does not exist. For example, suppose I believe that all good people are happy. For any world *w* in which I do not exist but all good people are happy, I have *being such that all good people are happy-at-w*. So, my belief fits every such world and thereby is true at every such world, which seems intuitively correct (even if we wish to maintain that any given subject exists in all of her belief worlds).

Let's finish up by applying this solution to the problem of Descartes considering his nonexistence in sentence (3) and then to Markie's original problem. One's direct consideration of nonexistence should be treated just like one's desire for nonexistence, and so sentence (3) is correctly understood in terms of (3a) after all. When Descartes considers its being the case that he does not exist, the content of his direct consideration is simply *nonexistence*. This is an impossible property (no thing could have it), but the property theorist can accommodate the intuition that Descartes considers something possible. This is because—as we have seen—there is a world *w* such that Descartes has *nonexistence-at-w*, and so Descartes' direct consideration fits *w*.

We can now extend this solution to cover Markie's objection that the property theory cannot give an adequate account of attribution (2), in which Descartes is said to consider someone's being wise while he himself neither exists nor has any properties. Just as (3a) provides the correct understanding of (3), Markie's (2a) gives the correct understanding of his sentence (2). The direct consideration attributed to Descartes in (2a) is a certain conjunctive property. It is something like the following impossible property: *not existing, and not having any properties, and being such that someone is wise.* The condition for Descartes' having this property, then, is the proposition *that it's not the case that Descartes has existence, and it's not the case that Descartes has any properties, and someone is wise.* For some possible world *w*, this proposition is true at *w*. So Descartes has the property *not existing, and not having any properties, and being such that someone is wise-at-w,* and so his attitude fits *w*. This is simply an extension of the solution to the puzzle raised by attitudes involving *nonexistence*, and captures the fact that (2) portrays Descartes as considering something possible. So, I conclude that the property theorist can in fact answer Markie's objection by understanding (2) along the lines of (2a).

There are other ways in which a property theorist might go about solving the problems considered here. My account does not posit nonexistent objects, and it plausibly implies that, necessarily, nothing has *nonexistence.* It also provides a uniform solution to the *de se* problems with nonexistence and the *de dicto* problems with attitudes like my desire that all good people are happy. I doubt that any other property-theoretic account has all of these benefits. It might be objected that my solution to the problems raised by Markie and Nolan is ad hoc, insofar as it employs properties of subjects in absentia. I do not think that this sort of objection carries much weight. First, I am not claiming that Descartes, for example, has any properties *in* a possible world where he does not exist. Second, it seems to me that the propositionalist needs to employ the very same kind of apparatus that I have employed here.[6] For example, suppose we were to claim that the content of Descartes' desire for nonexistence is the proposition *that Descartes does not exist.* It is plausible to think that this proposition exists only if Descartes exists (since Descartes himself, or perhaps some nondescriptive mode of presentation of Descartes that ontologically depends upon him, is a constituent of the proposition). If this is right, the proposition does not exist in any world where

---

6. This point is made by Turner (2006). My solution to the problem in this section was inspired partly by the solution that Turner offers to Nolan's problem. However, the account given by Turner does not seem to me to get the right results for *de dicto* cases.

Descartes does not exist. How, then, could it be true there? To get the correct results, the propositionalist must say that a proposition can be true *at a world* without existing in that world. And this is really all I have said about individuals, who in the same way can have properties *at worlds* without existing in them.

3. Stalnaker's Argument

Stalnaker (1981) presents an argument against the view that properties are the objects of our beliefs and other attitudes. His objection is directed against Lewis's version of the property theory, but it applies to any version of the general view. The argument is based upon the example of Rudolf Lingens, the amnesiac who is lost in the library and reads a biography of himself (see ch. 1, sec. 3). Stalnaker imagines that, according to the biography, Lingens is a cousin of a notorious spy (see ch. 3, sec. 3). He also adds the following twist to the Lingens saga:

> Lingens, still lost in the Stanford Library, meets Ortcutt. "I've lost my memory and don't know who I am," says Lingens. "Can you tell me? Who am I?" "You're my cousin, Rudolf Lingens," replies Ortcutt.
>
>   This seems to be a simple case of direct and successful communication. Lingens requested a certain piece of information; Ortcutt was able to provide it, and did. Ortcutt was sincere—he believed what he said—and Lingens believed what he was told. Furthermore, Ortcutt's reply was direct: he did not just say something from which Lingens was able to infer the right answer to his question. He *told* him the answer. (1981: 146)

On Stalnaker's view, as we have seen, the contents of belief and other cognitive attitudes are propositions. Stalnaker accounts for beliefs in much the same way that he accounts for assertions, the contents of which, on his view, are also propositions. For example, before Ortcutt replies to Lingens, there is a set of possible situations that represents the shared background knowledge of the two people. Ortcutt's answer then expresses a certain proposition that narrows down the members of this set by ruling out certain situations. Presumably, Ortcutt's assertion distinguishes between the situations in which Lingens himself is named "Lingens," is the subject of the biography he has read, and is a cousin of a spy, on the one hand, and those in which these things do not obtain, on the other.

On Stalnaker's account, Lingens has requested a certain piece of propositional information, which Ortcutt's reply subsequently expresses. The proposition expressed by Ortcutt's assertion is the very one that Lingens comes to believe. Stalnaker argues that Lewis cannot account for the case in this relatively simple and straightforward way, as follows:

> If Lewis holds that the objects of speech acts, as well as of attitudes, are properties—that to make an assertion is also to ascribe a property to oneself—then he will have to describe the case in something like the following way: Lingens asks which of a certain set of properties is correctly ascribed to himself. Ortcutt responds by ascribing a *different* property to *him*self. Lingens is then able to infer the answer to his question from Ortcutt's assertion.... The answer to the question is thus quite indirect, and this is not a special feature of this example. The account I am putting into Lewis's mouth must hold that *all* answers to questions are indirect in this way. If assertions are always self-ascriptions of properties, then people talk only about themselves. (1981: 146–147)

It seems, however, that it is open to Lewis, as a property theorist, to claim that the objects of speech acts and the objects of attitudes are of different sorts. In particular, the property theorist might say that, even though the objects of attitudes are properties, the objects of speech acts are propositions. But Stalnaker argues against this move as well:

> Alternatively, Lewis might hold that speech acts, unlike attitudes, have propositions rather than properties as objects. But then he must deny that speech is a straightforward expression of thought—that what a person says, when he believes what he says, is what he believes. If Lewis makes this move, then he may save the intuition that Ortcutt's reply is a direct answer to Lingens's question, but he cannot say that the content of the answer is the information that resolves Lingens's doubt. (1981: 147)

Stalnaker's objection is a dilemma for the property theorist. The property theorist has two choices, it seems, when it comes to assigning objects to assertions or speech acts: First, the objects of assertions might be self-ascribed properties; second, the objects of assertions might be propositions. The first choice unifies the objects of assertions and beliefs. However, according to Stalnaker, since this implies that people talk only about themselves, it makes all exchanges of information indirect. (For example, if I say to you "I am tired," the object of my assertion is the property *being tired*. However, a successful exchange of information would not culminate in your self-ascribing *this* property. You need to self-ascribe a property such as *talking to someone who is tired*. This makes the exchange indirect, since the object of my assertion is not what you come to believe.) The second choice takes the objects of assertions and the objects of beliefs to be different sorts of thing. On this choice, according to Stalnaker, assertion cannot be a straightforward expression of thought. What is said, even when it is said sincerely, cannot be what is believed. This also makes all exchanges of information indirect. So, each horn of the dilemma leads to the unwelcome conclusion that all exchanges of information are indirect. Intuitively, though, it seems that some exchanges of information are direct. It seems that, at least sometimes, even in cases relevantly similar to Stalnaker's example, what a speaker says is what her auditor comes to believe. This, according to Stalnaker, spells trouble for the property theory.

It seems that Stalnaker wishes to maintain that some exchanges of information are direct, in the quasi-technical sense that what the hearer comes to believe (or, at least, part of what the hearer comes to believe), in virtue of what the speaker asserts, is the very object (or, perhaps, one of the objects) of the speaker's assertion. Stalnaker offers the exchange between Ortcutt and Lingens as a case in point. When Ortcutt said "You're my cousin, Rudolf Lingens," the object of his assertion, according to Stalnaker, was a certain proposition that Lingens then came to believe, without inferring it from what Ortcutt said. If an exchange of information is indirect, on the other hand, what the hearer comes to believe is somehow inferred from what the speaker says (i.e., from the object of the assertion) along with facts about the context of the utterance.

How should the property theorist answer Stalnaker's objection? There are plausible responses, it seems to me, to both horns of the dilemma. First, let us suppose that the objects of assertion, like the objects of belief, are properties. (Perhaps this was Lewis's preference.) The problem is supposed to be that intuitively direct exchanges of information turn out to be indirect. Two responses are open to the property theorist here. One of them is to try to argue that direct exchanges of information are possible, after all, even if the objects of assertion are self-ascribed properties. The other is to admit that the exchanges are not direct in Stalnaker's sense, but to argue that this is not problematic. I shall consider each of these responses in turn.

Let's make use of a simpler example, which does not bring up issues that are independent of the current problem (in particular, issues involving the peculiarities of self-identification). For example, suppose that Valerie has amnesia and asks Joe what she does for a living. Joe answers "you are a spy." Stalnaker complains that, if Joe is self-ascribing a property in making this assertion, he is talking only about himself. This, in turn, entails that the exchange is indirect, since Valerie must self-ascribe a different property than the one Joe self-ascribes. However, maybe there is a sense in which Joe is not just talking about himself, and maybe this can allow the exchange to be direct.

For example, if Joe self-ascribes a property when he utters "you are a spy," he self-ascribes something like the property *addressing exactly one person who is a spy*. The property theorist might say that Joe's assertion has *two* objects: first, the entire property that he self-ascribes; and second, the property *being a spy*, which he ascribes to Valerie in making the assertion. (We might want to borrow some terms from Chisholm and say that the entire self-ascribed property is the *direct object* of the assertion and the other property is the *indirect object* of the assertion.) Joe's self-ascription is of the form *being an x such that x bears R to one and only one y such that y has F*. In Joe's case, R is the relation *x is addressing y*, and F is the property *being a spy*. In general, given a self-ascription of this form, the indirect object of the assertion will be the property F. The idea here is that Joe is (indirectly) talking about Valerie in virtue of (directly) talking about himself.

So, if *being a spy* is an object of Joe's assertion, and if Valerie comes to self-ascribe this property in virtue of what Joe asserts, the information exchange arguably turns out to be direct after all. On the present view, direct exchanges of information are possible even if properties are the objects of assertions. I think this strategy is plausible, but I am not convinced that it is the best property-theoretic response to Stalnaker. First, the strategy of positing multiple objects of assertion (if it is done simply for the sake of making direct information exchanges possible) might appear ad hoc. Second, perhaps the sense in which information exchanges are direct on this view is not strong enough. For example, Valerie needs to self-ascribe the indirect but not the direct object of Joe's assertion, and perhaps she must make some sort of inference from one to the other in order to do this.

We are still considering the horn of the dilemma according to which the objects of assertions are properties. The other property-theoretic answer to Stalnaker's objection is to admit the indirectness of information exchanges and explain away the problem. Can the property theorist plausibly deny that there is no direct exchange of information from Joe to Valerie, and claim that she must infer the information she requested from what he said? All that is needed to accompany this position is an adequate explanation of how the indirectness is not an impediment to ordinary, successful communication. It seems that such an explanation is available to the property theorist. I will provide a rough sketch, without exploring the mechanisms that underlie the successful conveying of information.

We might give such an explanation, for the present case, in the following way: Joe says to Valerie "you are a spy," and in so doing he self-ascribes a property, e.g., the property *addressing exactly one spy.* This property is the unique object of his assertion. Valerie hears and understands the words uttered by Joe, and believes that Joe is addressing her and her alone. Taking Joe to be sincere, Valerie concludes that she is talking with someone who is addressing a spy. Since she thinks she is talking with someone who is addressing only her, she infers that she is a spy. She comes to self-ascribe the property *being a spy.* This property was not the object (or even an object) of Joe's assertion, but she comes to it in a fairly natural and familiar way. Communication of thoughts, on this picture, need not require the hearer to come to believe what is said.[7] All that is required for communication is that the hearer come to grasp what is being said, partly in virtue of the semantic properties of the utterance, and form an appropriate belief.

The fact that the object of Joe's assertion is not identical with the information that Valerie requested, then, does not prevent her from acquiring it in a very natural way. It might seem from the explanation above that Valerie needs to infer the answer to her question in some laborious fashion from Joe's assertion. But even if this is the case, it seems that the property theorist can swallow this sort of indirectness. The intuitions, if they exist, that informational exchanges of this sort are direct in the sense intended by Stalnaker—i.e., are such that the object of the speaker's assertion becomes, without any inference, an object of the hearer's belief—can reasonably be discarded. In fact, it seems to me likely that there are no relevant intuitions about *this* sort

7. It need not, though it might. Clear cases of the expression of a *de dicto* belief might require the hearer to self-ascribe the content of the speaker's assertion. For a given proposition *P*, the speaker would self-ascribe the property *being such that P* in order to get the hearer to self-ascribe the very same property. Such exchanges of information, if they occur, might very well be direct in Stalnaker's sense. However, the information exchanges involved in Stalnaker's objection are of a quite different sort.

of directness at all. No serious problems, then, confront the property theorist on this horn of the dilemma.

Having said that, I am inclined to think that the property theorist should embrace the second horn of the dilemma. This would allow the object of an assertion to be the semantic content of the relevant utterance in the relevant context. If the property theorist were to embrace the second horn of the dilemma, a similar answer to Stalnaker would be available. Again, in this case, the objects of assertions are taken to be propositions, even though the objects of attitudes are properties. Stalnaker's complaint is that, in this case, assertion is not a straightforward expression of thought. But again, this should not worry property theorists, so long as we have an adequate explanation of how thoughts are communicated in the relevant cases. It seems to me that such an explanation would be available, and would be very similar to the kind of account given in the preceding paragraphs. Valerie grasps the linguistic meaning of Joe's utterance of "you are a spy," believes that he is addressing her, and so on. Again, the indirectness of communication in such cases is not a cause for concern. There is simply a rather loose connection between the contents of our thoughts, on the one hand, and the meaning of the language we use to express them, on the other.

I hope that I have shown that several plausible responses to Stalnaker's objection are available to the property theorist (even though I also think that the last one is the most plausible). I conclude that Stalnaker's argument does not constitute a devastating objection to the view of the attitudes taken by proponents of the property theory.

4. Propositionalist Arguments from Inference

In this section, I consider various inferences that might be thought to pull us toward the doctrine of propositions, and thereby away from the property theory. For example, one might argue that the property theory cannot make room for the intuitive validity of the following sort of argument:[8]

---

8. The argument is quoted from Bealer (1982: 23). Bealer uses the argument, and the next one to follow, to support the following claims: The predicates "is necessary" and "is true" are one-place predicates; "believes that" is a two-place predicate; and *that*-clauses work, in some way or other, as singular terms. See especially 23–25. Bealer does use other arguments to try to show that *that*-clauses are semantically correlated with propositions (26–29). However, these arguments do not favor propositions over other sorts of intensional entities, e.g., properties.

(I)   Whatever x believes is necessary.
        Whatever is necessary is true.
        $\therefore$ Whatever x believes is true.

Now, strictly speaking, the *validity* of this argument poses no threat to the property theory. The property theorist can readily admit that the conclusion of the argument would have to be true if both of its premises were true. But it seems that the property theory does have trouble allowing for *sound* instances of the argument, since the theory seems to entail that "believes" expresses a relation that relates subjects to entities—i.e., properties—to which the predicates "is necessary" and "is true" never literally apply. I concede that argument (I) is intuitively valid, and also that our inclination to regard the argument as possibly sound is best explained by the doctrine of propositions, which entails that belief contents can literally have the (seemingly monadic) properties *being necessary* and *being true*. However, for at least two reasons, there does not seem to be a weighty objection to the property theory here. First, the objection essentially amounts to the claim that we are willing to say that what is believed can be necessary and true—but the property theorist can make sense of these claims. Second, I think that the arguments against the doctrine of propositions are so convincing that we should be comfortable in accepting something less than the most straightforward account of (I)'s validity. I will briefly explain these points in turn.

Argument (I) contains claims to the effect that certain beliefs are necessary and true. We have already seen that the property theorist can say that a subject believes truly when she has the property that she self-ascribes. (Above, we have seen that the property theorist can also say that a subject's self-ascription of a property F is true at a given possible world w provided that she has F-at-w.) Talk of truth applies to properties, then, and in this way we can make sense of the notion of true belief. The same goes for talk of necessity. In fact, we can distinguish three slightly different senses in which a belief might be called "necessary." I will discuss each of these in turn, along with the associated understanding of argument (I).

First, we might say that what someone believes is necessary in the sense that the self-ascribed property is a necessary property, where a property F is necessary if and only if, necessarily, everything has F. (There are two sorts of necessary property in this sense. For example, the properties *being red or not red* and *being such that* $2 + 2 = 4$ both count as necessary on this definition.) This provides a way to understand argument (I) according to which it is valid and possibly sound. (Since we shall be tinkering with argument (I) a bit, perhaps we should say that it provides a *substitute* for argument (I) that has these features. I think this is a good enough response to the current objection.) In this case, the first premise says that whatever *x* believes is a necessary property, i.e., is necessarily true of everything. We can then take the second premise to say that whatever is a necessary property is true of everything, and the conclusion to say that whatever *x* believes is true of everything. This interpretation of (I) is valid and could be sound, and provides one possible account of the argument.

Second, we might say that what someone believes is necessary in the sense that the self-ascribed property is necessarily true of the believer, where a given property *F* is necessarily true of *S* if and only if, necessarily, if *S* exists then *S* has *F*. This gives us a slightly different way to make sense of argument (I). Here, the first premise says that whatever *x* believes is necessarily true of *x*. The second premise is understood to say that whatever is necessarily true of *x* is true of *x*. These premises entail the conclusion that whatever *x* believes—i.e., whatever *x* self-ascribes—is true of *x*. So this gives us another way to treat argument (I) according to which it is valid and possibly sound.

Finally, we might say that what someone believes is necessary in the sense that the self-ascribed property corresponds to a necessary proposition, where a property *F* corresponds to a necessary proposition if and only if there is a necessary proposition *P* such that *F* is the property *being such that P*. (Here, the relevant class of properties is only a proper subset of the class of necessary properties.) In this sense, we can even say that people sometimes believe propositions. For example, we might use "believes" to express a relation between subjects and propositions, and say that a subject believes a proposition if and only if she self-ascribes a property that corresponds to the proposition, i.e., *S* believes *P* if and only if *S* self-ascribes *being such that P*. This would provide us with perhaps the most natural account of argument (I). In this case, the argument can even be taken at face value. The first premise says that whatever *x* believes is necessary, the second that whatever is necessary is true, and the conclusion that whatever *x* believes is true. If we take locutions of the form "*x* believes *y*" to express a relation that holds only between persons and propositions, *in virtue of the self-ascription of the corresponding properties*, then we can simply help ourselves to the propositionalist's conception of (I).

I hope to have shown that the property theory has the resources to make sense of and account for the intuitive validity, and the possible soundness, of arguments like (I). Each of the cases outlined above corresponds to a natural sense in which what someone believes might be called "necessary," and each provides for a plausible understanding of argument (I). The last case even shows that the property theorist can make sense of the argument on the propositionalist's own terms. It seems to me that, even if the property-theoretic account of (I) needs to be more complicated than the propositionalist account, the overall case for the property theory is so strong that understanding (I) on its terms is a cost that is well worth accepting.

Let us turn now to another form of inference that might be thought to tell against the property theory. Consider the following argument:[9]

(II)   Whatever x believes is true.
         x believes that A.
         ∴ It is true that A.

This is also an intuitively valid argument (here, the schematic letter A is to be replaced with any formula). A complete analysis of this argument would require a worked-out treatment of *that*-clauses in attitude contexts, and that project is beyond the scope of this book. (On my view, claims of the form "S believes that P" can have different logical forms, e.g., "Joe believes that Valerie is a spy" has a more complex form than "Valerie believes that she [herself] is a spy" has. This will be explored in the following chapters.)

For now, it should be clear from the preceding discussion that the property theory can provide the resources for a plausible account of argument (II). For example, if the verb "believes" can have a sense according to which it expresses a (defined) relation to propositions, the propositionalist treatment of (II) can be accepted. Even if it has such a sense, however, that is certainly not the only sense it has. But truth talk about properties yields another, natural way for the property theorist to handle inference (II). The first premise can be taken to assert that whatever x self-ascribes is true of x. If the second premise is taken to assert (at least in part) that x self-ascribes a certain property, then the conclusion that this property is true of x follows immediately. Admittedly, this sense of the argument involves some departure from the most literal, straightforward account. But again, it seems to me that the overall case for the property theory makes it worth the extra complexity in the treatment of inferences along the lines of (II).

9. This argument is also quoted from Bealer (1982: 24).

It might also be worth pointing out that there are cases where the property theory has the most natural explanation of a given argument's intuitive validity, and where the doctrine of propositions stumbles. For example, consider this argument:

(III)   Venus wants to be famous.
         Serena wants everything Venus wants.
         ∴ Serena wants to be famous.

There is a clear sense in which (III) is valid, and this is probably the sense in which most speakers would be inclined to interpret the argument. On the property-theoretic account, the first premise has Venus wanting to have the property *being famous*, and the second has Serena wanting to have every property that Venus wants to have. The conclusion, that Serena wants to have *being famous* too, obviously follows. But this is not the case with the propositionalist's treatment, according to which the content of Serena's desire to be famous is a *different* proposition from the content of Venus's desire to be famous.[10]

This leads us to the final type of argument I would like to consider in defense of the property theory. This form of argument is quite similar to the form of argument (III) above, and can be seen below:

(IV) x believes that P.
         y believes everything x believes.
         ∴ y believes that P.

It is unclear that this form of argument undercuts the property theory in any way. The preceding argument seems to show that, if an instance of the first premise reports an irreducibly *de se* belief, then the property theory gives the most plausible account of a clear sense in which the argument is valid (assuming the second premise to say that y self-ascribes every property that x self-ascribes). And if the first premise reports a purely *de dicto* belief—i.e., a self-ascription of a property of the form *being such that P*—then it also seems that the argument poses no problem for the property theory.

However, many of our beliefs are not purely *de dicto* (indeed, much of what remains in this book will be devoted to showing that very few are), and belief reports do not always specify a proposition that the subject is said to believe. So it is possible that an argument with

10. Some of the preceding remarks in this section are based on section 4 of Feit (2001).

the form of (IV) could prove troublesome for the property theory. It might be argued, for example, that the following intuitively valid argument turns out to be invalid on the property theory:[11]

(V)   Rusty believes that Billy is riding a moped.
       Emily believes everything Rusty believes.
       ∴ Emily believes that Billy is riding a moped.

To see how this argument might be thought to tell against the property theory, we will need to see how the property theorist treats the first premise. For the usual reasons having to do with internalism, I do not take the first premise to say that Rusty believes the proposition *that Billy is riding a moped*, i.e., that he self-ascribes the property *being such that Billy is riding a moped*.[12] What, then, does the first premise say? In a nutshell, it says that Rusty ascribes the property *riding a moped* to Billy. This notion was introduced in chapter 2, section 4, and will be explored more fully in the next chapter. What it is for Rusty to ascribe *riding a moped* to Billy, roughly, is for there to be a suitable relation *R* that Rusty bears uniquely to Billy (perceptual relations such as *looking at* are paradigmatic examples, but not necessary) such that Rusty self-ascribes *bearing R to someone who is riding a moped*. On this account, the first premise says not only that Rusty self-ascribes a certain kind of property, but also that this property entails a suitable relation that he bears to Billy.[13]

Now, I have given a property-theoretic interpretation of the first premise. It says that Rusty ascribes *riding a moped* to Billy, where this implies that, for some suitable relation *R*, Rusty self-ascribes *bearing R to someone who is riding a moped* and in fact bears *R* to Billy. However, the most natural property-theoretic account of the second premise takes it to say that Emily self-ascribes every property that

11. This argument is taken from Richard (1990: 75). Richard uses the argument to object to a certain Fregean account of belief reports, and not to the property theory.

12. If we understood the first premise of the argument in this way, the argument would pose no problem for the property theory. For what it is worth, I think that there are reasons independent of internalism (e.g., Kripke's puzzle about belief) to think that the *that*-clause in the first premise of (V) does not specify a proposition that Rusty is alleged to believe. This issue will be discussed in chapter 6.

13. This account of property ascription will be examined more thoroughly in chapter 5. One might object that this account gives the first premise a *de re* reading rather than a *de dicto* one. I reply that, when it comes to belief reports containing proper names, something like this account is as *de dicto* as it gets. I will consider this point again in chapter 6.

Rusty self-ascribes. But given this reading of the second premise, the argument turns out to be invalid. This is because, from the two premises, we can deduce that Emily self-ascribes *bearing R to someone who is riding a moped*, but this is consistent with Emily's *not* believing that Billy is riding a moped, since she need not bear R to Billy. For example, Emily might bear R to Billy's molecule-for-molecule duplicate, Willy, or she might live on Twin Earth and bear R to Twin Billy, or she might be a brain in a vat and bear R to nobody at all.

This is clearly not a devastating objection, however, to the view that properties are the objects of beliefs. While it is true that, on the property theory, there is a clear sense in which (V) is invalid, there is a way for property theorists to save inferences of this sort. The idea is that the second premise is capable of another reading. On one reading, it does assert that Emily self-ascribes every property that Rusty self-ascribes, in which case the inference does turn out to be invalid. But there is another reading of the premise, according to which it asserts that Emily ascribes the same properties to the same things as Rusty, i.e., that for every *x* and every *F*, if Rusty ascribes *F* to *x* then so does Emily. (This might be put by saying that Emily has every *de re* belief that Rusty has, and so this strategy implies that there is a way to take the second premise to concern *de re* beliefs. More on this in the next chapter.) On this reading of the second premise, argument (V) is indeed valid. If Rusty ascribes *riding a moped* to Billy, and any property that Rusty ascribes to a thing is such that Emily ascribes it to the same thing, then Emily must ascribe *riding a moped* to Billy too. So, we can account in this way for the intuitive validity of the argument.

I hope to have shown that the sorts of inference considered here can be treated adequately from the property-theoretic perspective. My discussion of the final inference relied in part on a certain view of *de re* belief. I turn to this phenomenon, and its relation to the property theory of content, in the next chapter.

CHAPTER FIVE

THE PROPERTY THEORY
AND *DE RE* BELIEF

Many of our beliefs are, in some ordinary sense, *about* the various concrete particulars in our environment, i.e., they are so-called *de re* beliefs. For example, I have beliefs about my cat Virginia, my brother Fred, my car, the walnut tree in my neighbors' backyard, various buildings in my town, certain foreign cities, and so on. Any theory of *de re* belief must provide an account of what makes such a belief a singular thought, one that is directed toward, or about, a particular individual. In this chapter, I discuss and defend a property-theoretic picture of *de re* belief. This account takes the contents of *de re* beliefs to be self-ascribed properties of a certain kind, and is consistent with the internalist picture of the mind developed in the preceding chapters.

Philosophers have used the phrase "*de re* belief" in at least two different ways. First, it has been used to pick out a certain linguistic phenomenon, viz., a certain kind of attitude attribution. For example, the sentence "Joe believes of Valerie that she is a spy" can be called *de re* in this sense. This type of belief attribution has several interesting features, e.g., it is extensional and makes exportation valid. Second, the phrase has been used to pick out not a linguistic phenomenon but an allegedly psychological one, viz., a special sort of mental state that can be called *de re*. This sort of state is commonly taken to consist in the subject's believing a singular or object-dependent proposition. As I see it, we should admit *de re* attitude attributions, but not *de re* mental states. When we talk about a *de re* belief, then, we are talking about an ordinary belief or perhaps about a more complex state that includes a belief along with certain relations between the believer and some object in her environment. This view will be clarified and defended in due course.

In the first section of this chapter, I discuss Lewis's view of *de re* belief. I accept much of what Lewis has to say on the subject of *de re* belief, although (as we shall see later in the chapter) I will quibble with the details of his analysis. In the second section, I discuss an objection to Lewis's account given by McKay (1988), and defend the account from McKay's argument. In the third section, I give my own reasons to think that Lewis's account is not quite adequate. The reasons have to do with our intuitions about certain cases involving mistaken identity. I also try to replace Lewis's analysis of *de re* belief with a similar property-theoretic account. Finally, in the last section of the chapter, I discuss a few other worries about the notion of *de re* belief and make some concluding remarks on the project of theorizing about it.

1. Lewis's Account of *De Re* Belief

Lewis defends a view of *de re* belief in terms of the notion of self-ascription and the notion of a causal relation of acquaintance between a subject and another individual.[1] This individual is the res, or object, of the subject's belief. (However, it does not enter into the content of the subject's belief, and so we should not confuse the content of a belief with the object of a belief in the present sense.) According to Lewis, our *de re* beliefs are states of affairs that obtain only partly in virtue of our self-ascriptions, i.e., only partly in virtue of our beliefs, properly so-called. On his narrowly psychological view of belief, our beliefs are exhausted by our self-ascribed properties, which are determined by our intrinsic natures. Hence the following remark from Lewis: "Beliefs are in the head; but...beliefs *de re*, in general, are not. Beliefs *de re* are not really beliefs. They are states of affairs that obtain in virtue of the relations of the subject's beliefs to the *res* in question" (1983a: 152).

Property theorists should acknowledge the force of this remark. Suppose, for example, that Joe sees Valerie wearing a trench coat and takes her to be a spy. In this case, Joe is acquainted perceptually with

---

1. This section contains material drawn from section I of Feit (2000).

Valerie, and it is this acquaintance that leads him to believe what he does. The property theorist will distinguish two states of affairs here: (1) Joe's seeing Valerie, and nobody else, wearing a trench coat, and (2) Joe's self-ascribing the property *seeing just one person who is wearing a trench coat and who is a spy*. State (2) is a purely psychological state of affairs, and the property in question is the content of one of Joe's beliefs. On the other hand, state (1) consists in Joe's perceiving, in a certain way, a particular individual in his environment, and as such it is not purely a matter of his psychology. In ordinary circumstances, these two states determine that Joe has a *de re* belief, about Valerie, to the effect that she is a spy. The content of this belief is a property that Joe self-ascribes, viz., the property in (2) above.

According to Lewis, (1) and (2) are sufficient for Joe's belief to be about Valerie, partly because *seeing* (or *seeing-in-a-trench-coat*) is a "relation of acquaintance." It seems that any adequate account of *de re* belief will have to appeal to something like Lewis's notion of a relation of acquaintance. Lewis provides the following sketchy definition: "I and the one of whom I have beliefs *de re* are so related that there is an extensive causal dependence of my states upon his; and this causal dependence is of a sort apt for the reliable transmission of information" (1983a: 155).

Here, Lewis is talking of his beliefs about another person, but of course a subject can have *de re* beliefs about a wide array of various things. (In this chapter, I restrict my attention to beliefs about particular physical objects, i.e., to ascriptions of properties to single objects. Any account of such beliefs can easily be extended to more complex *de re* beliefs, e.g., the belief of Rochester and Syracuse that the first is west of the second.) In the example of Joe and Valerie, the relation of acquaintance that he bears to her is a perceptual relation, but Lewis (1986) reminds us that other sorts of relation can provide for belief *de re*: "A relation of acquaintance needn't be so very direct and perceptual. Other relations will do, so long as they afford channels for the flow of information. For instance there is the relation which obtains when one has heard of something by name" (1986: 33).

If we admit that we can have *de re* attitudes about things that we are not currently perceiving, as we certainly should, then we must also maintain that some relations of acquaintance convey information to us about things that we do not perceive directly. So, for example, the following dyadic relations should all count as relations of acquaintance: *x sees y*, *x remembers y*, *x has heard of y under the name "London,"* *x is reading about y*, *x is examining a letter written by y*, and so on. This kind of relation is thus a suitable causal dependence of thought upon some physical object, or perhaps upon the object's having certain properties. The self-ascription of such a relation plays (part of) the role of a *de re* mode of presentation under which the subject thinks of a given object.

Lewis's account of *de re* belief makes use of the notion of bearing a relation of acquaintance *uniquely* to an individual. As we have seen, this consists in the subject bearing the relation to the given individual *and to nothing else*. For example, I might be looking at a pair of birds and thereby fail to bear the relation *x is looking at y* uniquely to either bird, but in this case, there might be other relations of acquaintance that I do bear uniquely to each bird. In my discussion of examples, I will not always state that a given subject is acquainted *uniquely* with an object, but I shall suppose that this is the case.

In chapter 2, section 4, we saw that, on the property theory, to believe something *de re* of a given object is to ascribe a property to that object. (We also considered an account of *de re* belief—i.e., of what it is to ascribe a property to an object—that sufficed for our purposes in that section.) Joe, for example, ascribes *being a spy* to Valerie. He does this because he self-ascribes a property of a certain sort, a property entailing a certain relation of acquaintance, which he in fact bears uniquely to Valerie. We can take the following analysis to be Lewis's account of what it is for someone to ascribe a property to an object:

> *Lewis on De Re Belief (LDR)*: A subject S ascribes property F to object x if and only if there is a relation of acquaintance R such that (i) S bears R uniquely to x, and (ii) S self-ascribes the property *bearing R uniquely to something that has F*.[2]

Condition (i) of this analysis gives the nonpsychological part (or, at least, the not-wholly-psychological part) of a *de re* belief, whereas condition (ii) supplies the psychological part (the belief proper). In virtue of self-ascribing a property of the relevant kind, the subject is able to single out a particular individual and ascribe a property to it (given that condition (i) also obtains). On this property-theoretic view, properties of the form *bearing R to an F* play a role quite simi-

---

2. See Lewis (1983a: 155). I have ignored the fact that Lewis allows for a description that "captures the essence" of an object as well as a relation of acquaintance to the object, but Lewis (1983a: 155) himself claims that "it is unclear that anything is gained by providing for essence-capturing descriptions as well as relations of acquaintance. If we have the former, we will have the latter."

lar to the role played by propositions of the form *that the R is F* on other views, where *the R* is a description that corresponds to the relation of acquaintance. However, if the belief is *de re* rather than merely descriptive, this description will typically make reference to the subject—as in, for example, "the person *I* see wearing a trench coat"—and so there are good reasons to prefer the framework of self-ascribed properties of the form given in LDR.

On Lewis's view, then, *de re* reduces to *de se* in the sense that the content of the subject's belief in a *de re* belief state of affairs is a property that the subject self-ascribes. Moreover, the property will not in general correspond to a proposition, since it might be true of one inhabitant of a possible world and false of another. It might be helpful at this point to contrast the two property-theoretic content forms for *de dicto* and *de re* beliefs:

> *De dicto: being such that P*
> *De re: bearing R uniquely to something that has F*

This shows clearly that, according to the property theory (or Lewis's version of it, at any rate), *de dicto* belief and *de re* belief are subvarieties of *de se* belief, which consists in the self-ascription of any property at all. But not everyone thinks that Lewis's reduction of the *de re* to the *de se* is successful. In the next section, we shall consider an argument against LDR given by McKay.

2. McKay's Objection to Lewis

Suppose that a person bears some relation of acquaintance *R* uniquely to a certain thing *x*, and that she believes herself to bear *R* to something pretty. On Lewis's view, this person now has a *de re* belief about *x* to the effect that it is pretty. The res, or object, of this *de re* belief is *x*, because *x* is in fact the thing to which the person bears *R*. This is what directs the belief toward this particular thing, according to a view such as LDR. However, McKay (1988) presents an argument against Lewis's view of *de re* belief. The argument is based upon an example, which McKay describes as follows:

> Smith can stand in a relation of acquaintance to Wilson, yet believe that he (Smith) stands in that relation to Jones. Thus Wilson might be hatless and visible to the left of Smith; Smith might also see Jones, who is on his right, and believe (correctly) that Jones is wearing a hat. If Smith confuses left and right, the following will be true.

(i) Wilson (and only Wilson) is perceived from the left of Smith.
(ii) Smith self-attributes perceiving someone from his left who is wearing a hat.

Yet Smith's belief is about Jones, not Wilson, contrary to Lewis's analysis. (1988: 209)

I take it that McKay is arguing against Lewis's views about both the necessary and the sufficient conditions for *de re* belief. The idea is that (i) and (ii) above might be true even if Smith does not have a belief about Wilson, and also that Smith can have a belief about Jones even if he does not self-ascribe a property entailing a relation of acquaintance that he actually bears to Jones. However, it seems to me that McKay's argument does not succeed. I think that it suffers from a failure to make a certain sort of distinction, which we might take to be a distinction between Smith's belief, on the one hand, and the way in which Smith would express this belief, on the other. McKay's claim (ii), concerning the property self-ascribed by Smith, seems unjustified because it does not follow from the earlier stipulation that Smith confuses left and right.

It seems quite plausible to think that the only way to make sense of someone's confusing left and right, for example, is to construe it as some sort of linguistic or quasi-linguistic mistake. For instance, such a person might somehow use or understand the word "left" to mean what the word "right" in fact means, or vice versa. (This sort of explanation requires the familiar distinction between semantic meaning, and speaker or agent meaning.) So, in the example described above, although Smith might *express* his belief by saying "the person on my left is wearing a hat," it does not follow that he self-ascribes the property *perceiving someone from the left who is wearing a hat*. Because he confuses left and right, Smith would incorrectly express the property that he in fact self-ascribes, which might very well be the property *perceiving someone from the right who is wearing a hat*. There is thus little reason to think that McKay's claim (ii) really is true.

Suppose we accept McKay's premise that Smith has a belief about Jones to the effect that Jones is wearing a hat (and no belief about Wilson to that effect). It is then open to us—and it seems to me that something like this is correct—to hold that Smith really does self-ascribe the property *perceiving someone from the right who is wearing a hat* (or, more formally, *being an x such that x perceives from x's right a person who is wearing a hat*). As a result, we can agree with Lewis that this is how Smith has a belief about Jones to the effect that Jones is wearing a hat (given that Smith does actually see Jones from his right). If

McKay's claim (ii) is not true, moreover, Lewis's account does not entail the falsehood that Smith has a *de re* belief about Wilson to the effect that *he* is wearing a hat.

Although more could be said about the issues raised by McKay's argument and my objection to it, I think I have said enough to show that McKay's argument does not go through. On the other hand, I am inclined to think that LDR does not account correctly for all possible cases of *de re* belief, and in particular that the two conditions in LDR do not supply conditions that are sufficient for a given subject to have *de re* beliefs about something to which she stands in some relation of acquaintance. The trouble has to do with certain cases of mistaken identity, and I shall turn to these in the next section.

3. Mistaken Identity and the Case of the Shy Secret Admirer

Before discussing what seems to me to be a counterexample to LDR, I would like to consider a case that is similar in important respects to the example I shall present.[3] This is a case of mistaken identity given by Bach (1987). Bach describes the example as follows:

> Suppose you once knew the tennis player Tim Gullikson. You didn't know then and still don't know that he has a twin brother Tom, also a tennis pro, who is not quite identical: Tom is left-handed, Tim right-handed. One afternoon you show up late for a tournament and see what you take to be the player you remember (Tim) in the midst of a tennis match. To your amazement he is playing left-handed and winning, the scoreboard showing Gullikson leading Glickstein, 6–3, 4–1. What do you believe about whom? (1987: 29)

In this case, a subject mistakes one person for another because of a false identity belief. (The relevant sort of identity belief, on the property theory, consists in the self-ascription of a property of the form *bearing R to an x, and R* to a y, such that x = y*.) The subject in the Gullikson case, it seems, will ascribe the same properties to both Tim and Tom (in virtue of different relations of acquaintance, of course). For example, the subject might believe of Tim, and of Tom, that he is a tennis pro, that he is able to play tennis with either hand, that he is beating Glickstein, and that his name is "Tim." Bach suggests that "for each perception-based belief (about Tom)

---

3. This section draws on material in sections II and III of Feit (2000).

there is a memory-based belief (about Tim) with the same predicative content" (1987: 30). The property theorist could account for this by saying, e.g., that the subject self-ascribes the property *watching a tennis player (with such-and-such features) who is beating Glickstein*, and in virtue of the false identity belief, the subject also self-ascribes the property *remembering a tennis player (with so-and-so features) who is beating Glickstein*. In so doing, the subject seems to ascribe *beating Glickstein* to Tom and Tim, respectively.

I agree with Bach. It seems that, for each of the subject's *de re* beliefs about Tom, there is a corresponding belief about Tim (and vice versa, for that matter). When our subject self-ascribes the property *watching a tennis pro who can play with his right hand*, for example, she believes *de re* of Tom that he can play with his right hand (even though he cannot), because she is watching *him*. This is the case even though her evidence for the self-ascription comes from a belief about Tim. The Gullikson case, as a result, does not pose any problems for LDR, which seems to generate the pairs of *de re* beliefs about Tom and Tim with the same predicative content. However, I am inclined to think that LDR gives the wrong results in certain other cases of mistaken identity.

Consider the case of the shy secret admirer. Fran has a shy secret admirer, Frank. Frank convinces a friend of his—Fred—to write various letters on his behalf to Fran, signed simply "Your secret admirer." Let's suppose that Fred has written several of these letters, the material for which Frank has supplied to him. In addition to expressions of admiration for Fran, each letter contains a bit of information about Frank, the secret admirer. One of the things that Fred conveys to Fran about Frank is, let us suppose, the fact that he has an enormous bank account.

Like someone who has *de re* beliefs about the person whose biography she has read, Fran has *de re* beliefs about her secret admirer, Frank. One of them is her belief of Frank that he is wealthy. In this instance, Fran believes truly, because Frank is, in fact, wealthy. She also has some false beliefs about Frank, however. One of these is her belief of Frank that he wrote the letters she received. (Here and in what follows, I use "wrote" in the sense of "penned" or "inscribed." Frank is not the one who wrote the letters in this sense, even though there might also be a sense in which he is their author.) Like the subject in the Gullikson case, Fran mistakes one individual for another. She thinks that the one who wrote the letters is the one about whom they were written.

Does Fran also have a *de re* belief about Fred, who is not her secret admirer but the one engaged by him to write the various letters, to the effect that *he* is wealthy? My intuition is that she does not. The facts of the case, it seems to me, do not warrant such an attribution, despite the fact that Fran believes that the person who wrote the letters is the one about whom they were written. I would like to make two quick points about my claim here. First, I am not ruling Fred out completely as an object of belief for Fran. Suppose, for example, that she noticed certain smudges on the letters indicating that the writer was left-handed. In this case, Fran might believe of Fred that he is left-handed. (More on this shortly.) Second, my defense of the property theory's ability to provide a plausible account of *de re* belief would be simpler in the absence of my intuitions about the case of the shy secret admirer. Readers who do not agree with my intuitions, which tell against LDR, might just skip to the next section of this chapter and the summary of the property-theoretic account of *de re* belief given there.

I do think that an account in the spirit of LDR can handle the case of the shy secret admirer. Before discussing it, I would like to make the problem for LDR a bit more explicit. Suppose that Fran self-ascribes the property *having seen some letters of admiration written uniquely by someone who is wealthy.* She is likely to do this, since she has mistakenly identified two individuals with whom she is acquainted. (The false identity belief consists in Fran's self-ascribing something like the property *having read some letters about an x, and having seen some letters written by a y, such that x = y.*) Since the relation *x has seen some letters of admiration written by y* is a relation of acquaintance that Fran bears uniquely to *Fred*, LDR implies that Fran ascribes the property *being wealthy* to Fred, i.e., that she believes *de re* of Fred that he is wealthy. I have suggested, however, that this is mistaken. Although Fran believes *de re* of Frank that he is wealthy (in virtue of the relations that she bears to him), it seems that she does not have the corresponding belief about Fred.

As a result, it seems to me that the conditions for *de re* belief given by LDR are not sufficient. A subject (Fran) might stand in a relation of acquaintance R (*x has seen letters of admiration written by y*) uniquely to an individual (Fred), and self-ascribe the property *bearing R uniquely to something that has F* (*being wealthy*), without thereby having a *de re* belief about this individual to the effect that it has F. A new account of belief *de re* is therefore needed, if my intuitions about the present case are to be preserved. We should note that examples like the case of the shy secret admirer are puzzle cases for all approaches to *de re* belief, not just for property-theoretic ones (that is, if they are puzzle cases at all). For example, consider the view that to have a *de re* belief about an object is to believe a singular proposition about it. If my intuitions are correct, the proponent of such a view will have to try to find a way to say that Fran does not believe the singular proposition *that Fred is wealthy*.

Why doesn't Fran have a *de re* belief about Fred to the effect that he is wealthy? The answer to this question, I suggest, has two parts. The first has to do with the fact that Fran ascribes *being wealthy* primarily to the person about whom she has read, viz., Frank. What leads her to think that the person who *wrote* the letters is wealthy is her mistaken identification of the writer of the letters with the subject of the letters. But the Gullikson case shows that this cannot be the whole story. The subject in that case, for example, has a *de re* belief about Tim to the effect that he is beating Glickstein, even though the subject ascribes this property primarily to Tom, whom the subject is watching. So there seems to be a kind of symmetry in the Gullikson case that is not present in the case of the shy secret admirer.

It might be worthwhile to note that the present case could be revised in such a way that Fran does believe of Fred that he is wealthy. Suppose she takes a close look at the letters and concludes from the smudges that the writer is left-handed, and she also believes (for one reason or another) that anyone who is left-handed is wealthy. She puts these beliefs together and comes to self-ascribe the property *having seen some letters written by someone who is wealthy*. In this revised case, given that Fred wrote the letters, Fran believes *de re* that he is wealthy. I suggest the reason for this is that, in the revised case but not in the original one, the false identity belief does not play a role in Fran's coming to self-ascribe the relevant property, and so here she ascribes *being wealthy* primarily to the one who wrote the letters. The general idea here is that, when someone self-ascribes a property of the form *bearing R to something that has F*, she associates the property F with the relation R. And she associates them *primarily* provided that the association does not result from an identity belief (which identifies the object to which she bears R with the object to which she bears some other relation).

The second part of the answer to our question is needed to distinguish examples like the original secret admirer case from those like the Gullikson case. We need to determine just what prevents Fran's ascriptions to Frank from passing through the identity belief, so to speak, and attaching to Fred. This might lead us to a new, general account of *de re* belief to replace LDR. What is it about the original secret admirer case, then, that prevents Fran from believing of Fred that he is wealthy? Alternatively, what allows the subject in the Gullikson case to believe *de re*, say, of Tim (the righty) that he is beating Glickstein left-handed? I suggest that the answer to these questions has to do with the fact that the subject in the Gullikson case (mistakenly) identifies Tim and Tom *in virtue of* noticing that the player being watched shares many important features with the player being remembered: They are both named "Gullikson," they are both tennis pros, they share many physical attributes, and so on. These are features that make for an important kind of objective similarity. The subject's identity belief is explained by the fact that the subject associates so many salient properties with the person being watched and also with the person being remembered.

Things are different in the case of the shy secret admirer, however, since it is not in virtue of her thinking that the subject of the letters and the writer of the letters share many important features that Fran comes to identify them. The causal/explanatory order is different in the two cases. In Fran's case, she mistakes Fred for Frank *first*, perhaps because she thinks it is most likely that her secret admirer would at least write his own letters. It is in virtue of this (mistaken) identification that she believes that the one who wrote the letters shares the features of the one about whom they were written, not the other way around.

We are now considering cases in which a subject comes to self-ascribe a certain property because of a mistaken identity belief, i.e., a belief of the form *bearing R to an x, and R* to a y, such that x = y* (or, more simply, *bearing R and R* to the same thing*). In these cases, we should ask: Why does the subject have the relevant identity belief? If the answer is that the subject comes to have the identity belief because she thinks there is a similarity between the thing to which she bears R and the thing to which she bears R*, then *de re* belief is possible; otherwise, there can be no *de re* belief. Perhaps another example will make this clearer. Suppose that I am looking at Alex, who is moving his mouth, and also that I am hearing Bob's voice. However, Bob is a ventriloquist who is throwing his voice to Alex's mouth, and so despite the fact that I think Alex is talking, he really isn't saying anything at all. This seems like the secret admirer case insofar as I can have *de re* beliefs about Alex without corresponding ones about Bob—e.g., the belief of Alex that he has red hair—and vice versa.

And, in this case, my relations of acquaintance to Alex seem to be quite independent of my relations of acquaintance to Bob.

In this example, I believe that the person I see is the person I hear, but I do not believe this in virtue of associating the same or similar features with these two different relations. Rather, I believe that the person I see is the person I hear because I make a sort of inference to the best explanation of my experiences, e.g., the person I see seems to be moving his lips and sounds appear to be coming from his mouth. The fact that I don't identify Alex and Bob on the basis of a perceived similarity, I suggest, is what prevents my *de re* beliefs about Alex—e.g., my belief of him that he has red hair—from becoming *de re* beliefs about Bob. This is despite the fact that I believe that the person I see and the person I hear are identical, and hence self-ascribe properties like *hearing the voice of a man with red hair*.

Clearly, it would not be good practice, in general, to identify things on the basis of perceived shared features. For example, suppose that I see a nickel and then, a bit later, I see a dime. I should not identify them simply because both seem round and shiny. But certain features might be important or uncommon enough to make it reasonable for a subject, in an appropriate context, to identify things that she takes to instantiate them. In the Gullikson case, the subject is not being unreasonable or irrational in identifying Tim and Tom, because of their shared physical characteristics, name, profession, and so on. Since the subject makes the identification in virtue of noticing this similarity, a property that is ascribed primarily to one of the twin brothers will pass through the identity belief, so to speak, and attach to the other one.

Here is a way to make all of this somewhat more precise. The kind of mistaken identity at issue here consists in a subject taking one thing, under a certain relation of acquaintance, for a distinct thing, under another relation of acquaintance. The following definition of this notion will help us to formulate a new account of *de re* belief:

> S has a belief B that mistakes x, under R, for y, under $R* =_{df.}$
> (1) x is not identical to y, (2) S bears R uniquely to x,
> (3) S bears $R*$ uniquely to y, (4) B is the property *bearing R and R* to the same thing*, and (5) S self-ascribes B.

We may use this definition to replace LDR with a better principle about *de re* belief, while remaining squarely within the framework of the property theory. The new principle will also make use of the idea of thinking that the thing to which one is related in such-and-such a way is *similar* to the thing to which one is related in so-and-so a way. The kind of thinking here is not *de re*. All that is required is that one associate the same or similar features with the different relations. The subject in the Gullikson case does this by associating the same features with the different relations *watching* and *remembering*, but this is independent of the further fact that the subject actually bears these relations uniquely to Tom and Tim, respectively. This notion seems clear enough for my purposes here, and so we can state the modified view of *de re* belief as follows:

> *Modified Account of De Re Belief (MDR)*: S ascribes F to x if and only if there is a relation of acquaintance R such that (i) S bears R uniquely to x; (ii) S self-ascribes the property *bearing R uniquely to something that has F*; and (iii) if there is some object y and some relation of acquaintance $R*$ such that S's self-ascription in (ii) depends upon S's having a belief B that mistakes x, under R, for y, under $R*$, then S has B in virtue of associating the same or similar features with both R and $R*$.

I would like to say a few things about MDR. First, it contains the expressions "depends upon" and "in virtue of." I prefer to cash these out in causal/explanatory terms, so that a belief depends upon an earlier belief, for example, just in case the earlier belief plays an essential role in explaining why the subject comes to have the later one. Second, MDR generates the intuitively correct results when it is applied to the cases considered in this section. Unlike LDR, it does not wrongly entail that, in the secret admirer case, Fran believes *de re* of Fred that he is wealthy. Fran self-ascribes the property *having seen letters written by someone wealthy*, and she has seen letters written by Fred. But Fran does not have a *de re* belief about Fred to the effect that he is wealthy, since her self-ascription depends upon a mistaken identity belief, and Fran does not have this identity belief in virtue of thinking that the subject of the letters and the writer of the letters are similar, or share features. The subject in the Gullikson case, however, does believe *de re* of Tim (the righty) that he is playing left-handed. Although the relevant self-ascription depends upon a mistaken identity belief, the subject has this belief in virtue of thinking that the player being watched is similar to the one being remembered.

Consider a very ordinary case of mistaken identity. Suppose I have a friend, Red, who has short red hair and always wears a red shirt or a red jacket. One day, I notice that I am walking behind a man with short red hair who is wearing a red jacket. So, I hurry up to him and give him a friendly tap on the shoulder, but the man who turns around, to my surprise, is not Red. I apologize to the stranger, explaining that I believed he was a friend of mine. MDR lets us take my remark at face value. I *did* believe *de re* of this stranger that he was a friend of mine. But my self-ascription, whatever exactly it was, depended on a false identity belief (one that identified the person I saw with the friend I remembered). Since the identification was made in virtue of a perceived similarity (*having red hair, wearing red*, etc.), the account implies that I did in fact believe *de re* that this man was a friend of mine.[4] This example thus gets assimilated to examples like the Gullikson case rather than to examples like the case of the shy secret admirer.

I would like to conclude this section by considering a certain kind of attempt to defend LDR from putative counterexamples such as the secret admirer case. The idea is to claim that *de re* belief is a context-dependent affair, in the sense that a single subject might have *de re* beliefs in one context that she lacks in another. The imagined defender of LDR might say that, in the secret admirer case, the relations that Fran bears to Fred are somehow rendered unsuitable by the context in which we are attributing *de re* beliefs to her. And if we understand LDR implicitly to incorporate a contextually supplied restriction on which relations are suitable, the case of the shy secret admirer might turn out not to be a counterexample to LDR after all. This is because it need not imply that Fran has a *de re* belief about Fred to the effect that he is wealthy.

This defense of LDR is doomed to failure, however. There are two general reasons for thinking that *de re* belief is a context-dependent phenomenon, and thus two possible reasons for ruling out certain relations that a subject bears to a res in a given context. But neither reason has any bearing on the status of the case of the shy secret admirer as a counterexample to LDR. The first sort of reason is brought out in the following passage by Richard (who uses it in a discussion of the semantics of belief attributions):

> Consider Mutt and Jeff, who agree on what sentences Odile accepts. They agree about her dispositions to behavior. They agree on just about everything that seems relevant to the question Does Odile believe that Twain is dead?

---

4. The result would be no different if I were mistaken about the color of the stranger's hair or jacket, e.g., if my rose-colored glasses made these brown items appear to me to be red.

They don't agree on the answer. When Mutt was asked, it was
because someone wanted to know whether Odile would list Twain
under dead Americans. Mutt knew she accepted "Twain is dead" and
thus said yes. Jeff was asked by someone who couldn't understand
why Odile, who is pointing to Twain's picture, wants to meet him.
Doesn't she realize that Twain is dead? Jeff knew she rejected "He's
dead." He answered that, no, Odile didn't believe that Twain was
dead. (1990: 106)

Suppose we take Mutt and Jeff to be talking about what Odile
does and does not believe *de re*, and suppose we take both of their
assertions to be true. Then, it seems that we should say that, in Mutt's
context, Odile has a *de re* belief about Twain that she does not have
in Jeff's context. We would then be forced to admit that *de re* belief
depends in a certain way upon what we say, in addition to what we
believe and the things with which we are acquainted.

When Jeff said that Odile didn't believe that Twain was dead,
he was deliberately or inadvertently ignoring certain relations of
acquaintance that Odile bears to Twain (e.g., the relation *having heard
of a writer under the name "Twain"*) and thereby focusing on others
(e.g., the relation *looking at a picture of a man*). This is why it is plausible to take his assertion to be true, especially if his audience accom-
modates him. We might account for this by allowing interlocutors to
limit or restrict the domain of relations of acquaintance over which
they quantify in a given conversational context, so that some relations are not suitable in the context. However, when I claimed earlier that Fran did not believe *de re* that Fred was wealthy, I was not
ignoring any of the relations of acquaintance that she bears to him.
Indeed, I was attending to the fact that Fran was looking at certain
letters written by Fred, and also that she self-ascribed the property
looking at letters written by a wealthy person, but still it seemed that there
was no belief of Fred that he was wealthy.

The relations of acquaintance that Fran bears to Fred, as we have
seen, do provide her with various *de re* beliefs about him (e.g., that
he is left-handed, that he prefers blue ink, and so on). We may
attribute these beliefs to her in the same context in which we deny
her the belief that Fred is wealthy. It is not because we are ignoring
the relations that Fran bears to Fred, then, that we are unwilling to
attribute to her the *de re* belief that Fred is wealthy. So, the objection
that these relations are somehow not suitable in our context has no
bearing on the original argument against LDR.

The second kind of reason for thinking that *de re* belief is context-
dependent has to do with the vagueness of the notion of a relation of

acquaintance. Lewis, for example, says the following: "It will not be possible to say precisely which relations are suitable, since it is often quite vague whether some case should or should not count as an example of belief *de re*. The vagueness is partly resolved in context, but differently in different contexts" (1983a: 153).

Belief *de re* might very well be context-sensitive in this way. However, the foregoing considerations also show that this feature is irrelevant to the argument against LDR. We are willing to admit that certain relations that Fran bears to Fred allow her to have various *de re* beliefs about him (to the effect that he is left-handed, prefers blue ink, and so on). So, the case of the shy secret admirer is not a borderline case. Fran definitely has some *de re* beliefs about Fred, but she definitely does not have a *de re* belief about him to the effect that he is wealthy.

I conclude that the issues concerning the context-dependence of *de re* belief are independent of the sorts of consideration advanced in this section. The case of the shy secret admirer seems to me to be a counterexample to LDR, and so a more complicated account of belief *de re* is needed to replace it. MDR seems to do the work for which it is intended, and seems at least to be a step in the right direction. MDR is complex, and this might be thought to tell against it; but on the other hand, there is some reason to think that *de re* belief is not a simple and tidy affair. In the next section, I discuss a few other worries about belief *de re* and summarize my property-theoretic treatment of it.

4. Some Other Worries and Concluding Remarks

Lewis's view of *de re* belief and the modified account given in the previous section reject the *latitudinarian* view of *de re* belief. On the latitudinarian view, someone could have a *de re* belief about a given object without standing in any relation of acquaintance to the object. For example, if you were simply to form the *de dicto* belief that the shortest spy is a spy, you would thereby believe *de re*, of the shortest spy (given that there is one), that he or she is a spy. The mere fact that you have a description that singles out a given object suffices for your having a *de re* belief about that object. But it is implausible to think that *de re* belief comes so easily. Suppose that you are not acquainted with Valerie and that, unbeknown to you, she is the shortest spy.

Here, it doesn't seem right to say that if you simply form the (*de dicto*) belief that the shortest spy is a spy, you believe *de re* that Valerie is a spy. At the very least, there seems to be an ordinary notion of *de re* belief that is decidedly not latitudinarian.

However, some philosophers have argued that there is no real difference between the latitudinarian and nonlatitudinarian views of belief *de re*. Some have also taken this to be a reason to be skeptical about the very idea of *de re* belief. For example, Dennett argues that there is no principled way to pick out the phenomenon of *de re* belief. He asks us to imagine a scenario in which he is in a room with various people and has no idea which person is the youngest in the room. He forms the belief that the youngest person in the room (whoever that is) was born after the death of Franklin D. Roosevelt. This is *thought A*. He then looks at a particular person in the room, Bill, and wonders whether thought A is about *him*. This second thought is *thought B*. Dennett writes:

> Now *surely* (one feels) Thought B is *about* Bill in a much more direct, intimate, strong sense than Thought A is, even if Thought A does turn out to be about Bill.... This is, I think, an illusion. There is only a difference in degree between Thought A and Thought B and their relation to Bill. Thought B is (weakly) about whoever is the only person I am looking at and whose name I believe to be Bill and ... [so on] for as long as you like. Bill, no doubt, is the lone satisfier of that description, but had his twin brother taken his place unbeknownst to me, Thought B would not have been about Bill, but about his brother. (1982: 84)

Now, we might agree with Dennett that there is no special sub-variety of belief called "*de re* belief," if only because *de re* belief consists in more than just psychological content, i.e., belief proper. On the view defended here, a *de re* belief is a complex state of affairs, which includes *both* a belief *and* the instantiation of a relation of acquaintance between the believer and the res. It seems, however, that Dennett wants to make an even stronger claim, i.e., that the notion of (nonlatitudinarian) *de re* belief doesn't make sense. Dennett draws this conclusion by arguing that there are no plausible grounds for holding that thought B is a *de re* thought about Bill while thought A is not.

There are various ways in which the proponent of *de re* belief might respond to Dennett. The notion of a relation of acquaintance is essential to the property theorist's response, and something like it is probably essential to any adequate response. In the example

described by Dennett, thought A does not contain or imply any relation of acquaintance that Dennett bears to Bill. (The description
"the youngest person in the room," though it denotes Bill uniquely,
expresses no such relation.) On the other hand, thought B does contain or imply a relation of acquaintance that Dennett bears to Bill,
i.e., something like the relation *x is looking at y* or *x is attending to y*.
(On the property-theoretic view, whatever the exact content of
thought B is, it must contain a relation of acquaintance that holds
between Dennett and Bill.) So, there is more than a difference in
degree between thought A and thought B. In virtue of thought B,
one could truly say to Bill that Dennett is wondering whether a
certain thought is *about him*, but it would be incorrect to say to Bill
that Dennett believes *of him* that he was born after the death of FDR,
even if Bill were the youngest person in the room.

Of course, there might be some vagueness associated with the
notion of a relation of acquaintance, and hence some vagueness associated with the distinction between *de re* and non–*de re* thought. But
this does not entail that one ought to be skeptical about the very idea
of *de re* belief, since there are plenty of clear cases on each end of the
spectrum. The notion of *de re* belief also seems to be philosophically
useful, insofar as it captures one sense in which people can be said to
share beliefs. As we saw in chapter 4, section 4, for example, Emily
might share Rusty's belief that Billy is riding a moped even if she
does not self-ascribe the very same property that he does (Rusty
might see Billy riding down the street while Emily hears the char-
acteristic putt-putt of Billy's moped from her living room). I argued
that there is a reading of the premise that Emily believes everything
Rusty believes according to which Emily ascribes a property to an
object if Rusty does (i.e., Emily has every *de re* belief that Rusty
has). This reading provided an ordinary sense in which an intuitively
valid argument was valid. The considerations raised by Dennett do
not seem to me to justify any skepticism about the idea of *de re* belief,
nor to render inadequate attempts to account for it along the lines of
LDR or MDR.

Despite Dennett's concerns, then, we should make some theoretical room for our ordinary, pre-philosophical, useful notion of
de re belief. In what follows, I shall sum up the property-theoretic
account of *de re* belief defended here, and discuss a few lingering
worries about the adequacy of MDR as an analysis of the notion. I
hope my remarks make clear two points concerning *de re* belief. The
first is that the property theory can make just as much sense of our

ordinary, pre-philosophical notion of *de re* belief as any other theory of belief, and the same goes for the other attitudes. For example, any work that might be done with singular propositions can be done with the property-theoretic notion of ascribing a property to an individual (which appeals to nonpsychological facts about the believer's relations to the relevant individual as well as to psychological facts about his self-ascriptions). The second point is that any residual worries about property-theoretic analyses of ascribing a property to an individual, like MDR, are also worries about the correct analysis of *de re* belief from other theoretical perspectives. When it comes to the phenomenon of *de re* belief, the property theorist has no special problems that other theorists do not share.

So, here is the summary of the account of *de re* belief defended here. (Similar remarks will apply to the other cognitive attitudes, such as desire, that might be directed toward particular objects.) First, there are *de re* attributions of belief. The most explicit forms for such attributions are forms like *S believes of X that X is F*, *S believes X to be F*, and *X is believed by S to be F*. But this style of attribution can also come in other forms. This sort of belief attribution enjoys a sort of methodological primacy when it comes to the account of *de re* belief sketched here, in the sense that the main question the account seeks to answer is the question: What makes *de re* attributions of belief *true*?

Second, there are no *de re* belief contents. This means that there are no contents that are object-dependent in the strong sense that they contain either concrete particulars, haecceities, *de re* modes of presentation, or the like. This also means that, if we happen to be talking purely about psychological states, there are no *de re* beliefs. However, any theoretical work that might be done with *de re* belief contents can be done in other ways. For example, suppose that a triadic theorist attributes a belief to Joe the content of which is the singular proposition *that Valerie is a spy*. Here, we have a *de re* content, and the triadic theorist will wish to say that Joe has a *de re* belief about Valerie. In this case, property theorists can appeal to the (psychological) fact that Joe self-ascribes a property of the form *bearing R to a spy*, and to the (nonpsychological) fact that Joe bears R to Valerie. Property theorists, in so doing, can make sense of the way in which Joe's belief is about Valerie. All the facts for generating or determining the singular proposition *that Valerie is a spy* are at the property theorist's disposal; there is no need to claim that this proposition is actually the content of Joe's belief.

Third, if we happen to be talking about states of affairs that are broader or more complex than purely psychological states, then in a sense, there are *de re* beliefs as well as *de re* attributions. For example, according to LDR, a *de re* belief is a compound state of affairs in which a subject (i) bears a relation of acquaintance R uniquely to a given object, and (ii) self-ascribes *bearing R to something that has F* (for some property F). According to MDR, *de re* beliefs are slightly more complex, in that yet another state must obtain for a subject to have a *de re* belief. The compound states of affairs in question here are the states that make *de re* attributions true. So, such attributions are made true—in part—by facts that do not have to do with the subject's beliefs. Exactly which states or facts are needed might be controversial (especially if we waver between MDR and LDR, or if we have further worries about both of them, as I shall discuss below). But the point here is that, if we are careful, we can call things "*de re* beliefs" without committing ourselves to *de re* belief contents, which is exactly what I have been doing for much of this chapter.

I shall conclude by briefly discussing a few remaining worries about MDR, which apply to LDR as well. I would like to stress that my thoughts here are tentative and that the worries (if they are really worrisome) also apply to other accounts of *de re* belief; they are not just problems for the property-theoretic treatment. I have formulated MDR so that the conditions in it are necessary and sufficient for a subject to have a *de re* belief. I do think that conditions (i)–(iii) of MDR are sufficient for *de re* belief, but I am not so sure that they are necessary.

One worry has to do with uniqueness. Certain cases might seem to show that a subject can have a *de re* belief about an individual without standing in any relation of acquaintance *uniquely* to that individual. For example, suppose that Peter and Paul have made a recording of music on which both of them are playing the violin. It is a virtuoso performance, during which Peter and Paul keep perfect time with one another. Mary then listens to the recording and, because the violinists have played so perfectly, she believes she is listening to a single musician. She thinks to herself "*this* musician is a virtuoso," self-ascribing the property *listening to music played by one and only one virtuoso.*

I have some inclination to say that Mary believes of Peter that he is a virtuoso and also that she believes of Paul that he is a virtuoso. However, no relation of acquaintance relates Mary uniquely to either Peter or Paul. Every relation of acquaintance that she bears to Peter (e.g., the relation *x is listening to music played by y*) is such that she also bears it to Paul, and vice versa.[5] So, according to LDR and MDR, Mary does not have any *de re* beliefs either about Peter or about Paul. This case, then, might lead us to revise LDR or MDR in such a way that bearing a relation of acquaintance uniquely to an individual is not a necessary condition for having a *de re* belief about the individual. This might not be trivial, since we might not think that having non-unique acquaintance with a thing always allows the subject to have *de re* beliefs about it.

Another worry has to do with acquaintance itself. For example, consider the television commentator who says "I believe that *you*, the viewer, are smart enough to see through the administration's smoke screen." This seems to be a *de re* belief attribution to the commentator, despite the fact that the commentator is unacquainted with the viewer. However, even though *de re* attributions like this one are fairly standard, we can resist drawing the conclusion that they show acquaintance to be unnecessary for *de re* belief. As I see it, this is because the sort of attribution in question, although standard, is nonliteral. So there is no need to account for the literal truth of such attributions.

But other examples might provide stronger evidence against the acquaintance requirement. Such examples have to do with parts and wholes. Suppose that I see a red ball in perfectly ordinary conditions, and self-ascribe the property *looking at one and only one red ball*. It seems that I have a *de re* belief about the ball to the effect that it is red. However, it also seems that I am acquainted with the ball in virtue of being acquainted with a proper part of it (e.g., the ball's eastern hemisphere, which I see). I have some inclination, moreover, to say that I also have a *de re* belief about the western hemisphere of the ball, with which I am unacquainted, to the effect that it is red. The reasons for this seem to include the following facts: I have a *de re* belief about the whole ball, which includes the western hemisphere, to the effect that it is red all over; I might have a similar *de re* belief about the northern hemisphere, with which I am acquainted; I might have

---

5. Mary does bear the relation *x is listening to music played by y* uniquely to the plurality or collection of Peter and Paul. If she self-ascribes the property *listening to music played by one and only one virtuoso*, then LDR and MDR imply that she ascribes *virtuosity* to the plurality of Peter and Paul. It would seem odd to say that Mary has a *de re* belief about this plurality to the effect that *it* is a virtuoso, but given the strangeness of the example, perhaps this is an acceptable consequence of these views.

a similar *de re* belief about the southern hemisphere, with which I am acquainted; and the northern and southern hemispheres together include the western hemisphere. All of these facts, it seems to me, give at least some support to the claim that I believe of the western hemisphere that it is red, despite the fact that I do not see the western hemisphere and am otherwise unacquainted with it.

According to LDR and MDR, I do not have any *de re* beliefs about the western hemisphere of the ball, since I do not bear any relation of acquaintance to that part of the ball (let alone *uniquely* to that part of the ball). Cases like this, then, might lead us to revise LDR or MDR in such a way that certain *de re* beliefs about certain objects get transferred to certain *parts* of those objects. This might not be trivial, since we might not want to say that every time a subject has a *de re* belief about a thing that has proper parts, she thereby has *de re* beliefs, with the same predicative content, about the thing's parts.

A final worry has to do with the distinction between particular objects and kinds of objects. LDR and MDR are accounts of *de re* belief about particular objects, but there is reason to think that we can have *de re* beliefs about kinds of objects as well. For example, it seems that I can have a belief about aluminum, a kind of metal, to the effect that it is ductile. This might consist in my being acquainted in certain ways with various instances of aluminum, and taking myself to be acquainted in those ways with instances of a kind of metal that is ductile. If something along these lines is correct, our account of belief *de re* will have to be broadened to include such belief about kinds. I am inclined to think this is the case, and also that it shows that many of the beliefs commonly thought to be *de dicto*—e.g., the belief that aluminum is ductile—are actually *de re*. (This point is related to my earlier claim that we have far fewer *de dicto* or propositional beliefs than most philosophers have supposed, and I shall examine this claim more closely in ch. 7.)

I do not quite know what to make of all the worries discussed in this section, especially the worries about uniqueness and acquaintance. But that does not concern me a great deal. I shall conclude by repeating something that I stressed earlier. Whether or not these worries are well grounded enough to put property-theoretic accounts of *de re* belief like LDR and MDR into doubt, they apply not just to the property-theoretic perspective but to all other theoretical perspectives. For example, if Mary really does have a *de re* belief about Peter, say, even though she is not acquainted with him uniquely, then proponents of the other theoretical perspectives also will have to account for this fact. Triadic theorists, for example, will have to explain how Mary can believe a singular proposition about Peter without having a name for him and without a description that picks him out uniquely. More generally, triadic theorists will have to provide necessary and sufficient conditions for a given subject's believing a singular proposition. And it seems clear that this task is no easier than the property theorist's task of explaining just what makes it the case that a given subject ascribes a property to an object.

CHAPTER SIX

THE PROPERTY THEORY, RATIONALITY, AND KRIPKE'S PUZZLE ABOUT BELIEF

In this chapter, I apply the property theory to an important problem in the philosophy of mind and philosophical semantics, viz., Kripke's (1979) puzzle about belief.[1] Using the property theory and a related view about the semantics of certain attributions of belief, I provide a solution to Kripke's puzzle. The notion of contradictory beliefs, and the related notion of rationality, are essential to any adequate account of Kripke's examples. According to the position developed here, there are two senses in which a subject can be said to have contradictory beliefs. Just one of these senses threatens the rationality of the believer, but Kripke's puzzle is concerned only with the other one.

Kripke's widely discussed puzzle raises troublesome questions about the nature of the attitudes, the correct account of their attribution (at least with respect to a certain class of belief sentences), and, ultimately, the concept of rationality. The intuitively appealing answers to the questions associated with the puzzle seem to lead to unacceptable results. I shall argue that, if we take care to distinguish between the two different senses in which someone can be said to have contradictory beliefs, we can avoid the paradoxical

---

1. This chapter is drawn from sections 1–3 and section 5 of Feit (2001). I have made several modifications to the original paper, mostly in order to incorporate the material into this book.

consequences that seem to follow from the right answers to the puzzling questions. Unlike Kripke, then, I maintain that there are in fact correct answers to these questions, and that the apparently unacceptable consequences of these answers can be explained away.

In the first section, I review the details of the puzzle and the principles associated with it. Since I assume the reader's familiarity with Kripke's cases, I shall be fairly brief. The puzzle about belief gives rise to an argument that might be seen as an alleged reductio of one of the basic principles underlying our ordinary talk about what we believe. In the second section, I present a version of the argument, and suggest that, in addition to the principles discussed by Kripke, there are other, more dubious principles behind some of the premises. The third section contains a diagnosis of the argument, according to which each of the new principles is ambiguous, and each is false on one of its readings. The upshot is that there is a new way to solve the puzzle by rejecting the relevant readings of the principles. Finally, in the last section, I discuss some complications that arise when other forms of Kripke's puzzle are considered. These variants of the puzzle have to do with belief attributions containing empty names and kind terms.

1. Kripke's Puzzle about Belief

One of Kripke's (1979[1988]) goals is to refute a particular sort of argument for the conclusion that co-referential proper names are not substitutable in belief contexts. In this argument, a contradiction is derived from the assumption that such names are in fact governed by a substitutivity principle. Kripke accomplishes his goal by constructing a similar argument in which a similar contradiction is derived without any assumptions about substitutivity. Kripke's argument is based upon his puzzle about belief. A result of the entire enterprise is that the thesis of Millianism concerning proper names, insofar as it seems to entail a substitutivity principle for them, is not clearly refuted by facts about the attributions of belief.

The relevant substitutivity principle may be given as follows (ignoring contexts in which names are quoted, as well as other contexts in which names are mentioned rather than used):

Substitutivity: Co-referential proper names are interchangeable in all contexts *salva veritate*.

Some of Kripke's views about names, of course, seem to imply that this principle is true. In particular, it is a consequence, or so it appears, of the following thesis about names:

Millianism: The semantic content of a proper name is just its bearer.

I am not convinced that Millianism entails substitutivity, and I shall touch upon this issue later in the chapter.

According to Kripke, it would be a mistake to blame substitutivity for problems that would arise even if it were not presupposed. The argument based upon the puzzle about belief makes use of two other principles, each of which seems quite plausible. The first principle concerns the relation between belief and sincere assent to sentences:

Disquotation: If a normal English speaker, on reflection, sincerely assents to "*P*," then he believes that *P*.[2]

Clearly, analogous principles about speakers of other languages, stated in those languages, will be as plausible as disquotation.

The other principle essential to Kripke's puzzle involves the conventional or standard translation of one language into another:

Translation: If a sentence of one language expresses a truth in that language, then any translation of it into any other language also expresses a truth (in that other language).[3]

Translation, like disquotation, seems quite plausible. Some worries about it have been raised, but, as we shall see, it is ultimately not an essential assumption behind Kripke's argument.

At the beginning of this section I mentioned an argument against substitutivity. This argument is in a sense Kripke's target, and he presents it as follows:

Since a normal speaker—normal even in his use of "Cicero" and "Tully" as names—can give sincere and reflective assent to "Cicero

---

2. All page references to Kripke (1979) will be to the reprinted version in Salmon and Soames (1988). The content of the principle above is a quotation from Kripke (1979[1988]: 112–113). Kripke says: "'*P*' is to be replaced, inside and outside all quotation marks, by any appropriate standard English sentence" (1979[1988]: 112). Sentences that contain indexicals, pronouns, or ambiguous terms are not appropriate replacements for "*P*" (see 112–114).

3. The content of this principle is also a quotation from Kripke (1979[1988]: 114).

144 BELIEF ABOUT THE SELF

was bald" and simultaneously to "Tully was not bald," the disquo-
tational principle implies that he believes that Cicero was bald and
believes that Tully was not bald. Since it seems that he need not have
contradictory beliefs (even if he is a brilliant logician, he need not
be able to deduce that at least one of his beliefs must be in error),
and since a substitutivity principle for co-referential proper names in
belief contexts would imply that he does have contradictory beliefs,
it would seem that such a substitutivity principle must be incorrect.
(1979[1988]: 115)

By disquotation, the character in Kripke's story believes that
Cicero was bald. Substitutivity would entail that he believes that
Tully was bald, since "Cicero" and "Tully" are co-referential. However, the character also assents to "Tully was not bald." Hence,
assuming the truth of substitutivity leads to the character believing
that Tully was bald and that Tully was not bald. But this, according
to Kripke, would imply that the character in the story has contradictory beliefs (which contradicts his stipulation about the character's
logical acumen).

I will discuss the argument based on Kripke's puzzle about belief
in the next section. Since that argument is so similar to the argument just presented above, I will postpone a more careful examination of the premises until the next section. In the above argument,
disquotation and substitutivity together entail, given some auxiliary
assumptions, that a certain person both does and does not have contradictory beliefs. Clearly, this is not an acceptable result.[4] It might
be tempting to conclude that, since there is no reason to suspect
that disquotation leads to any trouble, the argument is a successful
reductio ad absurdum of substitutivity. However, as Kripke's puzzle
is intended to show, the same contradiction can be derived in a parallel fashion using only disquotation and translation.

The puzzle can be summarized as follows.[5] Pierre is a perfectly
rational, normal French speaker who lives in France. Pierre is monolingual, without a word of English or any other language save French.
He has heard of the famous city of London, but only under the
French name "Londres." Pierre has heard many good things about

---

4. That is, unless sentences of the form "*x* has contradictory beliefs" admit of
more than one reading. I will argue in what follows that such claims are indeed
ambiguous.

5. See Kripke (1979[1988]), 119–124 especially.

the appearance of London (perhaps he has also seen photographs, etc.) and so he sincerely assents to the French sentence "Londres est jolie." A principle of disquotation for French thus yields the truth, in French, of "Pierre croit que Londres est jolie." By translation, we may conclude that Pierre believes that London is pretty.

Somewhat later, Pierre moves to an unattractive part of London, a neighborhood in which nobody speaks French. He learns English directly, i.e., without any translation between English and French. In particular, Pierre does not come to know that the French name "Londres" conventionally translates the English name "London." He learns to call his new city "London," and since he rarely leaves his dismal neighborhood, he is inclined to assent sincerely to the sentence "London is not pretty." (Pierre does not, of course, withdraw his assent from the French sentence "Londres est jolie." He thinks he has moved to a city that is distinct from the one he calls "Londres.") Given Pierre's new status as a normal speaker of English and his sincere assent to "London is not pretty," disquotation allows us to conclude that Pierre believes that London is not pretty.

So, disquotation and translation—without substitutivity—apply to the story of Pierre in such a way as to generate the conclusion that Pierre believes that London is pretty and he also believes that London is not pretty. But this appears to conflict with our earlier assumption that Pierre is perfectly rational and hence does not have contradictory beliefs. In the next section, I will discuss the latter stages of this puzzling argument in greater detail.

For now, we should take Kripke to have shown indirectly that the previous argument concerning "Cicero" and "Tully" was not a successful reductio of substitutivity after all. And we might think about the general ways to respond to the puzzle, e.g., a Kripkean skepticism about the coherence of our general practice of belief attribution, the rejection of either disquotation or translation as stated above, or the reconciliation of the truth of the reports about what Pierre believes with his presupposed rationality. The last strategy itself might be divided into two substrategies: (i) maintain that Pierre's rationality need not preclude his having contradictory beliefs, or (ii) maintain that it does not follow that Pierre actually has contradictory beliefs from the facts that, e.g., he believes that London is pretty and believes that London is not pretty. I will try to motivate a certain combination of (i) and (ii).

Before concluding this section, I shall briefly discuss Kripke's revised puzzle, the Peter/Paderewski case,[6] in which no principle of (nonhomophonic) translation is used. In this example, Peter hears of Paderewski, under the name "Paderewski," as a famous pianist. At this time, Peter assents to the sentence "Paderewski had musical talent." Kripke continues the story:

> [I]n a different circle, Peter learns of someone called "Paderewski" who was a Polish nationalist leader and Prime Minister. Peter is skeptical of the musical abilities of politicians. He concludes that probably two people... were both named "Paderewski." Using "Paderewski" as a name for the *statesman*, Peter assents to, "Paderewski had no musical talent." (1979[1988]: 130)

In this case, only disquotation is needed to come to the suspicious conclusion that Peter believes that Paderewski had musical talent and also believes that Paderewski had no musical talent. So the revised puzzle shows that rejecting translation, or attempting somehow to reform translation practices concerning proper names, will be of no help in solving the general problem. I will not question translation, nor our ordinary practice of translation, nor even disquotation. Some philosophers have not accepted both of these principles,[7] but I am convinced that they are true (or at least that suitably restricted versions, which will do the work needed by Kripke, are true). Moreover, I suspect that disquotation itself is not essential to the argument based upon Kripke's puzzle. In other words, it seems to me that there are facts about Pierre that do not have to do with his assent to any sentences, which make true the suspicious pair of belief reports about him. I will proceed, then, without questioning either of these principles.

2. The Puzzle Argument

At one point in his paper, Kripke writes as follows: "[T]his is the puzzle: Does Pierre, or does he not, believe that London is pretty?" (1979[1988]: 124). And of course any answer to this question might seem to have intolerable consequences. I think it will be helpful to

---

6. See Kripke (1979[1988]: 130–131).

7. See, e.g., Barcan Marcus (1981) and Over (1983). Marcus questions *disquotation* (although she does accept the truth of the two basic reports about what Pierre believes), and Over questions (Kripke's use of) *translation*.

construe the puzzle as an argument, one that leads from apparently quite plausible and innocent assumptions into a contradiction. The task of solving the puzzle then becomes the task of supplying a satisfactory evaluation of the argument.

The argument might very well begin with premises about the sentences that Pierre accepts, and then proceed via principles of disquotation and translation to claims about what he believes. However, since these two principles are so plausible and since there are reasons *independent* of the principles (or so it seems to me) to accept the belief attributions to Pierre, I shall simply take the attributions to be among the premises of the argument.[8] We have already seen how these attributions could be supported by the principles of translation and disquotation. As a result, anyone who wishes to deny that Pierre has one of the attributed beliefs will, at the very least, be compelled to reject one of these principles.

We may then begin with the premises that attribute the relevant beliefs to Pierre:

(1) Pierre believes that London is pretty.
(2) Pierre believes that London is not pretty.

It would be futile, I think, to try to maintain that Pierre's past as a monolingual Frenchman gives us reason to deny (2), or that his current attitudes in England give us reason to deny (1).

So this appears to be where the trouble really begins. Kripke describes the situation at the present stage as follows: "[I]t seems that we must respect both Pierre's French utterances and their English counterparts. So we must say that Pierre has contradictory beliefs, that he believes that London is pretty *and* he believes that London is not pretty" (1979[1988]: 122).

From the above, it is clear that Kripke insists upon the truth of the following premise:

(3) If Pierre believes that London is pretty and Pierre believes that London is not pretty, then Pierre has contradictory beliefs.

Kripke, I suspect, thinks that (3) is analytic. I agree that there is a sense in which (3) is analytic, but as I noted earlier, I also think that the form "S has contradictory beliefs" is ambiguous. In the next

---

8. Sosa (1996) gives a couple of versions of the argument that begin with assumptions about the sentences to which Pierre assents. See especially 377–379. The argument in the text will otherwise be quite similar in structure to the ones presented by Sosa.

section, I shall try to describe how the ambiguity is such that there is also a sense in which (3) is false. This fact will ultimately help to resolve the puzzle.

Premise (3) may be viewed as a particular instance of a more general thesis, a statement of which might be helpful to have at hand. For lack of a better name, let's call it the *Principle of Contradictory That-Clauses*, or *PCT* for short:

> *PCT*: If ⌜*S* believes that *X* is *F*⌝ and ⌜*S* believes that *X* is not *F*⌝ are both true (where *S* and *X* are ordinary names, and *F* is an easy-to-understand predicate), then the bearer of *S* has contradictory beliefs.

If an explanation for premise (3) were wanted, it seems that something like *PCT* would have to play a role.

Kripke continues on to claim that problems lurk in the distance for anyone who admits that Pierre has contradictory beliefs:

> [T]here seem to be insuperable difficulties with this alternative as well. We may suppose that Pierre, in spite of the unfortunate situation in which he now finds himself, is a leading philosopher and logician. He would *never* let contradictory beliefs pass. And surely anyone, leading logician or no, is in principle in a position to notice and correct contradictory beliefs if he has them.... But it is clear that Pierre, as long as he is unaware that the cities he calls "London" and "Londres" are one and the same, is in no position to see, by logic alone, that at least one of his beliefs must be false. He lacks information, not logical acumen. He cannot be convicted of inconsistency: to do so is incorrect. (1979[1988]: 122)

Kripke maintains here that, if we admit that Pierre has contradictory beliefs, we are in some sense obliged to convict him of inconsistency—but Pierre is not inconsistent. Following Sosa (1996), I will use the more general concept of rationality here: Pierre's inconsistency would in any case entail that he is less than ideally rational. We then have the next premise:

(4) If Pierre has contradictory beliefs, then Pierre is not rational.

This claim, like premise (3), might be thought to be analytic.[9] It also might be taken to be an instance of a more general thesis about

---

9. Kripke seems to think so. Sosa (1996: 376) explicitly maintains that claims of this sort are analytic. Owens (1989: 289–295) argues that this is not the case, but Owens ultimately cannot explain why such claims *seem* analytic (or at least necessary). I hope to resolve this debate in the next section.

what is necessarily constitutive of rationality. Let's call it *PRC*, or the *Principle of Rationality and Contradiction*:

> *PRC*: Necessarily, rational agents do not have contradictory beliefs.

If an explanation for premise (4) were wanted, it seems something like *PRC* would play a role.

We may take *PRC* to report a necessary condition of being an *ideally* rational agent, one who is sufficiently reflective and whose thinking is not compartmentalized. Kripke's stipulation is that Pierre is rational, and we may take this to mean that he is ideally rational. What he lacks is "information, not logical acumen." Such a claim is, of course, perfectly legitimate. So, even though it follows from the premises given so far that

(5) Pierre is not rational

we nevertheless have as a basic assumption that

(6) Pierre is rational.

So much for the premises of the puzzle argument and the reasoning behind them. Let's take a quick look at the argument presented in its entirety:

1. Pierre believes that London is pretty.
2. Pierre believes that London is not pretty.
3. If Pierre believes that London is pretty and Pierre believes that London is not pretty, then Pierre has contradictory beliefs.
4. If Pierre has contradictory beliefs, then Pierre is not rational.
5. So, Pierre is not rational.
6. But Pierre is rational.
7. Therefore, Pierre is rational, and Pierre is not rational.

Given the rock-bottom assumptions and the structure of the puzzle argument, at least one of (1) through (4) must be false. If any general principles support the first two premises, claims like disquotation and translation do. I have suggested, however, that with respect to the puzzle argument as a whole, other principles are also at work, viz., *PCT* and *PRC*. In the next section, I shall argue that each of these two principles, suitably disambiguated, is considerably more questionable than either disquotation or translation. If I am right, we can accept all the basic assumptions involved with Kripke's puzzle, together with the relevant principles of disquotation and translation, without thereby falling into paradox and contradiction.

3. A Solution to the Puzzle

How can we accept that Pierre believes that London is pretty, that Pierre believes that London is not pretty, and also that Pierre is perfectly rational, and hence not inconsistent? In order to answer this question in as detailed a way as possible, we will have to be ready to answer a pair of more fundamental questions, viz.: What makes it true that Pierre believes that London is pretty? And what makes it true that Pierre believes that London is not pretty? And we will have to do this in such a way that the psychological facts that account for these truths are consistent with the additional fact that Pierre is rational.

What Kripke's puzzle appears to show, then, is that the statement "Pierre believes that London is pretty" does not attribute to Pierre a belief the content of which is the proposition *that London is pretty*, i.e., the proposition semantically expressed by the *that*-clause of the belief report. If the statement did attribute this belief to Pierre, it seems, we would be forced to conclude that Pierre is irrational, since the other true attribution "Pierre believes that London is not pretty" would then ascribe to Pierre a belief whose content directly contradicts the first.[10]

Perhaps we need to be a little bit more careful. We should not say that premises (1) and (2) above have Pierre believing the contradictory (singular) propositions *that London is pretty* and *that London is not pretty*, unless these beliefs themselves are somehow analyzable in a way that is consistent with the claim that Pierre is rational. For example, consider the triadic view of belief. According to this view, what makes belief attributions true is the three-place *BEL* relation among a conscious subject, a proposition, and a way of taking or grasping the proposition. The proponent of the triadic view of belief can say that premise (1) of the puzzle argument attributes to Pierre a belief in the proposition *that London is pretty*, and that (2) attributes a belief in the proposition *that London is not pretty*, and also that Pierre is rational. A rational subject can believe and disbelieve the same proposition provided that he takes the proposition in different ways. When the proposition that London is pretty is presented to Pierre through the French sentence "Londres est jolie," he assents to it, but

---

10. Lewis makes essentially this point when discussing the lesson of Kripke's puzzle. See Lewis (1981), especially 284–285.

when its negation is presented to him through the English sentence "London is not pretty," he assents to *it*, failing to recognize it as the negation of a proposition to which he also gives assent.

The triadic view provides a way for a rational agent to hold contradictory beliefs. As a result, the proponent of this view can reject the previously stated *PRC* and, with it, premise (4) of the puzzle argument. Although Pierre believes the propositions *that London is pretty* and *that London is not pretty*, his familiarity with each of these propositions is such that he is unable to determine that they are, at the same time, both contradictory and objects of his belief.[11] But I have rejected the triadic view, and hence I cannot accept this evaluation of the puzzle argument. I need instead a property-theoretic evaluation.

So, let's return to the question: What makes it true that Pierre believes that London is pretty? Part of what makes this true, I claim, is that Pierre self-ascribes a certain property, a property of the form *bearing R to something pretty*, where R is a relation of acquaintance that Pierre actually bears to London. Here, Pierre bears such a relation to London in virtue of his acquaintance with London while he was in France, and so the relation will be something like the relation *x has heard of y under the name "Londres."* This is a relation of acquaintance that Pierre bears to London, and under which he ascribes to it the property of being pretty.

Pierre, then, self-ascribes a property like the property *having heard of a pretty city under the name "Londres."* Since London is in fact the unique city of which he has heard under this name, Pierre ascribes the property *being pretty* to London. And this is what makes premise (1) true, it is what makes it true that Pierre believes that London is pretty. (In ch. 5, I suggested that the above conditions are not sufficient for Pierre to ascribe *being pretty* to London, but even if there are additional conditions, e.g., as in MDR, they seem to be satisfied in Pierre's case.)

Given a property-theoretic account of what it is for a subject to ascribe a property to an individual, such as LDR or MDR, we might consider the following account of the truth conditions for the sort of belief attribution at issue in this chapter:

Semantic Claim: ⌈S believes that X is F⌉ (where X is an ordinary proper name and F is an easy-to-understand predicate)

---

11. For more discussion, see Salmon (1989: 258–264).

is true if and only if the subject denoted by S ascribes the property expressed by F to the bearer of X.

As we have seen, to say that a subject ascribes a property to something is to quantify over relations of acquaintance, i.e., it is to say that there is some such relation that the subject bears (uniquely) to the thing, and so on. In our ordinary discourse about what we believe, there are often contextually supplied restrictions on which relations of acquaintance are admissible, and it seems that this is what accounts for the failure of substitutivity in belief contexts. For example, there are contexts in which one could say truly that Lois Lane does not believe that Superman wears glasses, even though she ascribes to Superman (= Clark Kent) the property *wearing glasses*. There are restrictions that arise, in such a context, to rule out the "Clark-Kentish" relations, and when we agree to ignore these relations, we can claim truly that Lois does not ascribe to Superman the property *wearing glasses*. Millianism, on this view, will entail that substitutivity holds for proper names in belief sentences only relative to a given context; a shift of context might result in substitutivity failure when different restrictions are operative, as they often are when the context changes. The tasks of identifying the contextual features that give rise to such restrictions, and explaining how they work, go well beyond the scope of this chapter.

I anticipate a Kripkean objection at this point. Could it be argued that I have not respected Kripke's explicitly stated intention that only *de dicto* readings, and hence not *de re* ones, are at issue in the puzzle about belief?[12] It seems to me that this cannot be argued in a persuasive fashion. Premises (1) and (2) are *de dicto* locutions, and there is nothing like the clearly *de re* locution "Pierre believes, of London, that it is pretty" among the premises of the puzzle argument. I claim that what makes the attribution "Pierre believes that London is pretty" true is that Pierre ascribes *being pretty* to London (given any restrictions on which relations of acquaintance between Pierre and London are admissible). With respect to belief sentences containing proper names, this is as *de dicto* as it gets.

We are finally in a position to consider my property-theoretic solution to Kripke's puzzle about belief. The solution hinges upon a distinction between two senses in which one can be said to have

---

12. See Kripke (1979[1988]: 104–106).

contradictory beliefs. In some (weak) sense, Pierre has contradictory beliefs when he ascribes to London—under two different relations of acquaintance, of course—the property *being pretty* and the property *being not pretty*. But there is also a (strong) sense in which Pierre does not have contradictory beliefs. He does not, for example, self-ascribe both the property *living in a pretty city* and the property *not living in a pretty city*.[13] With the framework of self-ascription, we may define the notion of having contradictory beliefs in this strong sense as follows:

Strong: S has contradictory beliefs (in the strong sense) $=_{df.}$ S self-ascribes contradictory properties.

Two properties are contradictory if and only if it is impossible for an individual (at a time) to instantiate both of them. It seems to me that this cashes out the important sense in which Pierre does not have contradictory or inconsistent beliefs.

The notion of having contradictory beliefs in the weaker sense may be characterized with the notion of property ascription as follows:

Weak: S has contradictory beliefs (in the weak sense) $=_{df.}$ S ascribes contradictory properties to a single thing.

Clearly, Pierre ascribes contradictory properties to a single thing. He ascribes *being pretty* and *being not pretty* to London. However, since he is ideally rational, Pierre does not self-ascribe contradictory properties. The self-ascribed properties in virtue of which he ascribes contradictory properties to London are themselves consistent. He self-ascribes properties such as the property *having heard of a pretty city under the name "Londres,"* and the property *living in a city (called "London") that is not pretty*. So Pierre has contradictory beliefs in the sense of weak above, but not in the sense of strong.[14]

---

13. Arguably, *nobody* (rational or not) has contradictory beliefs of this sort. If this is correct, there is yet another reason to think there is a sense in which Pierre does not have contradictory beliefs.

14. Brown (1992) defends the view that we believe certain propositions immediately or directly, while we believe others only indirectly. Although this sort of framework is not needed to explain the phenomena associated with Kripke's puzzle, it does allow for a distinction between having contradictory direct and indirect objects of belief, and so it is quite in the spirit of the view presented here.

Recall that premise (3) of the puzzle argument says that, if Pierre believes that London is pretty and believes that London is not pretty, then he has contradictory beliefs. Clearly, this premise is true only if the consequent has the reading given by weak. But the consequent of (3) is the antecedent of (4), which states that, if Pierre has contradictory beliefs, he is not rational. However, on the weak reading, (4) simply is not true. We have already seen how Pierre can ascribe contradictory properties to the same city without being irrational. What is essential to someone's being rational is not that he fails to *ascribe* contradictory properties to the same thing. Instead, what is necessary for rationality is that the subject refrains from *self-ascribing* contradictory properties. Since the ascription of contradictory properties to a single thing is partly a matter of what is going on outside of the subject's head, it can be done without having a system of belief that deserves epistemic censure of any kind.

Now, the truth of the following principle would suffice for the truth of premise (4):

PRC_{weak}: Necessarily, rational agents do not ascribe contradictory properties to the same thing.

But there is no good reason to think that this claim is correct. The discussion above, I hope, shows how the case of Pierre is a counterexample to PRC_{weak}. Pierre is rational, and things could be just the way he believes them to be, e.g., there could be distinct cities named "Londres" and "London," and so on. The property theorist will account for this aspect of Pierre's rationality by pointing to the fact that it is possible that he should have all of the properties he self-ascribes.

Of course, it remains true that, if Pierre did self-ascribe contradictory properties, he would be irrational. So premise (4) is true provided that the locution "Pierre has contradictory beliefs" is understood in the strong sense. As hinted above, however, if this is read in the strong sense, then premise (3) is incorrect. The reason for this is that the following reading of PCT turns out to be false:

PCT_{strong}: If ⌈S believes that X is F⌉ and ⌈S believes that X is not F⌉ are both true (where S and X are ordinary names, and F is an easy-to-understand predicate), then the bearer of S self-ascribes contradictory properties.

Once again, Pierre ascribes contradictory properties to the same city without self-ascribing contradictory properties, and so the case of Pierre shows that PCT_{strong} is false.

Let me sum up this evaluation of the puzzle argument. The sentence "Pierre has contradictory beliefs" is ambiguous between the weak and strong readings. If the argument is to be valid, the sentence must have the same reading in premises (3) and (4). But if the reading is strong, then premise (3) is false, and if the reading is weak, then (4) is false. On my view, the puzzle argument implicitly presupposes the truth of either PCT_{strong} or PRC_{weak} in addition, perhaps, to disquotation and translation. Since each of these principles is demonstrably false, we have a solution to the puzzle that does not force us to reject disquotation or translation and also allows us to maintain that our practice of belief attribution does not break down under the strain of cases like Pierre's.

In the Paderewski case, Peter uses descriptive information to "disambiguate" the relevant name. Here, Peter self-ascribes the property *having heard of a pianist called "Paderewski" with musical talent*, as well as the property *having heard of a politician called "Paderewski" with no musical talent*. In each case, the descriptive information is essential to the way in which Peter is acquainted with Paderewski. The properties that he self-ascribes are not contradictory, and so it would be a mistake to draw the conclusion that Peter is not rational from the premises about what he believes.

I would like to conclude this section by considering Sosa's diagnosis of Kripke's puzzle. Sosa takes the troublesome step to be premise (3) of the argument, viz., if Pierre believes that London is pretty and believes that London is not pretty, then he has contradictory beliefs. He also suggests that the following principle is essential to justifying the premise:

H: If a name in ordinary language has a single *referent* then it may correctly be represented logically by a single constant.[15]

The relevant name, of course, is "London," which we may suppose (at least for the sake of the present discussion) to have a single referent. Sosa claims: "[B]y combining (H) with the assumption that an agent has contradictory beliefs if and only if the agent has beliefs whose contents can be represented formally as ⌈Fa⌉ and ⌈~Fa⌉, we can justify [the premise that if Pierre believes that London is pretty and that London is not pretty, then he has contradictory beliefs]" (1996: 388).

---

15. The content of this principle is a quotation from Sosa (1996: 388). The name *H* stands for "hermeneutic."

Ultimately, Sosa argues that since (H) is essential to generating the contradiction in the puzzle argument, we should take the argument to be a reductio of (H). (H) also seems to be a consequence of Millianism, and for this reason Sosa claims that the correct solution to Kripke's puzzle actually leads us to take a Fregean position on names, according to which there may be a sort of semantic ambiguity—i.e., a plurality of senses—in a name with a single referent.

I reject the claim that anything like (H) is essential to justifying the relevant premise. In the quotation above, Sosa assumes that, e.g., the sentence "Pierre believes that London is pretty" attributes to Pierre a belief the content of which is the *proposition semantically expressed by the that-clause* "London is pretty." If *this* assumption were not made, (H) would not imply that Pierre has beliefs of the form *Fa* and ~*Fa*. It seems to me that the fault lies not in (H), but in the assumption. Indeed, the account provided earlier of what makes reports such as (1) and (2) true entails that the assumption is incorrect. Such reports say that someone ascribes a certain property to the named individual, not that someone has a particular *proposition* as an object of belief.

I conclude, then, that (H) plays no essential role in justifying the premises of the puzzle argument, and hence that the argument should not be taken as a reductio of (H). My view on the correct evaluation of the puzzle argument is consistent with (H) and also with Millianism (on the other hand, the general view is also compatible with a non-Millian view of names). In particular, the property theorist is able to borrow Fregean modes of presentation, in the form of relations of acquaintance, without being committed to the claim that names really have a Fregean sense or descriptive content, and without being committed to a Fregean treatment of indirect discourse.

The plausibility of the evaluation above seems to me to provide additional reason to believe that (H) is not the culprit. Instead, we may reject PCT_{strong} and PRC_{weak}, together with the assumption that any statement of the form "*S* believes that *P*" attributes a belief the content of which is the proposition semantically expressed by the *that*-clause.

4. Puzzles with Empty Names and Kind Terms

Kripke's puzzle may be taken to be a problem about proper names in belief reports. However, analogous puzzles arise for names without bearers, and also for kind terms. To some extent, these additional complications are acknowledged in Kripke's original paper, but they have received little attention in the literature. In this section, I try to adapt my general solution to the analogous puzzles.

Lewis very briefly discusses an example with empty names: "Pierre has been told in France that *'Pere Noel'* brings presents to all the children, and has been told in England that Father Christmas brings presents only to the good children. He reckons that good children get double shares" (1981: 288).

Given this story together with the conventional translation of "Pere Noel" into "Father Christmas," we are led to accept the following two belief reports:

(8) Pierre believes that Father Christmas brings presents to all the children.

(9) Pierre believes that Father Christmas doesn't bring presents to all the children.

Since "Father Christmas" is a name without a bearer, in this case we may not maintain that (8) and (9) are true in virtue of the fact that Pierre bears relations of acquaintance to Father Christmas. But the sad fact that there is no Father Christmas does not prevent poor Pierre from *thinking* that he bears such relations to someone who brings presents. So, it is still open to us to claim that what makes (8), for example, true is the fact that Pierre self-ascribes a property of the form *bearing R to someone who brings presents to all the children*, where R is a relation of acquaintance that Pierre does not actually bear to anything, but is such that it satisfies some contextually specified criteria. Roughly put, it must be a "Father-Christmas-ish" relation. The relation *having heard of a chubby and jolly present bringer under the name "Father Christmas"* might do, as might *having heard of someone under the name "Pere Noel."*

With respect to belief attributions of the form "*S* believes that *X* is *F*," the semantic claim considered earlier implies that the speaker is implicitly quantifying over (a restricted domain of) relations of acquaintance. It seems that when *X* is an ordinary proper name— i.e., when it is such that something bears it—one of the conditions on the relation of acquaintance is that it holds between the subject and the thing that bears the name. (For example, a person who is in no way acquainted with London could not believe that London is pretty.) When *X* is a name without a bearer, however, there can be no such condition. Instead, the relation must satisfy some other conditions, none of which implies that the subject bears the relation to an actual thing.

So, what makes it true that Pierre believes that Father Christmas brings presents to all the children, and that Pierre believes that Father Christmas doesn't bring presents to all the children? The following might suffice to make (8) and (9), respectively, true:

(8*) Pierre self-ascribes the property *having heard of someone, under the name "Pere Noel," who brings presents to all the children.*

(9*) Pierre self-ascribes the property *having heard of someone, under the name "Father Christmas," who does not bring presents to all the children.*

In this example, Pierre has neither of the two properties that he self-ascribes, but it is surely metaphysically possible that he should have both of them. So Pierre is consistent. He does not contradict himself, despite the fact that apparently contradictory sentences can be used, correctly, to attribute beliefs to him. The truth of both (8) and (9), in other words, does not entail that Pierre has contradictory beliefs in the strong sense, and hence does not conflict with the assumption that he is rational.

We might give a more general account of the primary function of names, with or without bearers, in belief reports as follows:

Revised Semantic Claim: An utterance of ⌈S believes that X is F⌉ (where S denotes subject s, X is a (possibly empty) proper name, and F expresses the property f) is true if and only if there is some *suitable* relation of acquaintance R such that s self-ascribes the property *bearing R uniquely to something that has f.*

This claim requires an account of what makes a relation of acquaintance *suitable* in a context of utterance. I cannot provide a full account here, but I will suggest a few conditions. First, in any context where the name X has a bearer, relation R is suitable only if s stands in R (uniquely) to the bearer of X. So, for example, "Pierre believes that London is pretty" cannot be true unless Pierre stands in some relation of acquaintance to London. (When the name has more than one bearer, it makes sense to say that contextual features will restrict the domain of relations to the ones that the subject bears to the contextually salient bearer of the name.) Second, a given relation is suitable only if contextually supplied restrictions don't rule it out. For example, such restrictions might rule out "Clark-Kentish" relations in the context of an utterance of "Lois does not believe that Superman is a journalist." Third, when the name X does not have a bearer, as in the case of "Father Christmas" and "Pere Noel," there might be conditions on suitability that are supplied by the identity of the name. And finally, there might be conditions that derive from the considerations discussed in the last chapter, e.g., the considerations that seemed to favor MDR over LDR.

The meaningfulness of names without bearers is taken by many, perhaps correctly, to tell against Millianism. Some advocates of a certain non-Millian theory of names have claimed that Kripke's puzzle does not arise for their view, or else that, given the view, it is easily solved.[16] On the view in question, a proper name X is semantically equivalent to a particular description that mentions the name, viz., "the bearer of X," or "the thing that is a bearer of X." Bach (1987) calls this view the "nominal description theory of names," and Katz (1994) calls it the "pure metalinguistic description theory" (PMT). Katz writes, of this view of names, that it "automatically provides a solution for Kripke's puzzle about belief. On PMT, there is no problem about the consistency of Pierre's beliefs because the subject term in the belief acquired in Paris is 'the thing which is a bearer of "Londres",' while the subject term of the belief acquired in London is 'the thing which is a bearer of "London"'" (1994: 16–17).

The present view of names is an interesting middle ground between the Millian and classical Fregean positions; however, by itself, the view does nothing to solve Kripke's puzzle. Solving the puzzle requires more than merely showing how Pierre's beliefs are consistent. It requires showing how Pierre's internal consistency is itself compatible with the truth of the attributions "Pierre believes that London is pretty" and "Pierre believes that London is not pretty." Since these attributions contain the name "London" but not "Londres," it is not at all clear what role PMT plays in solving Kripke's puzzle. PMT might have some advantages over a strictly Millian view of names—particularly with respect to negative existential claims—but providing a neat solution to Kripke's puzzle is not one of them. On the other hand, I see no reason that PMT could not be incorporated (with some additional assumptions) into the solution advanced in the previous section.

16. See Bach (1987), especially chapters 7–10, and Katz (1994).

I would like to conclude by adapting my account of Kripke's puzzle to similar examples with terms denoting natural kinds and artifacts. Kripke himself mentions a few such cases:

> [A] bilingual may learn "*lapin*" and "rabbit" normally in each respective language yet wonder whether they are one species or two, and … this fact can be used to generate a paradox analogous to Pierre's. Similarly, a speaker of *English* alone may learn "furze" and "gorse" normally (separately), yet wonder whether these are the same, or resembling kinds. … It would be easy for such a speaker to assent to an assertion formulated with "furze" but withhold assent from the corresponding assertion involving "gorse." … Yet "furze" and "gorse," and other pairs of terms for the same natural kind, are normally thought of as *synonyms*. (1979 [1988]: 134)

Suppose that Martin uses the term "woodchuck" to pick out a certain kind of rodent commonly found in his neighborhood. Martin believes that woodchucks are pests. If you and I were members of some community in which the term "groundhog" was used instead of "woodchuck," I could correctly report what Martin believes to you by saying that he believes that groundhogs are pests. Moreover, Martin could subsequently move into our community, learn the term "groundhog," and use it normally to pick out a certain kind of rodent, but fail to learn that it is synonymous with "woodchuck." Martin might now maintain that groundhogs are not pests, and the following pair of belief attributions would be true:

(10)   Martin believes that groundhogs are pests.

(11)   Martin believes that groundhogs are not pests.

It is well known that natural kind terms are similar in important respects to proper names. On my view, a propositional attitude verb functions to introduce an existential quantifier, over relations of acquaintance, for each occurrence of a name within its scope. The same should be true for terms that denote natural (and artificial) kinds. So, for example, to say that Martin believes that groundhogs are pests is to say, roughly, that there is a relation of acquaintance R such that Martin bears R to groundhogs, and self-ascribes the property *bearing R to pests*.

What makes it the case that a subject bears a relation of acquaintance to a *kind* of thing? Clearly, the subject need not be acquainted with every member or instance of the kind. He merely needs to be acquainted with at least one member or instance, and perhaps only in virtue of being at the end of some chain of communication that goes back to such a thing (as someone might be acquainted with Socrates, for example). Acquaintance with kinds, like acquaintance with individuals, may be in virtue of being able to use a certain linguistic item competently. We might say that a subject, S, bears a relation of acquaintance to a kind of thing, K, provided that there is another relation of acquaintance that S bears to a member (or an instance, or a sample) of K. More, I think, would be required for the subject to have a *belief* about the kind. This will be considered in the next chapter.

Consider again the story about Martin. He bears two distinct relations of acquaintance to woodchucks or groundhogs. Let us say that he is *w-related* and *g-related* to the species (e.g., he has seen woodchucks and has heard of them called "woodchucks," and he has also heard of them under the term "groundhog"). The facts that make sentences (10) and (11) true, then, might be given as follows:

(10*) Martin is w-related to groundhogs, and self-ascribes the property *being w-related to things that are pests*.

(11*) Martin is g-related to groundhogs, and self-ascribes the property *being g-related to things that are not pests*.

Martin's situation is significantly like that of Pierre. Sentence (10) asserts that Martin ascribes the property *being pests* to groundhogs, and (11) says that he ascribes *being non-pests* to them. Martin ascribes these contradictory properties to groundhogs under two different relations that he bears to them, as represented in (10*) and (11*), and so he, like Pierre, does not have contradictory beliefs in the strong sense.

What goes for groundhogs will go for other kinds as well.[17] For example, I bear many relations of acquaintance to aluminum: I have heard of it as a metal called "aluminum," I have seen bits of it on the sides of various houses, and so on. I believe that aluminum is ductile, and what this means (given that aluminum exists) is that I ascribe *ductility* to aluminum. It does not mean that I believe the proposition that is semantically associated with the English sentence "aluminum is ductile" (unless, of course, we have stipulated that to believe this

---

17. In the groundhog case, there is some temptation to say that Martin ascribes the properties to a *plurality* of things rather than to a *kind* of thing. Perhaps this is how we ought to think of beliefs about kinds in general. To ascribe a property F to a kind of thing would involve bearing a relation R to a plurality of things—in virtue of bearing another relation to at least one of the things in the plurality—and self-ascribing the property *bearing R to some things, each one of which has F*.

proposition is simply to ascribe *ductility* to aluminum). And I ascribe *ductility* to this kind of metal in virtue of the same sorts of facts that make true my ascriptions of properties to individual things, i.e., I bear some relation of acquaintance R to aluminum, and self-ascribe the property *bearing relation R to something ductile*.

My (narrow) psychological twin on some other planet might self-ascribe the very same property but bear the relation of acquaintance to some other metal, distinct from aluminum but superficially similar to it, making different belief attributions true of him. For example, he might believe that twin aluminum is ductile, but he would not believe that aluminum is, since he is simply not acquainted with that kind of thing. This is one way in which different *attributions* of belief may be true of subjects who are microphysical, and hence psychological, duplicates and who therefore have the same *beliefs*. (More on this in the next chapter.)

Should empty kind terms be treated in a way that is analogous to the treatment of empty names? How should we treat reports such as the claim that Priestley believed that phlogiston was emitted by burning wood? It is possible, after all, to dream up Kripke-style puzzles that turn upon such items. Should the empty kind term "phlogiston" be assimilated to a name without a bearer, like "Father Christmas," just as kind terms with extensions were assimilated to names with bearers? I am inclined to think that such an account would be plausible, but I shall not fill in the details here. Some of them will be discussed in the next chapter.

My main goal in this chapter has been to piece together an adequate solution to the relevant puzzles about belief. The solution advanced here does not require us to reject principles like disquotation and translation, nor to regard people like Pierre as irrational, nor to maintain that from the fact that a subject is (ideally) rational, we cannot infer that there is a sense in which it would be correct to say that she does not have contradictory beliefs. Moreover, the general solution does not require us to take a stand on the precise semantic analysis of the relevant belief attributions, although I have formulated the solution in terms of the framework that seems to me to be the most plausible. Finally, the solution does not logically require a particular account of the meaning of names, and, given the tangled cluster of problems surrounding the role that names play in belief contexts (among others) this is surely a virtue. The puzzles considered here involve someone who has contradictory beliefs in the weak sense, but only when one has contradictory beliefs in the strong sense is rationality threatened.

CHAPTER SEVEN

THE PROPERTY THEORY, TWIN EARTH, AND BELIEF ABOUT KINDS

Despite the size of the literature on Twin Earth cases, as in Putnam (1973, 1975a), interesting things can be said about the issues that they raise. In this chapter, I present a collection of answers to various metaphysical and semantic questions associated with these issues. The account that I defend is a property-theoretic version of internalism about the mind, which I defend in part by examining the standard arguments that draw externalist conclusions from our intuitive judgments about Twin Earth cases.[1] In the first section, I review Putnam's classic example and distinguish two versions of internalism, one semantic and the other psychological. In the second section, I discuss the general Twin Earth argument against psychological internalism. I then present an internalist response, within the framework of the property theory, in two stages. Finally, in the fifth section, I make some concluding remarks about self-ascription and belief about kinds.

1. It is well known that Putnam himself did not use the Twin Earth thought experiment to argue for a conclusion about mental or psychological content. Putnam's claim concerned the external basis of the linguistic meaning of natural kind terms, like "water" and "gold." This point will be discussed briefly in the text. Although I shall describe various Twin Earth scenarios, I assume the reader's basic familiarity with the literature concerning them.

1. Twin Earth and Two Kinds of Internalism

Putnam argued that the meaning of a natural kind term is not determined by the (narrow) psychological state of a speaker who uses the term. In other words, linguistic meaning is not always in the head. This conclusion amounts to a rejection of *semantic* internalism, the view that the meaning of any given word is determined by the intrinsic psychological properties of a person who understands or uses it (or perhaps by all of the intrinsic psychological properties of those who belong to a community in which the word is used). Putnam's Twin Earth scenario serves as the basis of his argument for semantic externalism (as I understand it, this is simply the denial of semantic internalism).

Twin Earth, as we know, is just like Earth in every respect except that, wherever water—i.e., H_2O—is located on Earth, Twin Earth has a similar but distinct liquid, with a different chemical composition. We can call this other liquid "twater" (or, if you prefer, "twin water") and, following Putnam, we can abbreviate its chemical formula as "XYZ." Twater is imagined to be qualitatively indistinguishable from water at the macroscopic level; it behaves, looks, feels, and tastes just like water. The time is 1750, before the rise of modern chemistry on both Earth and Twin Earth. Each person on Earth has an exact duplicate on Twin Earth (and vice versa). We imagine two duplicates: Oscar and Twin Oscar. (It has often been pointed out that, since we are in large part composed of water, nobody on Twin Earth could be an exact duplicate of anybody on Earth. Putnam claims only that Oscar and Twin Oscar are "exact duplicates in appearance, feelings, thoughts, interior monologue, etc." (1975a: 141). In order for a Twin Earth argument to have a chance of refuting *psychological* internalism, a different example must be used.) Oscar uses the word "water" to denote samples of water—i.e., H_2O—although of course Oscar is ignorant of the chemical details. Twin Oscar uses "water" to denote samples of twater—i.e., XYZ—and of course Twin Oscar is similarly ignorant.

According to the basic argument advanced by Putnam, anything that is not H_2O is not water, since water is H_2O. Hence, twater is not water. Putnam concludes that "water" as used by English speakers on Earth differs in extension from "water" as used by Twin English speakers on Twin Earth. And it does seem clear that the utterances of Oscar and Twin Oscar differ with respect to their semantic properties. On the plausible assumption that two natural kind terms could have the same meaning only if they share the same extension, it follows that the meaning of "water" on Twin Earth is not the same as the meaning of "water" on Earth. Since there are no narrow psychological differences between Oscar and Twin Oscar (or between Earthers and Twin Earthers generally), the meaning of "water" is not determined by the narrow psychological properties of those who use the word.

Again, Putnam's conclusion is an externalist semantic thesis about natural kind terms. It is not my aim to explore or evaluate Putnam's reasoning for this conclusion (although, for the record, I do find it persuasive). My main topic here is *psychological* rather than *semantic* internalism. Psychological internalism, as we have seen in chapter 1, section 4, and elsewhere, is the view that one's psychological properties are determined by one's intrinsic, physical properties. The denial of this view is psychological externalism. Putnam's original argument has been extended in a variety of ways, and, in particular, many philosophers would have us think that the contents of Oscar's *beliefs* differ from those of Twin Oscar.[2] My question, then, is this: Can Twin Earth examples serve as the basis for a persuasive argument against psychological as well as semantic internalism?

Psychological internalism amounts to the thesis that psychological properties supervene locally on physical (e.g., neural) properties, which implies that psychological properties are themselves intrinsic properties of the subject. Examples of psychological properties are things like the property of experiencing a given sensation, the property of having a certain sort of perceptual experience, or the property of having a belief with a particular content. (Hereafter, I may omit the qualifier "psychological" and continue to refer to this view about psychological properties simply with the label "internalism.")

To say that psychological properties supervene locally on physical properties is to say that any two individuals who have exactly the same physical properties must also have exactly the same psychological ones (or, if you prefer, it is to say that, necessarily, no two individuals share all of their physical properties but not all of their psychological ones).[3] We may take any view that entails this kind of

---

2. Again, Putnam (1973, 1975a) did not draw any such conclusion, but the general style of argument was soon extended into the psychological realm. See, e.g., Burge (1979, 1982) and McGinn (1982).

3. My view, again, is that internalism is true not only when the relevant modality is that of nomological necessity, but also when it is metaphysical necessity. So, I think that, if the instantiation of certain neural properties actually determines or realizes a given mental property, then this is metaphysically necessary. A defense of this view is far beyond the scope of this chapter. For some discussion, see Yablo (1992).

local supervenience of the mental upon the physical to be a version of internalism, e.g., Putnam's characterization that "no psychological state, properly so called, presupposes the existence of any individual other than the subject" (1975b: 220), or Segal's characterization that "being in a state with a specific cognitive content does not essentially involve standing in any real relation to anything external" (2000: 11). According to internalism, then, psychological content is *narrow* in the usual sense of this term. Any theory according to which some such content is *wide* (or *broad*) is a version of psychological externalism, although of course there might be significant differences between particular externalist accounts.

2. The Twin Earth Argument

We need to describe a nomologically possible pair of situations in which intrinsic duplicates differ with respect to their relational properties. Segal (2000) provides a Twin Earth case involving two very similar kinds of gemstone: (yellow) topaz and citrine. He describes them as follows:

> They are different kinds of stone, in the sense of being composed of different chemical compounds. Topaz is $Al_2SiO_4(OH, F)_2$ and citrine, a type of quartz, is SiO_2. Typical samples of yellow topaz and citrine are indistinguishable to the eye and other unaided senses. But they are easily distinguished by their different refraction indices. (2000: 26)

Let us roll back the clock appropriately, and imagine a planet—called "Earth" for simplicity—on which there is plenty of topaz but no citrine. English speakers on Earth use the word "topaz" as a natural kind term to talk about samples of topaz. In particular, Oscar uses this word to denote these gemstones. Suppose that Oscar is a competent, reflective speaker of English who has a belief that he sincerely expresses by uttering "topaz is yellow." Now consider Twin Oscar, Oscar's duplicate on Twin Earth. Twin Oscar has never seen topaz nor interacted with it in any way, however indirect. This is because there is no topaz on Twin Earth; Twin Earth has citrine wherever there is topaz on Earth. Of course, as any good molecule-for-molecule duplicate does, Twin Oscar uses the word "topaz" as a natural kind term to talk about samples of citrine, with which he has exactly the same sort of familiarity that Oscar has with topaz. He also has a belief that he expresses with the words "topaz is yellow."

It seems clear that Oscar believes that topaz is yellow. Granted, he doesn't know much about microstructure, but you don't have to know that water is H_2O to believe that water is wet, or is thirst quenching, or fills the rivers. We may imagine that Oscar has seen many instances of topaz, has examined them quite thoroughly, etc. On the other hand, it also seems clear that Twin Oscar does *not* believe that topaz is yellow. He *says* "topaz is yellow," but his word "topaz" does not mean what Oscar's word means. Twin Oscar, again, has never seen topaz nor interacted with it in any way, and so it seems hard to imagine that he could believe that topaz is yellow. (Twin Oscar really believes that citrine is yellow, but, of course, he would not express his belief in those terms.) These considerations form the basis of the standard Twin Earth argument for psychological externalism. Let's examine the formally valid version of the argument presented below:

First Formal Twin Earth Argument

1. (a) Oscar believes that topaz is yellow, but (b) Twin Oscar does not believe that topaz is yellow.
2. If (1), then Oscar and Twin Oscar do not share all of their beliefs.
3. If Oscar and Twin Oscar do not share all of their beliefs, then internalism is false.
4. Therefore, internalism is false.

This argument makes use of the simplifying assumption that the relevant Twin Earth story is true. But, of course, the same line of reasoning could be presented in a more complicated form, since internalism entails that *if* the story were true, the duplicates would have all of the same psychological properties.

I have already reviewed the reasoning behind the claims made in premise (1). Perhaps the most common internalist strategy, when it comes to dealing with Twin Earth arguments, has been to reject this premise and its analogues. One way to implement the strategy is to maintain that Oscar could believe that topaz is yellow only if he had the concept *topaz* (i.e., the concept expressed by our word "topaz"), but since he lacks the concept, he does not have the relevant belief. Segal (2000) has defended this sort of account. Consider the following passage, in which Segal is discussing the Twin Earth scenario involving water and XYZ: "In Oscar's case the ascriptions are wrong: he does not have the concept *water*, so he has no *water* beliefs.

And I think it is simply wrong for us to use the word 'water' in the content sentences of our discourse on his thoughts" (2000: 123).

On Segal's view, the first formal Twin Earth argument is unsound because part (a) of the first premise is false. Oscar does not believe that topaz is yellow, on this view, because he does not have the concept *topaz*. Here, however, I agree with the externalist. It might be difficult to assess the belief attribution in premise (1a) in the absence of a semantic account of belief sentences, but it does seem deeply counterintuitive to deny that Oscar believes that topaz is yellow. If an internalist strategy like Segal's is correct, then we almost always speak falsely when we attribute beliefs to non-experts by using content sentences that contain natural kind terms. Nobody in 1750, for example, would then have believed that water filled the rivers. Certainly, this is difficult to swallow. As I see it, denying the truth of the belief attributions in Twin Earth cases has been an unfortunate internalist trend. It seems to me that the intuitions in favor of their truth are too clear and strong to explain away. We would do better, I think, to accept the truth of premise (1) and locate the real problem with the argument elsewhere.

Before doing this, I would like to consider briefly another possible way to deny premise (1), which involves rejecting (1b) instead of (1a). Lewis (1994) suggests that it would be acceptable to say of *Twin* Oscar—in the water/XYZ case—that he believes that water is wet, falls from the clouds, and so on:

> Like any up-to-date philosopher of 1955, I think that "water" is a cluster concept. Among the conditions in the cluster are: it is liquid, it is colourless, it is odourless, it supports life. But, *pace* the philosopher of 1955, there is more to the cluster than that. Another condition in the cluster is: it is a natural kind. Another condition is indexical: it is abundant hereabouts. Another is metalinguistic: many call it "water." Another is both metalinguistic and indexical: *I* have heard of it under the name "water." When we hear that XYZ off on Twin Earth fits many of the conditions in the cluster but not all, we are in a state of semantic indecision about whether it deserves the name "water." . . . So if some philosopher, call him Schmutnam, invites us to join him in saying that the water on Twin Earth differs in chemical composition from the water here, we will happily follow his lead. (1994: 424)

On Lewis's view, there is a kind of indeterminacy in claims of the form "*S* believes that water is *F*." The term "water" expresses a cluster concept, and our semantic decisions have not settled the question as to exactly which, or how many, of the conditions in the cluster need to be satisfied in order for the term to apply. Consider the sentence "Twin Oscar believes that water fills the rivers." According to Lewis, we are permitted to follow the externalist's lead and deny it, e.g., because twater—the liquid with which Twin Oscar happens to be acquainted—is not abundant hereabouts, and we have not heard of it under the name "water." But in other contexts, it would be permissible to accept it, since twater does satisfy many of the conditions in the cluster. Lewis's view might seem to provide internalists with a plausible way to deny the externalist premise that Twin Oscar does not believe, say, that water fills the rivers. On a more disappointing note, his view seems to be that there really might be no fact of the matter about the truth of belief reports like "Twin Oscar believes that water fills the rivers."[4]

For several reasons, I am not at all convinced that this is a suitable route for the internalist to take. First, I find the Kripke-Putnam semantics for natural kind terms to be preferable to the cluster concept view taken by Lewis (although a defense of this position is beyond the scope of this chapter). So, it seems to me to be clearly correct to say, for example, that there is no water on Twin Earth and, as a result, that Twin Oscar does not believe that water fills the rivers. Second, on Lewis's view, there is a perfectly acceptable interpretation of a sentence like "Twin Oscar believes that water fills the rivers" on which it is *false*, just as a Twin Earth argument for psychological externalism might claim. Therefore, the view cannot provide a fully general strategy for the internalist to take in diagnosing the failure of Twin Earth arguments. Finally, the strategy suggested by Lewis does not seem at all plausible when applied to the first formal Twin Earth argument. Can we really deny premise (1b), according to which Twin Oscar does not believe that topaz is yellow? The only way to do this is to say that there is topaz on Twin Earth. However, that is just wrong. On Twin Earth, there is plenty of citrine, but there is no topaz. It is surely incorrect to say that topaz exists on Twin Earth and has the formula SiO_2, the very same formula that citrine has here on Earth, where the laws of nature are no different.

So I plan to defend an internalist objection to the first formal Twin Earth argument that lets the externalist have premise (1). Sure, Oscar believes that topaz is yellow, but Twin Oscar does not. In

4. See Lewis (1994: 423–425) for more on his view about the lessons of Twin Earth.

the next two sections, I try to show why these facts do not entail psychological externalism. But first, I shall conclude this section by taking a look at the externalist's case for the remaining premises of the argument.

According to the second premise, if the belief reports about the twin Oscars in premise (1) are correct, then they do not share all of their beliefs. There are a number of things to say in support of premise (2), and the reasoning might seem straightforward enough. Belief sentences report what we believe. If we can report one of Oscar's beliefs with the complement sentence "topaz is yellow," but we cannot use this same sentence correctly to report one of Twin Oscar's beliefs, then it seems that there is at least one belief they do not share. Moreover, one might maintain that the twins believe what they say.[5] Given that the argument for semantic externalism is successful, the contents of the twins' utterances are different. What Oscar says is true if and only if topaz is yellow, but what Twin Oscar says is true if and only if citrine is yellow. Twin Oscar never says that topaz is yellow. If the twins believe what they say—if the contents of their beliefs are the contents of their utterances—then they believe differently.

Premise (3) moves from a difference in beliefs to a difference in psychological properties, and hence to the falsehood of internalism. Again, it claims that, if Oscar and Twin Oscar do not share all of their beliefs, then internalism is false. The idea here is that belief content properties are psychological properties par excellence. To believe something is to have a certain property, the property of having a belief with a particular content. Such properties are psychological properties. So it seems that, if the two Oscars do not share all their beliefs, they must not share all their psychological properties. If internalism were true, however, it would be impossible for them to differ psychologically without some intrinsic, physical difference between them. Oscar and Twin Oscar are duplicates. All of their intrinsic, physical properties are the same. As a result, if they don't share all of their psychological properties, then psychological internalism must be false. So much for this line of reasoning; let's turn to an evaluation of the argument.

5. See Stalnaker (1993) and Segal (2000: 23–25) for discussion of this line of thought.

3. An Internalist Response (Stage One)

In granting the Twin Earth externalist premise (1) of the argument, I
am agreeing that psychological externalists are correct in their semantic assessment of belief reports in Twin Earth cases. Why doesn't
psychological externalism follow? The simplest and best internalist
response—and one that is correct as far as it goes, I think—is as follows: It is true that Oscar believes that topaz is yellow and also true
that Twin Oscar doesn't believe that topaz is yellow. Nevertheless,
Oscar and Twin Oscar share all of their beliefs. Each of them believes
everything that his twin believes. In a nutshell, premise (2) is false.[6]

Many internalist views about the nature of belief, and many views
about the semantics of belief sentences, are consistent with the denial
of premise (2). Of course, I favor views that incorporate the property
theory. For the time being, however, I would like to be as neutral as
possible. How can an internalist about the mind deny premise (2)?
What needs to be done is to reject the following claim about belief
reports: An utterance of ⌈S believes that P⌉ is true only if the semantic
value of P (i.e., the proposition that is semantically expressed by P) is
the content of one of the beliefs held by the referent of S.[7] An utterance of "Oscar believes that topaz is yellow," then, does not attribute
to Oscar a belief in the proposition *that topaz is yellow* (i.e., the proposition semantically expressed by the sentence "topaz is yellow").

Happily for internalists, independent considerations refute the
claim that needs to be rejected. As we saw in chapter 6, in one of
Kripke's puzzles about belief, Peter believes that Paderewski had
musical talent and he also believes that Paderewski had no musical
talent, but Peter is perfectly rational and does not have contradictory
beliefs. So, the two belief reports about Peter must not entail that he
believes the contradictory propositions expressed by the two *that*-
clauses. The upshot is that, on the externalist view, there is too close
a connection between the *that*-clauses used to attribute beliefs, on

---

6. Jackson (2003) and Loar (1988) defend responses to Twin Earth reasoning
along these lines. Loar's positive view resembles an account of narrow content suggested by Dennett (1982). Interesting critical discussions of the views of Dennett and
Loar can be found in Stalnaker (1989, 1990), respectively.

7. Bach (1997) calls this claim the "specification assumption" and argues that it
is incorrect. He maintains that complement sentences describe beliefs rather than
specify them.

the one hand, and the psychological content of the beliefs that make those attributions true, on the other.[8]

We can use the sentence "topaz is yellow" correctly to report one of Oscar's beliefs, but not one of Twin Oscar's beliefs. However, we cannot conclude that the two Oscars believe differently. The general reason for this is that the belief reports about the Oscars are made true not only by their systems of belief, which on the internalist view are identical, but by external factors as well.[9] Roughly put, what makes it true that Oscar believes that topaz is yellow is that Oscar thinks of topaz in a certain way, and associates this way with the concept or property *being yellow*. Twin Oscar thinks of something in this very same way, and he also associates this way with the concept or property *being yellow*. This is why Twin Oscar has the same belief that Oscar has. What Twin Oscar thinks of in the relevant way, however, is not topaz but citrine, and so it is not the case that Twin Oscar believes that topaz is yellow.

One who favors the combination of semantic externalism and (psychological) internalism, as I do, should probably claim that what the twins *say* is not quite what they believe. The semantic contents of their utterances, at any rate, differ from the contents of their beliefs. Again, this should not surprise us. In Kripke's puzzle, Peter utters the words "Paderewski had musical talent" and also "Paderewski had no musical talent" (without retracting the first statement). But Peter is a logician who would never let contradictory beliefs pass. Since Peter says contradictory things—unbeknown to him—but doesn't believe contradictory things, what he says must differ from what he believes.

The general approach taken so far is applicable to Burge's version of the Twin Earth argument as well, although Burge's example raises several new issues. Burge presents the following case:

> A given person has a large number of attitudes commonly attributed with content clauses containing "arthritis" in oblique occurrence.

---

8. Loar (1988) uses convincing examples to argue that intentional psychological states are not individuated by the wide, social content expressed by many of our ordinary, oblique *that*-clauses. Social content (i.e., the conventional linguistic meaning of *that*-clauses), Loar argues, cannot distinguish between belief contents that are clearly distinct, and also mistakenly distinguishes states that are psychologically alike, thereby failing to capture explanatory generalizations.

9. This way of thinking about the matter is discussed by Lewis (1979, 1986: 32–36).

For example, he thinks (correctly) that he has had arthritis for years, that his arthritis in his wrists and fingers is more painful than his arthritis in his ankles, that it is better to have arthritis than cancer of the liver, ... and so forth. In short, he has a wide range of such attitudes. In addition to these unsurprising attitudes, he thinks falsely that he has developed arthritis in the thigh. ... The person might have had the same physical history and non-intentional mental phenomena while the word "arthritis" was conventionally applied, and defined to apply, to various rheumatoid ailments, including the one in the person's thigh, as well as to arthritis. (1979: 77–78)

Let's take Burge's actual situation to be Earth, and his counterfactual situation to be Twin Earth. In order not to multiply names beyond necessity, let's use a common name for Burge's patient, "Alf." We can imagine the two Alfs walking into their doctors' offices and saying "I have arthritis in my thigh." Thereafter, their mental lives diverge, e.g., Alf is corrected by his doctor whereas Twin Alf is not. In Burge's example, the important difference between Earth and Twin Earth is a sociolinguistic one. Members of the medical community and well-informed individuals on Twin Earth use the term "arthritis" in a broader way than people do on Earth. Hence Twin Alf's word "arthritis" does not mean what our "arthritis" means, indeed he has no word that means what our "arthritis" means. Burge summarizes the argument as follows: "However we describe the patient's attitudes in the counterfactual situation, it will not be with a term or phrase extensionally equivalent with 'arthritis'. So the patient's counterfactual attitude contents differ from his actual ones" (1979: 79).

Burge's general argument differs in several ways from the earlier water/twater and topaz/citrine arguments. There is the obvious fact that, in Burge's example, the two situations are the same with respect to the natural kinds in the subjects' environments. All the cases allegedly show that at least some belief content is wide, i.e., not determined by the intrinsic nature of the believer. However, the earlier cases allegedly show that the content properties of beliefs can depend upon the kinds of things in the environment, while Burge's case allegedly shows that they can depend upon linguistic practices. So, Burge's argument would seem to have externalist implications for many beliefs over and above beliefs about natural kinds.[10] In

---

10. Indeed, "arthritis" itself is probably not a natural kind term. See Segal (2000: 62–65) for an interesting discussion of this issue.

terms of the structure of Twin Earth arguments, these differences are relatively minor. I do think it will be useful, though, to present a new formal version of the present argument, since it seems to me that other features of the argument raise issues that must be confronted by internalists about the mind. We could formulate the argument in many ways. Here is a simple version that is analogous to the earlier Twin Earth argument:

Second Formal Twin Earth Argument

1. (a) Alf believes that he has arthritis in his thigh, but (b) Twin Alf does not believe that he has arthritis in his thigh.
2. If (1), then Alf and Twin Alf do not share all of their beliefs.
3. If Alf and Twin Alf do not share all of their beliefs, then internalism is false.
4. Therefore, internalism is false.

I would like to discuss two new considerations brought out by our second formal argument. The first has to do with the fact that premise (1) concerns *de se* belief. This is no doubt an artifact of the particular way in which the argument is stated. For example, the belief that arthritis sometimes occurs in the thigh could have been used instead. The important question that is raised is whether Alf and Twin Alf *would* share the same belief *if* each one believed himself to have arthritis in the thigh. If the answer is no—if, for example, the content of Alf's belief is the proposition *that Alf has arthritis in his thigh*, but the content of Twin Alf's belief is the proposition that *Twin Alf has arthritis in his thigh*—then externalists do not need Twin Earth scenarios to establish their view. They could simply imagine two twins here on Earth, each of whom believes himself to be a millionaire, say. If their belief contents differ, externalism is true. The conclusion we should draw, then, is that one who uses an argument like the second formal Twin Earth argument presupposes that the content of the twins' *de se* beliefs could be shared. Since this is an accidental by-product of our particular version of the argument, I will not say more about it just now; however, this issue will be important in what follows.

The second consideration has to do with a reason to believe premise (1b) that does not have an analogue in our version of the earlier topaz/citrine argument. Premise (1b) states that Twin Alf does not believe that he has arthritis in his thigh. The reason in favor of this claim is that, if he did believe that he had arthritis in his thigh, his belief would be false (just as Alf's belief is false). Arthritis simply cannot occur in the thigh. But Twin Alf's belief—i.e., the one he expresses by saying "I have arthritis in my thigh"—is true. So, he must not believe that he has arthritis in his thigh. This line of reasoning cannot be pursued in the earlier case, because if Twin Oscar believed that topaz is yellow, his belief would still be true. (However, the earlier argument might be modified so as to give rise to this sort of divergence in truth value.)

The truth of premise (1b) is no problem in itself, since I accept the externalist's assessment of belief reports in Twin Earth cases. However, if Alf's belief is false and Twin Alf's is true, the case for premise (2) becomes much stronger. It seems that the Alfs must not share all of their beliefs. For example, we may stipulate that all of Twin Alf's beliefs are true. Then, since Alf has at least one false belief, the twins do not share all of their beliefs. The background assumption here, of course, is that propositions are the contents of beliefs. If Alf and Twin Alf reside in different possible worlds, one might try to use the fact that the very same proposition can be true at one world and false at another to block the conclusion that they have different beliefs. It is clear, however, that the story can be told in such a way that there is a single possible world in which, for example, Alf and Twin Alf inhabit distinct regions.

If we maintain that the Alfs share all of their beliefs, but admit that Alf believes falsely while Twin Alf believes truly, we must conclude that the contents of some of their beliefs are not propositions. And, of course, this is exactly what property theorists should say about Burge's example.

On Lewis's view, for example, Alf and Twin Alf stand in the same relation—viz., the relation *having heard of something under the name "arthritis"* or, for short, the relation *being "arthritis"-acquainted with something*—to different things.[11] Alf bears this relation to arthritis, but Twin Alf bears it to something different (perhaps to rheumatism). However, they both self-ascribe the same property, viz., *being "arthritis"-acquainted with a disease that he has in his thigh* (this is the property *being an x such that x is "arthritis"-*

---

11. Lewis (1986: 27–36) discusses Burge's case briefly but explicitly. See especially 33.

acquainted with a disease in x's thigh). They self-ascribe the same property because they share all of their beliefs; they self-ascribe all of the same properties. But Alf lacks this property, since he is not "arthritis"-acquainted with anything he has in his thigh, and so Alf believes falsely. On the other hand, Twin Alf has the property and hence his belief is true. This is how premise (2) of the second formal Twin Earth argument can be false. Alf believes that he has arthritis in his thigh because he bears a certain relation to arthritis, and his belief is false because arthritis (necessarily) occurs in the joints. His belief is false because he lacks the property that he self-ascribes, or takes himself to have. Twin Alf does not believe that he has arthritis in his thigh, because he bears no relation of acquaintance to arthritis. But Twin Alf self-ascribes the very same property that Alf does, and his belief is true because he is related in the specified way to something he has in his thigh (rheumatism, "tharthritis," or whatever we might call it).

The important point for the internalist is that the two Alfs do indeed share all of their beliefs (i.e., at the relevant time, before their doctors reply to their inquiries). Their systems of belief are constituted by the properties they self-ascribe, and they both self-ascribe exactly the same properties. Taking belief to be a matter of ascribing properties reflexively to oneself also allows us to answer the earlier question about the Alfs' *de se* beliefs. If each twin believes himself to have arthritis in his thigh, the twins can indeed share beliefs, since they can self-ascribe exactly the same property. The differences in the status of our belief reports about the Alfs, and in the correctness of their beliefs, stem from their different relational properties and not from differences in the contents of their beliefs. In the final section, I will return to these considerations in greater detail.

4. An Internalist Response (Stage Two)

I am inclined to think that it would be best if the response given in the previous section were supplemented in a way that I will try to make clear below. In particular, the externalist is now in a position to charge me with holding views that are inconsistent with the validity of what appears to be an intuitively valid pattern of inference. Consider the argument below, which concerns a Twin Earth example discussed above and resembles argument (V) from chapter 4, section 4:

1. Oscar believes that topaz is yellow.
2. Twin Oscar believes everything Oscar believes.
3. Therefore, Twin Oscar believes that topaz is yellow.

Thus far, I have committed myself to the premises of this argument, insofar as the second premise seems clearly to follow from the claim that the Oscars share all of their beliefs. And the argument does appear to be valid; at the very least, it seems that there is an interpretation of the argument according to which it is valid. However, I have also denied that the conclusion is true. An internalist might just bite the bullet and deny the validity of the argument. On my view, this would be partly correct. There is a sense in which the argument is invalid. However, it would be better to admit that there is also a sense in which the argument is valid, as it intuitively seems to be.

Given that the first premise is true but the conclusion is not, the validity of the argument entails that Oscar believes something that Twin Oscar does not believe. If we wish to say that the argument has a reading on which it is valid, then, we must also say that there is a sense in which it would be true to say that the two Oscars do *not* share all of their beliefs. The natural way to do this is to talk about their *de re* beliefs (assuming that we have *de re* beliefs about kinds of thing in addition to individual things—a point that will be discussed in a bit more detail later). For example, Oscar has many beliefs about topaz that Twin Oscar lacks, including his belief, of topaz, that it is yellow. We might use the following pair of neutrally formulated definitions to distinguish the sense in which the Oscars do share all of their beliefs from the sense in which they do not:

i. S and $S*$ share all of their beliefs $=_{df.}$ For every c, S has a belief with content c if and only if $S*$ has a belief with content c.

ii. S and $S*$ share all of their beliefs $=_{df.}$ For every x and for every F, S believes of x that x has F if and only if $S*$ believes of x that x has F.

If we use reading (i), we should say that Oscar and Twin Oscar share all of their beliefs, and we should agree with the second premise in the argument above. If we use reading (ii), however, we can say that the twins don't share all of their beliefs, and we may go on to reject the second premise. (For example, Oscar believes of topaz that it is yellow, but Twin Oscar does not believe of topaz that it is yellow.) So, we can make room for the validity of the argument if we take definition (ii)—or perhaps a combination of (i) and (ii)—to provide an acceptable reading of the premises. I will take this strategy.

The strategy makes the evaluation of the Twin Earth arguments somewhat more complicated, since these arguments make claims about the sharing of beliefs, which we are now taking to be equivocal. With respect to this issue, the differences between our two Twin Earth arguments are irrelevant. So, let's focus on the first formal Twin Earth argument. Premise (2) of that argument claims that, if Oscar believes that topaz is yellow but Twin Oscar does not, then they do not share all of their beliefs. And premise (3) says that, if they do not share beliefs, then psychological internalism is false. If *this* argument is to be valid, the phrase "share all of their beliefs" must have the same meaning in both premises. However, the argument is unsound whichever reading we give to this phrase. Let's take the reading provided by definition (i) first.

On this interpretation, internalists should evaluate the argument in the way that was detailed in the previous section, i.e., we should reject premise (2). In that section, I was essentially assuming that the notion of sharing beliefs is to be understood along the lines of definition (i), i.e., in terms of identical belief content. From the facts that Oscar believes that topaz is yellow and that Twin Oscar does not believe that topaz is yellow, it does not follow that one twin has a belief with a content that is not also the content of one of the other twin's beliefs. On my view, of course, the contents in question are simply properties that are self-ascribed by the twins. For example, each twin might self-ascribe the property *being "topaz"-acquainted with a yellow gemstone*. Since Oscar is "topaz"-acquainted with topaz but Twin Oscar is not, only Oscar believes that topaz is yellow. Nevertheless, they share all of their beliefs according to definition (i).

An externalist might object to all of this by saying that the twins have beliefs with different wide contents. Of course, to say this would simply be to assume exactly what Twin Earth arguments are designed to show. Perhaps, however, such wide contents must be taken to characterize the way in which the twins do not share all of their beliefs. This leads us directly into the second interpretation of the argument, which employs our other way of understanding the notion of sharing beliefs, viz., definition (ii).

It seems that, on the second interpretation of the argument, premise (2) is true. From the fact that Oscar believes that topaz is yellow, it seems to follow that he believes of topaz that it is yellow.[12] And from the fact that Twin Oscar does not believe that topaz is yellow, it might seem to follow that it is not the case that he believes of topaz that it is yellow—in any case, Twin Oscar clearly does not believe anything of topaz. According to definition (ii), then, Oscar and Twin Oscar do not share all of their beliefs, just as the consequent of premise (2) maintains. I am willing to grant all of this. However, we do not yet have a refutation of internalism. What remains is the task of evaluating premise (3) of the argument, given the relevant sense of "share all of their beliefs."

Since definition (ii) is formulated in terms of explicitly *de re* attributions of belief, it should already be reasonably clear that the externalist is not going to get the desired result. (Remember that I introduced definition (ii) in order to account for the intuitive validity of a certain form of inference.) But let us see if there is anything to be said for premise (3) of the Twin Earth argument on the relevant interpretation. Essentially, the premise now makes this claim: If there is some (kind of) thing, such that one of the twins believes of this thing that it has a certain property, but the other does not believe of this thing that it has the same property, then internalism is false. However, the fact that only one of the twins believes of topaz that it is yellow does not seem to entail that there are any psychological differences between them, i.e., that Oscar and Twin Oscar differ with respect to their psychological properties.

According to premise (3) in this version of the argument, differences in *de re* belief imply differences in belief content or psychological state. But *this* is something that is denied not only by those who take the internalist view of the mind, but by many externalists as well.[13] What the externalist needs here is the general principle that, if a person believes of a given thing that it has a certain property, then the *proposition* about the thing to the effect that it has the property (presumably, a singular or object-dependent proposition) is the psychological content of one of the person's beliefs. Unless this is true, externalism simply does not follow from the failure to share beliefs in the sense of definition (ii). But the case for this principle is not compelling, just as the case for identifying the wide, social content

---

12. Perhaps this follows only given the additional fact that topaz exists (i.e., that there are instances of topaz). Since topaz exists, premise (2) still seems safe.

13. For example, see the opening passages of Burge (1982).

of (oblique) *that*-clauses with the psychological content of beliefs is not compelling.

Twin Earth arguments, and especially Burge's, were supposed to show that the contents of many (*de dicto*) attitudes, including attitudes ascribed with a wide range of expressions over and above natural kind terms, depend partly on external conditions. I suggest, however, that the foregoing considerations show that Twin Earth cases involve differences in *de re* attitudes only. Since *de re* attitudes, as we have seen in chapter 5, are in fact complex states of affairs with a nonpsychological, relational component in addition to a psychological one, such differences do not threaten internalism about the mind.

5. Self-Ascription and Belief about Kinds

Recall the case of Oscar and Twin Oscar, in which the environments differ with respect to the presence of topaz and citrine. Earlier, I spoke of the seemingly obvious fact that Oscar and Twin Oscar think of different things in the same way. According to the property-theoretic perspective, these ways of thinking of something (or some kind of thing) are relations of acquaintance that believers take themselves to bear to something. Oscar, for example, bears many such relations to topaz. He has heard of it as a gemstone called "topaz," he has seen samples of it in museums and jewelry stores, and so on. (Recall the earlier discussion of Alf's "arthritis"-acquaintance with arthritis.) When Oscar believes that topaz is yellow, the content of his belief is a property that he self-ascribes. It is the property of being acquainted in a given way with something yellow. So the property in question will have roughly this form: *bearing relation R to a kind of thing that has F.* For example, Oscar might self-ascribe the property *having heard of a gemstone called "topaz" that is yellow.*

The precise form of the relevant sort of property might vary somewhat from case to case. In the present example, it may be something like this: *bearing relation R to a kind of thing, K, such that instances of K are yellow.* It might be possible to construe these sorts of relations as holding between subjects and *fusions* or *aggregates* of things, and to take instances to be constituents of the fusions. In certain cases, it might be more natural to take a relation of acquaintance to hold between a subject and a *plurality* of things. For example, Ben might believe that horses have tails in virtue of self-ascribing a property of the form *bearing R to a plurality X, such that each one of X has a tail,* where R is a relation of acquaintance that Ben bears to horses. In what follows, I shall speak in terms of a person being acquainted with a kind of thing, leaving open the possibility that this may be understood somewhat differently in different cases.

On my view, a person is acquainted with (i.e., bears a relation of acquaintance to) a *kind* of thing provided that she is acquainted in some way with an instance or sample of that kind. This acquaintance need not consist in the perception of the instance by the person; it could be indirect, mediated by the perceptions, beliefs, and intentions of others. However, being acquainted with a natural kind in this sense is not sufficient for having beliefs about the kind rather than about the particular instance or sample of the kind. To take oneself to be acquainted with a given yellow gemstone, for example, is not to take oneself to be acquainted with a kind of gemstone instances of which are yellow. In order for somebody to have a belief about a kind of thing, as distinguished from a belief about an instance or sample of the kind, she must take herself to be related to the kind in virtue of self-ascribing a property of the form above (italicized in the preceding paragraph). For example, Oscar could believe that topaz is yellow if he self-ascribes the property *having heard of a kind of stone called "topaz" such that samples of it are yellow.*

These considerations suggest a view about the information carried by attributions of belief about natural kinds. Consider an utterance of ⌈*S believes that K is F*⌉, where S is a referring expression, K a kind term, and F a predicate that expresses the property f. To make an attribution of this form is to assert that there is some relation of acquaintance, R, such that the referent of S self-ascribes the property *bearing R to a kind of thing that has f*. In typical cases, where K succeeds in picking out a natural kind, a belief attribution of the above form will be true only if the referent of S also bears R to the kind of thing picked out by K. On this view, then, at least two facts make it true that Oscar believes that topaz is yellow: First, Oscar bears a certain relation of acquaintance R to topaz; and second, Oscar self-ascribes a certain property, i.e., the property *bearing R to a kind of thing that is yellow*. Only the second fact is purely psychological. It consists in Oscar's having a certain psychological property, one that he shares with Twin Oscar.

We might give a preliminary statement of this account of belief reports containing natural kind terms along the following lines: An utterance of ⌈*S believes that K is F*⌉ is true if and only if there is a relation of acquaintance R such that the referent of S bears R to the kind denoted by K, and self-ascribes the property *bearing R to a kind of thing that has f* (where f is the property expressed by the predicate *is F*). This view bears obvious similarities to Lewis's account of *de re* belief, LDR. I am suggesting, however, that this sort of view—with certain modifications, to be discussed shortly—provides the correct account of *de dicto* attributions of belief containing kind terms. In fact, it seems to me that the truth conditions given above are correct for explicitly *de re* reports of belief about kinds, e.g., attributions of the form "S believes, of K, that it is F." The modifications will result in a view that is appropriate for the sort of *de dicto* locution that appears in the Twin Earth arguments for psychological externalism.

The need for the first modification is most clearly illustrated with belief reports containing proper names. (This issue came up briefly in ch. 6.) Consider the familiar Superman story, in which Lois Lane is ignorant of the fact that Superman disguises himself as Clark Kent. Suppose that the story is true. Lois bears many relations of acquaintance to Superman (= Clark Kent), some of which involve bearing the name "Superman" or having attributes such as *wearing a blue and red suit*, and others of which involve bearing the name "Clark Kent" or having attributes such as *wearing eyeglasses*. Let's call relations in the first group "Superman-ish relations" and those in the second group "Kent-ish relations." Lois, of course, bears all of these relations to the same individual, but she mistakenly thinks she bears the relations in the first group and the relations in the second group to different people.

Now, it seems quite clear that the belief report "Lois believes that Clark Kent can fly" might be false on a given occasion of utterance, even though there exists some relation of acquaintance R—a Superman-ish relation—such that Lois bears R to Clark Kent (= Superman) and self-ascribes the property *bearing R to somebody who can fly*. How could this be? I suggest that there are contextually supplied restrictions that, in this example, serve to eliminate Superman-ish relations of acquaintance from the domain of discourse or otherwise prevent them from making the utterance true. If the participants in the conversation are not quantifying over Superman-ish relations, or if such relations are somehow not suitable in the context, then there is no (suitable) relation of acquaintance that would make the attribution true. This is because there is no Kent-ish relation R such that Lois self-ascribes the property *bearing R to somebody who can fly*. So, the first modification consists in the possibility of a shrinking domain of discourse (with respect to relations of acquaintance) or the unsuitability of certain relations that are present in the domain. (I am inclined to go with the first option but leave open the possibility that the second might be better.) This is how the *de dicto* attribution "Lois believes that Clark Kent can fly" might be false while the *de re* attribution "Lois believes, of Clark Kent, that he can fly" is true. The psychological content that makes the *de re* attribution true might contain a relation of acquaintance that, in the context of the *de dicto* one, is not included within the domain of discourse or is somehow not suitable if it is so included.

The need for the second modification, as I see it, is brought about by so-called empty kind terms, or kind terms that lack an extension. Consider, for example, the phlogiston theory of combustion. Many people in the seventeenth and eighteenth centuries believed that phlogiston was emitted by burning wood. Since phlogiston does not and never did exist, however, nobody ever stood in a relation of acquaintance to phlogiston. Given that "phlogiston" is a kind term, then, we cannot always require that a subject bear a relation of acquaintance to a kind of thing in order for an attribution of belief to the subject to be true. I think we can give a general account of the relevant sort of belief report that is consistent with the externalist assessment of such reports in Twin Earth cases, which I have accepted, and also with the commonsense assessment of reports containing empty kind terms.

The idea is as follows: The form "S believes that K is F" entails "if K exists, then S is acquainted with K." (To say that K exists is simply to say that there are instances or samples of K.) However, if the term K does not denote an existing kind, a belief report of this form might still be true, provided that the subject self-ascribes a property of an appropriate sort. The property will, as before, be a property of the form *bearing R to a kind of thing that has f*, where R is a relation of acquaintance. In examples of the present sort, of course, the subject will not actually bear R to any kind of thing. But if R satisfies certain conditions, conditions that are supplied by the context of utterance and the identity of the kind term itself, the belief report might be true. Joseph Priestley, for example, might have self-ascribed the property *having observed the effects of a fiery substance called "phlogiston" that is emitted by burning wood* (or some such property). As a result, the *de dicto* attribution "Priestley believed that phlogiston was emitted by burning wood" can be true, whereas the *de re* claim "Priestley believed, of phlogiston, that it was emitted by burning wood" cannot.

In this case, I must say that the relation of acquaintance *having observed the effects of a fiery substance called "phlogiston"* somehow satisfies whichever conditions are relevant. I offer no theory on exactly why this is so, but it clearly has something to do with the descriptive information contained in the relation. In this case, the alleged kind is described as something fiery and as something called "phlogiston." Perhaps neither of these is necessary. Perhaps the characteristics of colorlessness and weightlessness would also suffice. But not just any descriptive information will do. If somebody were to self-ascribe the property *having seen fairy dust given off by burning wood*, we should not want to say that this person believes that phlogiston is emitted by burning wood.

The final, if not completely precise, account may be given as follows (this is analogous to the revised semantic claim from ch. 6, sec. 4):

> *Semantic Claim for Kind Terms*: An utterance of ⌈*S believes that K is F*⌉ (where *S* denotes subject *s*, *K* is a (possibly empty) kind term, and *F* expresses property *f*) is true if and only if there is some suitable relation of acquaintance *R* such that *s* self-ascribes *bearing R uniquely to a kind, k, such that instances of k have f.*

Again, in order for a relation of acquaintance *R* to be *suitable* in the relevant sense, the subject must bear it to the kind picked out by the term *K*, if indeed there is such a kind. In addition to this condition, there might also be other, contextually supplied conditions. For example, *R* might have to be in the domain of discourse or might have to be suitable in some other relevant way (recall the Superman example, although of course neither "Superman" nor "Clark Kent" is a kind term). And in cases where the term *K* fails to pick out an existing kind, *R* will have to satisfy certain conditions of the sort discussed above.

On this account, *de dicto* belief attributions are made true not only by what the subject believes (i.e., by what properties she self-ascribes), but also by facts concerning the relation of acquaintance that the subject takes herself, correctly or incorrectly, to bear to an existing kind of thing. This is a desideratum that arose from the earlier diagnosis of the failure of Twin Earth reasoning. I would like to conclude by discussing how the present account applies to some of the cases discussed in this chapter.

It is true that Oscar believes that topaz is yellow, since there is a relation of acquaintance *R* that he bears to topaz—he must bear it to topaz, given that topaz exists—and he self-ascribes the property *bearing R to a kind of thing that is yellow*. Twin Oscar also self-ascribes this property, but he does not bear any relation of acquaintance to topaz, and so it is not true that Twin Oscar believes that topaz is yellow. Relation R is not suitable with respect to this belief report about Twin Oscar.

In the case of our sample belief attribution to Priestley, the truth conditions are satisfied. Since phlogiston does not exist, Priestley need not bear any relation of acquaintance to it. Yet there is nothing to stop him from thinking that he is acquainted with a fiery substance called "phlogiston" that is given off by burning wood. The descriptive information contained in the relation he takes himself to bear to a kind of thing that is emitted by burning wood is sufficient for the suitability of the relation in the context of utterance.

In this section, I have proposed a semantic account of belief reports with kind terms, which incorporates the framework of the property theory. This account seems to give plausible results for the examples considered in this chapter, including examples involving empty kind terms, which are especially problematic in a variety of ways for externalists.[14] The account also seems to help explain why psychological externalism does not follow from differences in the truth values of belief attributions to subjects in Twin Earth cases. Where there is no difference in the intrinsic, physical nature of a pair of subjects, the twins will self-ascribe all of the same properties. Insofar as they do this, they will not differ with respect to which belief content properties they have. Some of these self-ascribed properties, however, will contain or entail relations of acquaintance, i.e., they will be of the form *bearing R to a kind of thing that is such-and-such*. Since it is possible that one twin should bear such a relation to one kind of thing while another bears it to something else or to nothing at all, an attribution that is true of one might not be true of the other. Internalism deserves to be the commonsense view of the attitudes and of psychological properties generally, and Twin Earth reasoning does not show that, on this point, common sense is mistaken. The property theory of content helps to show why this is the case.

---

14. For a thorough and (to my mind) convincing examination of many of these issues, see Segal (2000).

REFERENCES

Almog, J., J. Perry, and H. Wettstein, eds. 1989. *Themes from Kaplan* (New York: Oxford University Press).

Austin, D., ed. 1988. *Philosophical Analysis: A Defense by Example* (Dordrecht: Reidel).

Bach, K. 1997. "Do Belief Reports Report Beliefs?" *Pacific Philosophical Quarterly* 78: 215–241.

———. 1987. *Thought and Reference* (New York: Oxford University Press).

Bealer, G. 1998. "Propositions," *Mind* 107: 1–32.

———. 1993. "A Solution to Frege's Puzzle," *Philosophical Perspectives* 7: 17–60.

———. 1982. *Quality and Concept* (Oxford: Clarendon).

Boghossian, P. 1997. "What the Externalist Can Know a Priori," *Proceedings of the Aristotelian Society* 97: 161–175.

Brown, C. 1992. "Direct and Indirect Belief," *Philosophy and Phenomenological Research* 52: 289–316.

———. 1986. "What Is a Belief State?" *Midwest Studies in Philosophy* 10: 357–378.

Brueckner, A. 1992. "What an Anti-Individualist Knows a Priori," *Analysis* 52: 111–118.

Burge, T. 1988. "Individualism and Self-Knowledge," *Journal of Philosophy* 85: 649–663.

———. 1982. "Other Bodies," in A. Woodfield, ed., *Thought and Object* (Oxford: Oxford University Press), 97–120.

———. 1979. "Individualism and the Mental," *Midwest Studies in Philosophy* 4: 73–122.

Castañeda, H. N. 1968. "On the Logic of Attributions of Self-Knowledge to Others," *Journal of Philosophy* 65: 439–459.

Chisholm, R. 1981. *The First Person* (Minneapolis: University of Minnesota Press).

———. 1979. "The Indirect Reflexive," in C. Diamond and J. Teichman, eds., *Intention and Intentionality: Essays in Honour of G. E. M. Anscombe* (Brighton, England: Harvester), 39–53.

Crane, T. 1991. "All the Difference in the World," *Philosophical Quarterly* 41: 1–25.

Davidson, D. 1988. "Reply to Burge," *Journal of Philosophy* 85: 664–665.

Dennett, D. 1982. "Beyond Belief," in A. Woodfield, ed., *Thought and Object* (Oxford: Oxford University Press), 1–95.

Evans, G. 1982. *The Varieties of Reference* (Oxford: Oxford University Press).

Feit, N. 2006. "The Doctrine of Propositions, Internalism, and Global Supervenience," *Philosophical Studies* 131: 447–457.

———. 2001. "Rationality and Puzzling Beliefs," *Philosophy and Phenomenological Research* 63: 29–55.

———. 2000. "Self-Ascription and Belief *De Re*," *Philosophical Studies* 98: 37–51.

Fodor, J. 1987. *Psychosemantics: The Problem of Meaning in the Philosophy of Mind* (Cambridge, MA: MIT Press).

Forbes, G. 1987. "Indexicals and Intensionality: A Fregean Perspective," *Philosophical Review* 96: 3–31.

Frege, G. 1918. "Der Gedanke." Translated as "Thoughts" in N. Salmon and S. Soames, eds., *Propositions and Attitudes* (New York: Oxford University Press, 1988), 33–55.

Geach, P. 1957. "On Beliefs about Oneself," *Analysis* 18: 23–24.

Grim, P. 1985. "Against Omniscience: The Case from Essential Indexicals," *Nous* 19: 151–180.

Grimm, R., and D. Merrill, eds. 1988. *Contents of Thought* (Tucson: University of Arizona Press).

Heil, J. 1988. "Privileged Access," *Mind* 97: 238–251.

Jackson, F. 2003. "Narrow Content and Representation—or Twin Earth Revisited," *Proceedings and Addresses of the American Philosophical Association* 77: 55–70.

———. 1998. *From Metaphysics to Ethics* (Oxford: Oxford University Press).

Kaplan, D. 1989. "Demonstratives," in J. Almog, J. Perry, and H. Wettstein, eds., *Themes from Kaplan* (Oxford: Oxford University Press), 481–564.

Katz, J. 1994. "Names without Bearers," *Philosophical Review* 103: 1–39.

Kripke, S. 1979. "A Puzzle about Belief," in A. Margalit, ed., *Meaning and Use* (Dordrecht: Reidel), 239–283. Reprinted in N. Salmon and S. Soames, eds., *Propositions and Attitudes* (New York: Oxford University Press, 1988), 102–148.

Lewis, D. 1994. "Reduction of Mind," in S. Guttenplan, ed., *A Companion to the Philosophy of Mind* (Oxford: Blackwell), 412–431.

———. 1986. *On the Plurality of Worlds* (Oxford: Blackwell).

——. 1983a. *Philosophical Papers*, vol. 1 (Oxford: Oxford University Press).

——. 1983b. "New Work for a Theory of Universals," *Australasian Journal of Philosophy* 61: 343–377.

——. 1981. "What Puzzling Pierre Does Not Believe," *Australasian Journal of Philosophy* 59: 283–289.

——. 1979. "Attitudes De Dicto and De Se," *Philosophical Review* 87: 513–545. Reprinted in D. Lewis, *Philosophical Papers*, vol. 1 (Oxford: Oxford University Press, 1983), 133–159.

Loar, B. 1988. "Social Content and Psychological Content," in R. Grimm and D. Merrill, eds., *Contents of Thought* (Tucson: University of Arizona Press), 99–110.

——. 1976. "The Semantics of Singular Terms," *Philosophical Studies* 30: 353–377.

Marcus, R. B. 1981. "A Proposed Solution to a Puzzle about Belief," *Midwest Studies in Philosophy* 6: 501–510.

Markie, P. 1988. "Multiple Propositions and 'De Se' Attitudes," *Philosophy and Phenomenological Research* 48: 573–600.

——. 1984. "*De Dicto* and *De Se*," *Philosophical Studies* 45: 231–237.

McDowell, J. 1984. "*De Re* Senses," *Philosophical Quarterly* 34: 283–294.

McGinn, C. 1982. "The Structure of Content," in A. Woodfield, ed., *Thought and Object* (Oxford: Oxford University Press), 207–258.

McKay, T. 1988. "De Re and De Se Belief," in D. Austin, ed., *Philosophical Analysis: A Defense by Example* (Dordrecht: Reidel), 207–217.

McKinsey, M. 1991. "Anti-Individualism and Privileged Access," *Analysis* 51: 9–16.

McLaughlin, B. 1997. "Supervenience, Vagueness, and Determination," *Philosophical Perspectives* 11: 209–230.

——. 1996. "Supervenience," in D. Borchert, ed., *Encyclopedia of Philosophy, Supplement* (New York: Simon & Schuster Macmillan), 558–560.

Moltmann, F. 2003. "Propositional Attitudes without Propositions," *Synthese* 135: 77–118.

Nolan, D. 2006. "Selfless Desires," *Philosophy and Phenomenological Research* 73: 665–679.

Nozick, R. 1981. *Philosophical Explanations* (Cambridge, MA: Belknap Press of Harvard University Press).

O'Brien, L. 1995. "Evans on Self-Identification," *Nous* 29: 232–247.

——. 1994. "Anscombe and the Self-Reference Rule," *Analysis* 54: 277–281.

Over, D. E. 1983. "On Kripke's Puzzle," *Mind* 92: 253–256.

Owens, J. 1989. "Contradictory Belief and Cognitive Access," *Midwest Studies in Philosophy* 14: 289–316.

Peacocke, C. 1992. *A Study of Concepts* (Cambridge, MA: MIT Press).

——. 1983. *Sense and Content* (Oxford: Oxford University Press).

——. 1981. "Demonstrative Thought and Psychological Explanation," *Synthese* 49: 187–217.

Perry, J. 2006. "Stalnaker and Indexical Belief," in J. Thomson and A. Byrne, eds., *Content and Modality: Themes from the Philosophy of Robert Stalnaker* (New York: Oxford University Press), 204–221.

——. 1980. "Belief and Acceptance," *Midwest Studies in Philosophy* 5: 533–542.

——. 1979. "The Problem of the Essential Indexical," *Nous* 13: 3–21. Reprinted in N. Salmon and S. Soames, eds., *Propositions and Attitudes* (New York: Oxford University Press, 1988), 83–101.

——. 1977. "Frege on Demonstratives," *Philosophical Review* 87: 474–497.

Putnam, H. 1975a. "The Meaning of 'Meaning'," *Minnesota Studies in the Philosophy of Science* 7: 131–193.

——. 1975b. *Mind, Language and Reality* (Cambridge: Cambridge University Press).

——. 1973. "Meaning and Reference," *Journal of Philosophy* 70: 699–711.

Recanati, F. 1993. *Direct Reference: From Language to Thought* (Oxford: Blackwell).

Richard, M. 1990. *Propositional Attitudes* (New York: Cambridge University Press).

——. 1983. "Direct Reference and Ascriptions of Belief," *Journal of Philosophical Logic* 12: 425–452. Reprinted in N. Salmon and S. Soames, eds., *Propositions and Attitudes* (New York: Oxford University Press, 1988), 169–196.

Robbins, P. 2004. "To Structure, or Not to Structure?" *Synthese* 139: 55–80.

Russell, B. 1918. "The Philosophy of Logical Atomism," reprinted in R. C. Marsh, ed., *Logic and Knowledge* (London: Allen and Unwin, 1956), 177–281.

——. 1913. *Theory of Knowledge* (London: Routledge).

——. 1912. *The Problems of Philosophy* (London: Williams and Norgate).

Salmon, N. 1989. "Illogical Belief," *Philosophical Perspectives* 3: 243–285.

——. 1986. *Frege's Puzzle* (Cambridge, MA: MIT Press).

Salmon, N., and S. Soames, eds. 1988. *Propositions and Attitudes* (New York: Oxford University Press).

Schiffer, S. 1978. "The Basis of Reference," *Erkenntnis* 13: 171–206.

Segal, G. 2000. *A Slim Book about Narrow Content* (Cambridge, MA: MIT Press).

——. 1989. "The Return of the Individual," *Mind* 98: 39–57.

Shier, D. 1996. "Direct Reference for the Narrow Minded," *Pacific Philosophical Quarterly* 77: 225–248.

Sider, T. 1999. "Global Supervenience and Identity across Times and Worlds," *Philosophy and Phenomenological Research* 59: 913–937.

Sosa, D. 1996. "The Import of the Puzzle about Belief," *Philosophical Review* 105: 373–402.

Stalnaker, R. 2006. "Perry, 'Stalnaker and Indexical Belief'," in J. Thomson and A. Byrne, eds., *Content and Modality: Themes from the Philosophy of Robert Stalnaker* (New York: Oxford University Press), 285–289.

——. 1996. "Varieties of Supervenience," *Philosophical Perspectives* 10: 221–241.

——. 1993. "Twin Earth Revisited," *Proceedings of the Aristotelian Society* 93: 297–311.

——. 1990. "Narrow Content," in C. A. Anderson and J. Owens, eds., *Propositional Attitudes: The Role of Content in Logic, Language and Mind* (Stanford, CA: CSLI), 131–146.

——. 1989. "On What's in the Head," *Philosophical Perspectives* 3: 287–316.

——. 1984. *Inquiry* (Cambridge, MA: MIT Press).

——. 1981. "Indexical Belief," *Synthese* 49: 129–151.

Thau, M. 2002. *Consciousness and Cognition* (New York: Oxford University Press).

Thomson, J., and A. Byrne, eds. 2006. *Content and Modality: Themes from the Philosophy of Robert Stalnaker* (New York: Oxford University Press).

Turner, J. 2006. "Fitting Attitudes *De Dicto* and *De Se*," unpublished manuscript.

Woodfield, A., ed. 1982. *Thought and Object* (Oxford: Oxford University Press).

Wright, C., B. Smith, and C. Macdonald, eds. 1998. *Knowing Our Own Minds* (New York: Oxford University Press).

Yablo, S. 1992. "Mental Causation," *Philosophical Review* 101: 245–280.

INDEX